THE PRACTICAL GUIDE TO PUBLIC INQUIRIES

This practical guide provides legal practitioners, participants, witnesses and all those with an interest in public inquiries, with stage-by-stage 'hands on' guidance on the process of public inquiries into matters of public concern.

With its user-friendly format of summaries, checklists, 'top tips' and flow charts, this book looks at the setting up of a public inquiry through to its close. It includes information on:

- the appointment of the chair and inquiry team;
- the choice and significance of the venue;
- the drawing up of inquiry procedures, protocols and rulings;
- the appointment and role of core participants;
- evidence taking;
- conducting and attending hearings;
- the role of experts;
- the writing and publication of the inquiry report.

Drawing on the authors' extensive experience as public inquiry lawyers, working on inquiries such as the Bloody Sunday Inquiry, Mid Staffordshire NHS Foundation Trust Inquiry, Leveson Inquiry and Grenfell Tower Inquiry, together with contributions from a number of other eminent practitioners in the field, this book provides valuable, comprehensive guidance on the public inquiry process.

The Practical Guide to Public Inquiries

Isabelle Mitchell
Peter Watkin Jones
Sarah Jones
and
Emma Ireton

•HART•
OXFORD • LONDON • NEW YORK • NEW DELHI • SYDNEY

HART PUBLISHING
Bloomsbury Publishing Plc
Kemp House, Chawley Park, Cumnor Hill, Oxford, OX2 9PH, UK
1385 Broadway, New York, NY 10018, USA
29 Earlsfort Terrace, Dublin 2, Ireland

HART PUBLISHING, the Hart/Stag logo, BLOOMSBURY and the Diana logo are trademarks of Bloomsbury Publishing Plc

First published in Great Britain 2020

Reprinted 2022

A catalogue record for this book is available from the British Library.

Library of Congress Cataloging-in-Publication data

Names: Mitchell, Isabelle, author. | Jones, Peter Watkin, author. | Jones, Sarah, author. | Ireton, Emma, author.

Title: The practical guide to public inquiries / Isabelle Mitchell, Peter Watkin Jones, Sarah Jones, and Emma Ireton.

Description: Oxford, UK ; New York, NY : Hart Publishing, an imprint of Bloomsbury Publishing, 2020. | Includes bibliographical references and index.

Identifiers: LCCN 2020043501 (print) | LCCN 2020043502 (ebook) | ISBN 9781509928347 (hardback) | ISBN 9781509928330 (pdf) | ISBN 9781509928323 (Epub)

Subjects: LCSH: Governmental investigations. | Legislative auditing.

Classification: LCC K3321 .M58 2020 (print) | LCC K3321 (ebook) | DDC 352.8/80941—dc23

LC record available at https://lccn.loc.gov/2020043501

LC ebook record available at https://lccn.loc.gov/2020043502

ISBN: HB: 978-1-50992-834-7
ePDF: 978-1-50992-833-0
ePub: 978-1-50992-832-3

Typeset by Compuscript Ltd, Shannon
Printed and bound in Great Britain by TJ International Ltd, Padstow, Cornwall

To find out more about our authors and books visit www.hartpublishing.co.uk. Here you will find extracts, author information, details of forthcoming events and the option to sign up for our newsletters.

CONTENTS

ABOUT THE AUTHORS

Isabelle Mitchell
As a Principal Associate in Eversheds Sutherland's Inquiries and Investigations team, Isabelle Mitchell has extensive experience working on behalf of inquiries (Mid Staffordshire, Independent Jersey Care Inquiry, Trojan Horse, Telford CSE) and core participants to inquiries (Leveson, IICSA, Grenfell). Isabelle has been recognised by Legal 500 as a 'Rising Star' (2020 and 2021) for her public inquiry work.

Peter Watkin Jones
Peter Watkin Jones created the Eversheds Inquiries and Investigations team in 1997. He led the team acting for the following inquiries; Bloody Sunday; Shipman; Rosemary Nelson; Mid Staffordshire Hospital; and Independent Jersey Care Inquiry. He led teams acting for clients involved with the Leveson, Grenfell, and numerous child abuse inquiries. A partner for 33 years, Peter is now a consultant with the firm.

Sarah Jones
Sarah is a partner in Eversheds Sutherland and heads up the Inquiries and Investigations team, having worked on various statutory and non-statutory inquiries (acting on behalf of inquiries and interested parties) for over 15 years. The Inquiries and Investigations team consists of 12 lawyers and paralegals who work solely on inquiry and investigations matters. Sarah was recognised by The Lawyer as one of the "Hot 100" lawyers for 2017 and again in 2020.

Dr Emma Ireton
Dr Emma Ireton is a solicitor (non-practicing) and Senior Lecturer at Nottingham Trent University, with a research specialism in public inquiries. While in practice, she was a member of the evidence gathering team for the Bloody Sunday Inquiry. Emma's work focuses on bridging the gap between legal academia and practice; she works closely with leading members of the legal profession on research, curriculum design, teaching, and academic and practitioner publications.

1

Public Inquiries

Introduction

In recent years, public inquiries have become an increasingly prominent feature of administrative justice. There have been well in excess of 50 statutory and non-statutory government-sponsored inquiries in the UK and its crown dependencies over the last 25 years. The last few years alone has seen the establishment of public inquiries with extremely wide-ranging subject matter. These have included the Independent Inquiry into Child Sexual Abuse; the Litvinenko Inquiry into the death of Alexander Litvinenko; the Undercover Policing Inquiry into covert police operations; the Renewable Heat Incentive Inquiry into a failed renewable heat incentive scheme in Northern Ireland; the Leveson Inquiry into press reporting; the inquiry into the circumstances surrounding the fire at Grenfell Tower; and the Infected Blood Inquiry into the circumstances in which thousands of NHS patients were given infected blood and infected blood products. What all public inquiries have in common is that they are investigations into significant matters of public concern.

Understanding the nature of public inquiries and how they are run in practice is essential for those conducting an inquiry and for participants. This guide provides practical guidance on public inquiry procedure for inquiry teams, legal practitioners, participants, witnesses and all those interested in the public inquiry process, drawn from lessons learned and best (and worst) practice from past inquiries, and the expertise of experienced public inquiry practitioners.

Unlike the court system or tribunals system, there is no permanent 'system of inquiries' nor any permanent secretariat or 'inquiries service'. Individual public inquiries are convened as and when necessary. In the case of a statutory inquiry, the minister sets the inquiry's terms of reference, sometimes with input from the chair, and often after consulting others. Staff have to be found, premises located and set up, and systems, protocols and procedures put in place before the inquiry's work on the substance even begins. Once a public inquiry has fulfilled its terms of reference, it is then closed down and ceases to exist.

Every public inquiry differs from those that have come before, depending on its subject matter, terms of reference and exercise of discretion by the chair. There is no detailed and prescriptive rulebook for public inquiry procedures[1] and this guide is not intended to be that rulebook, but instead to provide guidance.

[1] The Inquiries Act 2005 and Inquiry Rules 2006 (SI 2006/1838) do provide a statutory framework, but this framework gives the chair or panel a wide discretion when conducting an inquiry.

The chair of an inquiry determines the inquiry's procedures, which are specific to the needs of that inquiry. Those involved in setting up and chairing public inquiries have frequently expressed frustration at finding themselves reinventing the wheel each time a new inquiry is set up, for example when devising protocols. It is equally challenging to those who find themselves giving evidence to, and participating in, a public inquiry for the first time, given the absence of any detailed guidance as to public inquiry procedure.

Quote

Speaking at a seminar on the future of public inquiries, Sir Robert Francis QC, Chair of the Mid Staffordshire NHS Foundation Trust Public Inquiry commented:

'there is a need not to reinvent the wheel. The extraordinary thing is that every inquiry is reinventing the wheel in regard to procedure, the collection of resources and generally how to go about its business. It seems to me that the more inquiries we have ... the more there needs to be a common resource available that enables those who conduct inquiries to get off to a better start'.

Those who have had previous involvement in public inquiries will know that lessons about how best to set up and manage an inquiry are frequently overlooked. Too often practitioners look to previous inquiries only to learn about what not to do, rather than what to do.

Currently, the only formal written guidance for sponsoring departments of public inquiries is the Inquiries Guidance produced by the Cabinet Office in 2012 ('the Cabinet Office Guidance'), which is still in draft form.[2] It is written as 'best practice guidance for all types of inquiry commissioned by government – whether statutory or non-statutory ...' although it is 'not binding on inquiry teams.[3] It is, however, very brief and general. In accordance with that guidance, at the conclusion of every inquiry, the inquiry secretary should submit a 'Lessons Learned' report to the Cabinet Office, which should include details of successes and failures, and information to help inform the setting up of future inquiries.' In practice, this has rarely been done (see chapter fifteen).[4] Even when reports are

[2] Cabinet Office, *Inquiries Guidance: Guidance for inquiry chairs and secretaries, and sponsor departments: Draft version* (2012), available at www.parliament.uk/documents/lords-committees/Inquiries-Act-2005/caboffguide.pdf (accessed 12 August 2020).

[3] Cabinet Office, *Inquiries Guidance* (n 2) 2.

[4] The Home Office established its own dedicated inquiry sponsorship team in 2017. Its aim is to improve the management of inquiries, whilst maintaining their independence, by supporting inquiry secretariats in the setting up of inquiries. It covers areas such as human resources, finance and IT, and provides links with other government departments and non-Home Office inquiries.

submitted, the content of such reports are not publicised, and they are not generally prepared in consultation with all those involved in the inquiry concerned.

There are, however, many examples of good, common practice that have evolved over the years, and valuable lessons to be learnt from past public inquiries. The following chapters draw these lessons together, to provide practical guidance on the setting up of an inquiry; the appointment and roles of those running and participating in an inquiry; the choice of venue and setting up of premises, protocols and procedures; the taking of evidence and conducting hearings; what to expect as a participant in an inquiry; and also the writing and publication of the inquiry report, the costs of an inquiry and the closing down of the inquiry.

> **Quote**
>
> At a 2012 conference into public inquiries, Sir William Gage, Chairman of the Baha Mousa Inquiry, described public inquiries as 'one of the fastest growing areas of the law and practice.'
>
> This comment was made nearly 10 years ago, but it continues to be the case.

What is a Public Inquiry?

In many ways, public inquiries may appear to resemble a court. The majority of public inquiries are chaired by a judge or retired judge; a solicitor and counsel to the inquiry are appointed and many participants have legal representation. Some public inquiries are held in court buildings. Evidence is often taken during oral hearings and many statutory public inquiries have the power to compel witnesses to give evidence on oath.

However, public inquiries are not a court and do not have the power to determine any person's civil or criminal liability. They cannot make awards for damages nor determine any criminal sanctions.

Whilst being a major instrument of accountability, and an important component of our administrative justice system, public inquiries are, in fact, part of the political process. They are convened by a minister to inquire into a matter of public concern. The report ultimately produced by a statutory public inquiry is delivered to the minister who convened the inquiry and is subsequently laid before Parliament. A public inquiry's recommendations are not legally binding and it is for the Government, or other relevant bodies or organisations, to decide what action will be taken in response to the report. Where the Government or other bodies fail to implement the recommendations of a public inquiry, any influence or pressure brought to bear on that failure derives not from legal pressure, but from political pressure from Parliament, or from the public, the media and others, such as non-governmental organisations (NGOs), victims, survivors and their families.

The Role of a Public Inquiry

Public inquiries may serve a number of different purposes. They inquire into and establish the facts and may provide answers about matters of public concern, and failings in public systems and services, in a way that the court system does not. They provide accountability (though not civil or criminal liability). They may produce lessons learned, make recommendations to prevent recurrence and suggest improvements for the future. An inquiry can therefore look both backwards and forwards. They can restore public confidence and provide catharsis for those deeply affected by the subject matter of the inquiry, as well as playing a role in developing public policy and discharging investigative obligations under Articles 2 and 3 of the European Convention on Human Rights.[5] An inquiry report may be the catalyst for civil and criminal proceedings to follow.

The role of an inquiry will differ depending on its subject matter and terms of reference. For example, not all inquiries are required to make recommendations, and not all inquiries will have an element of catharsis. What is considered to be the primary role of an inquiry may differ depending on the capacity in which a person has an interest in an inquiry. For many victims, survivors or bereaved family members, a public inquiry offers a long sought-after opportunity for their voices to be heard and for those in authority to be held to account; for others the key role might be learning lessons and preventing recurrence. The inquiry has to balance effectively all aspects of its role, and the interests of all those involved, but ultimately it is governed by its terms of reference.

The Basis upon which an Inquiry may be Convened

Public inquiries into matters of public concern may be convened by a minister under statute. Prior to the Inquiries Act 2005 coming into force, inquiries were held either under its predecessor, the Tribunals of Evidence (Inquiry) Act 1921, or under pieces of subject-specific legislation (eg the Marchioness Inquiry under s 258 of the Merchant Shipping Act 1995).

[5] The right to life and the right to not be subjected to torture or to inhuman or degrading treatment or punishment. See also Jason Beer and others, *Public Inquiries* (Oxford University Press 2011) paras 1.02–10 on the role of public inquiries.

Almost all statutory inquiries are now convened under the Inquiries Act 2005.[6] Examples include the Mid Staffordshire NHS Foundation Trust Public Inquiry, the Baha Mousa Inquiry, the Independent Inquiry into Child Sexual Abuse, the Grenfell Tower Inquiry and the Infected Blood Inquiry. The 2005 Act and the Inquiry Rules 2006 confer on these inquiries certain powers and obligations, including the power to compel witnesses to provide documents and attend to give evidence on oath, and the obligation to warn those who may be criticised in the inquiry report. The 2005 Act also introduced a rebuttable presumption that hearings will be held in public.[7]

A minister has a very broad discretion to convene a 2005 Act public inquiry. Section 1(1) of the 2005 Act provides that a minister 'may' cause an inquiry to be held under the Act. There is no formula or criteria in the Act for convening a statutory inquiry beyond that stated in s 1(1):

> … where it appears to him that –
>
> (a) particular events have caused, or are capable of causing, public concern, or
> (b) there is public concern that particular events may have occurred.

Public inquiries into matters of public concern can also be set up by a minister on a non-statutory basis, outside of the strictures of the legislation, under the prerogative powers of the government. These may include parliamentary inquiries, counsels of Privy Councillors, independent reviews with public hearing elements and Royal Commissions.[8] Examples include the Iraq Inquiry; the Morecambe Bay Investigation; the Detainee Inquiry; the Harris Review; the Magnox Inquiry examining the award of the Magnox decommissioning contract by the Nuclear Decommissioning Authority and its subsequent termination; and the Independent Inquiry into Ian Paterson. Again, the minister has a very broad discretion over whether to convene a non-statutory inquiry and, for non-statutory inquiries, there are no criteria that have to be applied. These non-statutory inquiries are often very similar in nature and form to a statutory public inquiry. However, they do not have the power to compel the giving of evidence or to take evidence on oath, and there is no presumption that the inquiry's hearings or its findings will be public. The justification for establishing some inquiries as

[6] One of the main purposes of the Inquiries Act 2005 was to consolidate numerous pieces of subject-specific legislation, to provide a single comprehensive statutory framework for inquiries convened by ministers into matters of public concern. Two statutory provisions, relating to health and safety at work and financial services continue to apply independently of the 2005 Act (Health & Safety at Work Act 1994, s 14 and Financial Services Act 2020, ss 68–72).

[7] Inquiries Act 2005, s 18.

[8] Royal Commissions appear to have fallen out of use in the United Kingdom. The most recent was convened in 2000 and, prior to that, they tended to be used to deal with broader policy issues rather than specific incidents or series of incidents of public concern. They are still used in Australia, Canada and New Zealand.

non-statutory inquiries is that matters of intelligence may need to be examined in private.[9]

Inquiries are not restricted to those convened by ministers into matters of public concern. Essentially, inquiries can be held by any person or body, whether they be public or private, to look at any issue which they consider requires investigation. Private organisations have established their own inquiries when things have gone wrong; for example, the review of the culture and practices of the BBC in connection with the Jimmy Savile scandal.[10] Local authorities have also commissioned their own inquiries, such as the Independent Inquiry into Child Sexual Exploitation in Rotherham established by Rotherham Metropolitan Borough Council in 2013 and the Independent Inquiry into Telford Child Sexual Exploitation established by Telford & Wrekin Council in 2019, both of which were (and at the time of writing for the Telford & Wrekin Inquiry are) tasked with examining issues concerning the sexual exploitation of children in the respective local area. Many standing statutory bodies also have powers of inquiry, such as the Commons Committee on culture, media and sport or the Banking Standards Commission, but with different powers to those of public inquiries convened by ministers into matters of public concern.

This guide focuses on statutory and non-statutory public inquiries convened by ministers into matters of public concern. However, many of the principles and procedures that apply to those public inquiries will apply equally to other forms of inquiry. This guide examines the processes and procedures involved in an inquiry, from the point that it is announced.

The Challenges

The challenges facing any public inquiry is to conduct a searching inquiry, usually on an inquisitorial rather than an adversarial basis, to fulfil its terms of reference, and to do so:

- expeditiously;
- effectively;
- fairly;
- transparently; and
- in a cost-effective manner.

[9] Decisions taken by ministers not to convene a public inquiry have been challenged in the past, in some cases successfully, by way of judicial review, and this is discussed further in chapter fourteen.

[10] *The Jimmy Savile investigation report* by Dame Janet Smith DBE, available at http://www.damejanetsmithreview.com/ (accessed 12 August 2020).

Checklist – Immediate issues and challenges at the start of an inquiry

Conducting an inquiry

Those conducting an inquiry, including members of the inquiry team, need to address a wide variety of issues and challenges, which include but are not limited to:

- Appointing an inquiry team (chair, counsel, solicitors, secretary, administrators, assessors, experts); ensuring there are sufficient resources to support the inquiry's work; and establishing internal communication systems and protocols.
- Sourcing a venue for the inquiry's operations and managing its set up, possibly at several locations (IT, security, stationery, furniture, telephones, email, office layout, hearing room layout).
- Establishing and managing the budget and dealing with applications for costs and expenses.
- Setting up appropriate management systems for the conduct of the inquiry's work including, crucially, IT systems, and the security around those systems.
- Identifying what is relevant material, what is key material, any material missing and likely witnesses.
- The storage and analysis of large volumes of relevant material.
- Data protection, freedom of information, confidentiality and redaction issues.
- Providing public access and managing security issues.
- Liaising with core participants and other interested parties.
- Managing vast quantities of correspondence, dealing with disclosure and evidence and disclosing material to parties.
- Liaising with a large number of witnesses with differing needs and challenges; this includes fostering their confidence, providing support during the process and where necessary overcoming language barriers. Dealing with witnesses in other jurisdictions and obtaining evidence from reluctant witnesses.
- Liaising with the sponsoring department – understanding how the 'Whitehall machinery' works and fostering a good working relationship with the sponsoring department while maintaining independence and not allowing discretion to be fettered.
- Putting protective measures in place for vulnerable or anonymous witnesses and providing for the open, anonymous or private giving of evidence as required.

- Arranging and conducting daily oral hearings; setting up the hearing room; timetabling witnesses; preparing and disseminating evidence in advance of the hearings; preparing for a mix of public and private hearings; managing the attendance and subsequent questioning of witnesses; and formally recording the oral evidence and publishing transcripts.
- Managing the relationship with the media, establishing clear procedures and dealing with press statements and engagement with the media and the public.
- Maintaining a full audit trail of all of the inquiry's work and its interactions.
- Working under tight timescales and significant budgetary pressures.
- Establishing counselling services as appropriate, possibly to include ongoing support.

Participants to an inquiry

Those participating in an inquiry also need to address a wide variety of issues and challenges, which include, but are not limited to:

- Considering whether to make an application for core participant status.
- Issues relating to funding and legal representation.
- Familiarisation with:
  - the role of the public inquiry, its terms of reference, its powers and also its limitations, in order to manage expectations.
  - the role of those involved in the public inquiry process, including the chair, panel members, counsel, solicitors, secretary, administrative staff, assessors and experts.
  - how an inquiry works – its protocols and procedures.
  - the venue of the inquiry: any entrances allocated to a specific category of participants; security arrangements for entering the venue and hearing room; the location of the hearing room, meeting rooms and waiting rooms, and other rooms as relevant, such as a family room, media room and other facilities.
  - the layout of the hearing room including the 'witness box' and allocated seating for core participants, the media and the public.
  - the process for giving oral evidence to the inquiry and how to access the hearing timetables.
  - the inquiry's approach to redacting documents, and considering that in light of their own position and the protection of any confidential or commercially sensitive information.

- Identifying methods for communication with the inquiry team and the process for engagement with the inquiry team and the inquiry.
- Accessing, and familiarisation with, the inquiry website and any IT systems that are available to core participants, if appropriate.
- Understanding the process for providing documents, witness statements and oral evidence to the inquiry.
- Considering likely witnesses who may be called to provide evidence, and the individual needs of such witnesses and how their evidence may need to be managed (eg anonymity, evidence to be given in private, witness support to be provided).
- Considering the documents that may be requested by the inquiry, ensuring such evidence is preserved and prepared in readiness for the inquiry's work and that the inquiry's procedures for disclosing documents is understood.
- Accessing interpreters or other support services for witnesses.
- Considering potential for engagement with the media.

In some cases, for example where non-statutory inquiries or inquests are converted to 2005 Act inquiries, some of these challenges may already have been addressed, but considering whether any adjustments to the original arrangements are required for the statutory inquiry forum will still be important.

This guide examines all of these issues and challenges and provides practical guidance from the announcement of an inquiry through to the production and publication of the report and the subsequent archiving of material and the closing down of an inquiry.

Table of UK Public Inquiries Convened by a Minister

Inquiry	**Statutory/ Non-statutory**[a]	**Dates**
The Saville Inquiry (Bloody Sunday Inquiry)	*Statutory* – pre-2005 Act Tribunals of Inquiry (Evidence) Act 1921	January 1998 – March 2010
Sierra Leone Arms Investigation	*Non-statutory*	May 1998 – July 1998
Bristol Royal Infirmary Inquiry	*Statutory* – pre-2005 Act NHS Act 1977, s.84	June 1998 – July 2001

(continued)

(Continued)

Inquiry	Statutory/ Non-statutory[a]	Dates
Thames Safety Inquiry (into the Marchioness-Bowbell disaster)	*Non-statutory*	August 1999 – January 2000
Royal Liverpool Children's Hospital Inquiry	*Statutory* – pre-2005 Act NHS Act 1977, s 2	January 2000 – January 2001
MV Derbyshire Inquiry	*Statutory* – pre-2005 Act Merchant Shipping Act 1995, s 269(1)	April 2000 – November 2000
Ladbroke Grove Inquiry	*Statutory* – pre-2005 Act Health and Safety at Work Act 1974, s 14(2)(b)	May 2000 – September 2001
Joint Inquiry into Train Protection Systems	*Statutory* – pre-2005 Act Health and Safety at Work Act 1974, s 14(2)(b)	September 2000 – March 2001
Marchioness Inquiry	*Statutory* – pre-2005 Act Merchant Shipping Act 1995, s 268	February 2000 – March 2001
Inquiry into issues arising out of the identification of the victims following major transport accidents	*Non-statutory*	November 2000 – March 2001
Victoria Climbié Inquiry	*Statutory* – pre-2005 Act Children Act 1989, s 81; NHS Act 1977, s 84; and Police Act 1996, s 49	May 2001 – January 2003
Shipman Inquiry	*Statutory* – pre-2005 Act Tribunals of Inquiry (Evidence) Act 1921	January 2001 – January 2005
'The Three Inquiries': Ayling, Neale, Kerr/Haslam	*Statutory* – pre-2005 Act NHS Act 1977, s 84	July 2001 – July 2004
Foot and Mouth Disease 2001: Lessons to be learned Inquiry	*Non-statutory*	April 2001 – July 2002
Equitable Life Inquiry	*Non-statutory*	August 2001 – March 2004
Investigation surrounding the death of Dr David Kelly	*Non-statutory*	July 2003 – January 2004
Holyrood Inquiry	*Non-statutory*	June 2003 – September 2004

(continued)

(Continued)

Inquiry	Statutory/ Non-statutory[a]	Dates
Bichard Inquiry (Soham murders)	*Non-statutory*	December 2003 – June 2004
FV Gaul Inquiry	*Statutory* – pre-2005 Act Merchant Shipping Act 1995, s 269	April 1999 – December 2004
Review of intelligence on weapons of mass destruction (the Butler Review)	*Non-statutory*	February 2004 – July 2004
Zahid Mubarek Inquiry	*Non-Statutory*	April 2004 – June 2006
The Billy Wright Inquiry	*Statutory* Inquiries Act 2005 (converted from an inquiry under s 7 of the Prisons Act (Northern Ireland) 1953)	July 2004 – September 2010
The Robert Hamill Inquiry	*Statutory* Inquiries Act 2005 (converted from an inquiry under s 44 of the Police (Northern Ireland) Act 1998)	November 2004 – February 2011
Rosemary Nelson Inquiry	*Non-statutory* Police (Northern Ireland) Act 2005	November 2004 – May 2011
E.coli Inquiry	*Statutory* Inquiries Act 2005	March 2006 – March 2009
Contaminated Blood and Blood Products Inquiry	*Non-statutory*	March 2007 – February 2009
Human Tissue Analysis in UK Nuclear Facilities	*Non-statutory*	April 2007 – November 2010
Bernard (Sonny) Lodge Inquiry	*Statutory* Inquiries Act 2005	February 2009 – December 2009
ICL Inquiry	*Statutory* Inquiries Act 2005	January 2008 – July 2009
Baha Mousa Inquiry	*Statutory* Inquiries Act 2005	August 2008 – September 2011
Fingerprint Inquiry	*Statutory* Inquiries Act 2005	October 2008 – December 2011

(continued)

(Continued)

Inquiry	**Statutory/ Non-statutory**[a]	**Dates**
Inquiry into the outbreak of C.difficile in Northern Health and Social Care Trust Hospitals	*Statutory* Inquiries Act 2005	October 2008 – March 2011
Penrose Inquiry	*Statutory* Inquiries Act 2005	April 2008 – March 2015
Mid Staffordshire NHS Foundation Trust Independent Inquiry	*Non-statutory* NHS Act 2006	July 2009 – February 2010
Iraq Inquiry	*Non-statutory*	June 2009 – July 2016
FV Trident	*Non-statutory* Merchant Shipping Act 1995, s 269	October 2009 – February 2011
Vale of Leven Hospital Inquiry	*Statutory* Inquiries Act 2005	April 2009 – November 2014
Al-Sweady Inquiry	*Statutory* Inquiries Act 2005	November 2009 – December 2014
Mid Staffordshire NHS Foundation Trust Public Inquiry	*Statutory* Inquiries Act 2005	June 2010 – February 2013
Detainee Inquiry	*Non-Statutory*	July 2010 –December 2013
Azelle Rodney Inquiry	*Statutory* Inquiries Act 2005 (converted from an inquest)	June 2010 – July 2013
Inquiry into Culture, Practices and Ethics of the Press (the Leveson Inquiry)	*Statutory* Inquiries Act 2005	July 2011 – November 2012
Office of Inquiry into Child Sexual Exploitation in Gangs and Groups	*Non-statutory* Children Act 2004, s 3	October 2011 – November 2013
The Morecambe Bay Investigation	*Non-statutory*	September 2013 – March 2015

(continued)

(Continued)

Inquiry	Statutory/ Non-statutory[a]	Dates
Inquiry into Historical Institutional Abuse 1922–1995	*Statutory* Inquiry into Historical Institutional Abuse Act (Northern Ireland) 2013[b]	May 2012 – June 2017
Independent review of self-inflicted deaths of young adults in custody aged between 18 and 24	*Non-statutory*	February 2014 – July 2015
Litvinenko Inquiry	*Statutory* Inquiries Act 2005 (converted from an inquest)	July 2014 – January 2016
Committee of Inquiry into the Banking Crisis	*Statutory* Houses of the Oireachtas (Inquiries, Privileges and Procedures) Act 2013	December 2014 – January 2016
Edinburgh Tram Inquiry	*Statutory* Inquiries Act 2005	May 2015 – present
Independent Inquiry into Child Sexual Abuse	*Statutory* Inquiries Act 2005	February 2015 – present
Undercover Policing Inquiry	*Statutory* Inquiries Act 2005	March 2015 – present
Scottish Child Abuse Inquiry	*Statutory* Inquiries Act 2005	October 2015 – present
Anthony Grainger Inquiry	*Statutory* Inquiries Act 2005 (converted from an inquest)	March 2016 – July 2019
Renewable Heat Incentive Inquiry	*Statutory* Inquiries Act 2005	January 2017 – March 2020
Magnox Inquiry	*Non-statutory*	March 2017 – present
Grenfell Tower Inquiry	*Statutory* Inquiries Act 2005	June 2017 – present
Infected Blood Inquiry	*Statutory* Inquiries Act 2005	July 2017 – present

(continued)

(Continued)

Inquiry	**Statutory/ Non-statutory**[a]	**Dates**
Independent Inquiry into Ian Paterson	*Non-statutory*	December 2017 – February 2020
Public inquiry to examine the new Royal Hospital for Children and Young People and the Queen Elizabeth University Hospital sites	*Statutory* Inquiries Act 2005	September 2019 – present
Public inquiry into the Manchester Arena terror attack	*Statutory* Inquiries Act 2005 (converted from an inquest)	October 2019 – present
Public inquiry into the mistreatment of detainees at Brook House immigration removal centre	*Statutory* Inquiries Act 2005 (converted from an independent investigation by the Prisons and Probation Ombudsman)	November 2019 – present
Public inquiry into the circumstances of the death of Jermaine Baker	*Statutory* Inquiries Act 2005 (converted from an inquest)	February 2020 – present

Notes

[a] See definition of statutory and non-statutory inquiries post the Inquiries Act 2005 on pages 5 and 6.

[b] This legislation was specifically enacted for the purposes of this inquiry. The 2013 Act was closely modelled on the Inquiries Act 2005, with many of its provisions exactly replicating corresponding provisions in the 2005 Act.

The last time there were no active public inquiries was 27 years ago and since 1997 there have never been fewer than three running at any one time and often significantly more.[11]

[11] See https://www.instituteforgovernment.org.uk/explainers/public-inquiries (accessed 12 August 2020).

2

Appointments

Introduction

Following the announcement of an inquiry, certain appointments have to be made. This chapter examines the key appointments and the roles and responsibilities of the appointees, including the chair, counsel to the inquiry, solicitor to the inquiry and secretary to the inquiry, as well as examining the role of the sponsoring department.

The Chair and Panel

Public inquiries can be undertaken by a chair alone, as was the case in the Leveson Inquiry, and the Mid Staffordshire NHS Foundation Trust Inquiry, or by a chair together with one or more other persons forming an inquiry panel,[1] as was the case in the Billy Wright Inquiry, the Grenfell Tower Inquiry and the Independent Inquiry into Child Sexual Abuse. The chair of an inquiry must be appointed before the inquiry can start any work or make any decisions.

During the course of a public inquiry, selecting the chair of the inquiry is possibly one of the most important decisions that has to be made. The chair sets the tone and direction of an inquiry. Often, as with the Leveson and Iraq Inquiries,[2] an inquiry is identified by, and inextricably linked with, the identity of the chair.[3] It is being seen more and more often that the chair becomes the public figure of the recommendations and the messages that an inquiry wants to convey (subject to the view of any other panel members and with the benefit of advice from any assessors appointed). The identity of the chair may also be the subject of controversy, for example if a campaign group perceives the chair as being inappropriate for the task or subject matter. The chair is at the heart of the inquiry and

[1] Panel members adopt a different role to assessors or experts appointed by an inquiry chair. This is discussed in more detail in chapter twelve.

[2] Inquiry into the culture, practices and ethics of the press and the inquiry to identify lessons that could be learned from the Iraq conflict.

[3] The Iraq Inquiry is often referred to as the 'Chilcot Inquiry': it being chaired by Sir John Chilcot. Similarly, the inquiry into culture, practices and ethics of the press is more commonly known as the 'Leveson Inquiry', the chair being Lord Justice Brian Leveson (now Sir Brian Leveson).

the choice of chair has a major influence on the operation of the proceedings, the degree of engagement from stakeholders and the overall success of the inquiry.

The chair is responsible for discharging the inquiry's terms of reference and has a broad discretion to determine its procedure and conduct (subject to the provisions of the Inquiries Act 2005 and the Inquiry Rules 2006, if presiding over a statutory inquiry).[4] The chair supervises the running of the inquiry and, at its conclusion, delivers a report to the minister who convened the inquiry, setting out findings of fact and any recommendations[5] for the future.

Following consultation with the chair,[6] the minister may decide that an inquiry panel is also required. The panel members' role is to provide support to the chair as necessary in order to share the workload. Often panel members will be required to undertake an advisory function and to ensure that the chair's decision-making and thought processes are clear (sometimes referred to as 'sense-checking'). Panel members are usually selected specifically for their relevant expertise or knowledge of the subject matter of the inquiry and the different perspective they may be able to offer on the issues in hand. Examples of the range of backgrounds from which panel members have been drawn include a professor of prison studies and the Bishop of Hereford, who were panel members for the Billy Wright Inquiry;[7] a military historian, Professor of War Studies, a cross bencher, a member of the Joint Committee on Human Rights, a chair of the Judicial Appointment Commission and a British diplomat, who were panel members for the Iraq Inquiry; and a professor of public international law, a barrister with experience in child protection, human rights and family law, and a barrister who was previously Chief Crown Prosecutor in the London Area, who are panel members for the Independent Inquiry into Child Sexual Abuse.

Although the appointment of a panel member is ultimately a decision for the relevant minister with the consent of the chair, a chair may feel that operating as a panel is not necessary and may wish to lead the inquiry alone. The chair may be supported by assessors at various stages of the inquiry, as chosen by the chair; these assessors will also be individuals with appropriate expertise. The appointment and use of assessors is discussed in more detail in chapter twelve.

Process of Appointing a Chair and Panel Members

The minister appoints the chair and, where there is a panel, each member of the panel.[8] Neither the Inquiries Act 2005 nor the Inquiry Rules 2006 provide a formal process for the appointments.

[4] Inquiries Act 2005, ss 17, 18 and 21. See chapter eight.

[5] Either when required to do so by the terms of reference or where the chair or panel otherwise see fit to do so, Inquiries Act 2005, s 24(1).

[6] Inquiries Act 2005, s 4(3) for statutory inquiries. There is no such requirement for non-statutory inquiries, though consultation may still take place.

[7] Inquiry into the death of Billy Wright, an Ulster loyalist, in HM Prison Maze.

[8] Inquiries Act 2005, s 4(1).

Chair

The chair is appointed by the minister. The minister is not required to apply any specific criteria. Draft cabinet office guidance, which is non-binding, states that the minister may seek advice from professional, regulatory or other bodies in the appropriate field when selecting a chair.[9] Advice is also likely to be sought from people who have handled inquiries and who have dealt with the proposed chair in the past. Where a minister wishes to appoint a serving judge, the consent of the appropriate senior member of the judiciary should first be obtained. In politically contentious matters, the prime minister may be consulted.

Concern is often expressed about the lack of transparency of the appointment process as neither the details of the selection process, nor the criteria and reasoning applied in any given case, are in the public domain. There has been a recent trend of challenges to appointments, possibly fuelled by the secrecy of the appointment process.

Panel Members

The Inquiries Act 2005 provides that the process for appointing panel members to a statutory inquiry is as follows:

- The minister must consult the person appointed (or proposed to be appointed) as the chair before appointing any panel member (s 4(3)).
- In making such an appointment, the minister must have regard to the need to ensure the inquiry panel as a whole has the necessary expertise to undertake the inquiry and the need for balance in the composition of the panel (s 8(1)), as well as the assistance that may be provided to the inquiry panel by any assessor whom the minister proposes to appoint, or has appointed (s 8(2)).

There are no specific requirements for non-statutory inquiries.

Similar steps may be taken by the minister and the chair to seek advice on the appointment of panel members as those taken for the chair of the inquiry. Again, as with the position of chair, there is a lack of transparency to the selection process for panel members. This perceived secrecy around appointments means there are sometimes concerns raised, and challenges made, to such appointments.

The decision around appointing a panel is not necessarily one that needs to be taken at the early stages of an inquiry, and it may be one that evolves as an inquiry's work progresses. For example, in the Grenfell Tower Inquiry, the chair sat

[9] Cabinet Office, *Inquiries Guidance: Guidance for inquiry chairs and secretaries, and sponsor departments: Draft version* (2012), available at www.parliament.uk/documents/lords-committees/Inquiries-Act-2005/caboffguide.pdf (accessed 12 August 2020).

alone during phase 1 of the inquiry's proceedings, with panel members not being appointed until phase 2 of the inquiry's work.[10]

Conflicts

An issue that must be considered, both when appointing a chair and panel members to an inquiry, is whether any conflicts of interest exist. Section 9(1) of the Inquiries 2005 Act states that the minister must not appoint a person as a member of the inquiry panel:

> … if it appears to the Minister that the person has –
>
> (a) a direct interest in the matters to which the inquiry relates, or
>
> (b) a close association with an interested party,
>
> unless, despite the person's interest or association, his appointment could not reasonably be regarded as affecting the impartiality of the inquiry panel.

Issue – Conflicts and impartiality

In order to establish and maintain public confidence, the choice of chair must be considered carefully. Ensuring that no conflict of interest exists, whether personal or commercial, actual or perceived, will form an important part of that choice. However, this can present a challenge. An experienced and knowledgeable individual, with the necessary status and expertise in an area relevant to the inquiry's subject matter, may often have interests or associations (or both) with particular parties or organisations relevant to the inquiry.

For example, Sir Robert Francis QC and Sir Ian Kennedy QC both chaired health-related public inquiries and both had backgrounds as barristers practising in medical law. In the same way, Lord Laming's background in social care made him a very suitable candidate as chair to the Climbié Inquiry.

The test is often a difficult one to apply: 'a direct interest in the matters to which the inquiry relates, or a close association with an interested party'.[11]

[10] The appointment of one panel member was affected by conflict concerns, which are referred to further below. The son of one of the Grenfell Tower residents who died in the fire sought to judicially review the Prime Minister's decision not to appoint a panel at the outset of the inquiry, although permission to review the decision was refused: *R (on the application of Daniels) v Prime Minister and Another* [2018] EWHC 1090 (Admin).

[11] Inquiries Act 2005, s 9.

How far should this test go, given the need for an inquiry chair to have expertise and knowledge in a particular area in order to be effective?

The application of this test has proved problematic in recent years. For example, the appointment of the chair to the Independent Inquiry into Child Sexual Abuse was beset with problems. The inquiry's subject matter is all-encompassing, involving churches and other religious organisations, the police, prosecuting authorities, prisons, local authorities, politicians, government departments, health services, schools and the armed forces. Therefore identifying an individual who was not conflicted but who had the necessary expertise and the necessary standing to foster public confidence proved difficult.

Although the first choice of chair, Baroness Butler-Sloss, resigned due to ill health, as sister of the former Lord Chancellor, and Attorney General in the 1980s, she faced calls to resign, from the media and victim and survivor groups, due to her links to the establishment. This was despite the fact her background in many ways made her an ideal candidate, being the first female Lord Justice of Appeal and an expert in the field of child protection.

The next appointee, Fiona Woolf, a solicitor and former President of the Law Society and Lord Mayor of London, also faced calls to resign, due to a personal association with the former Home Secretary, Lord Brittan, who was likely to be called by the inquiry to give evidence. She too resigned soon after her appointment.

Dame Lowell Goddard, a New Zealand High Court Judge with no links to the 'British establishment', was appointed as the third chair of the Inquiry, but after serving as chair for 18 months she resigned, citing a 'legacy of failure which has been very hard to shake off'. Professor Alexis Jay, a social worker and academic, who was already a panel member was subsequently appointed. While many welcomed this appointment, some core participants objected to her appointment on the basis of lack of independence, since the actions of social workers were under the scrutiny of the inquiry.

Lord Leveson's appointment as chair to the Leveson Inquiry was also called into question by the media due to his alleged social connections with News Corporation and the fact he had attended two parties at the home of Rupert Murdoch's son-in-law. Lord Leveson responded to the allegations, setting out in full his contact with relevant individuals, and said:

'I do not believe I have any conflicts of interest that would prevent me from looking at the evidence dispassionately and fairly. However I will declare any conflicts should they arise in the future and willingly withdraw from any necessary hearings.'[12]

[12] The Leveson Inquiry: see http://webarchive.nationalarchives.gov.uk/20140122145147/http:/www.levesoninquiry.org.uk/wp-content/uploads/2011/11/Declaration-Lord-Justice-Leveson.pdf (accessed 12 August 2020).

In June 2017, the decision to appoint Sir Martin Moore-Bick, a retired Court of Appeal judge, to chair the Grenfell Tower Inquiry was met with dismay by some of the survivors and families of the victims of the fire, with one Labour MP questioning the appointment of a 'white, upper-middle class man' who has 'never' visited a tower block.[13] Questions were also raised around a judicial decision made in 2014 by Moore-Bick to allow Westminster council to rehouse a tenant in Milton Keynes, 50 miles away from her home.

The prime minister's appointment of Benita Mehra as a panel member for the Grenfell Tower Inquiry in late 2019 was also met with controversy due to her former role as chair of the Women's Engineering Society. The Society had accepted funding from the charitable arm of the organisation that had made the cladding that was blamed for accelerating the spread of the fire at Grenfell Tower, with this organisation also being a core participant to the inquiry. The perceived conflict and concern around this, along with widespread media scrutiny, ultimately led to her resignation.

The question of conflicts can mean that an individual who is extremely well suited and experienced for the role is challenged due to a perceived bias or interest. The likelihood is, no matter who is appointed, questions may be raised by some interested party or the media.

Ultimately public confidence in the chair who is appointed is key. This adds a further dimension to the appointments process.

The guidance for making chair and panel member appointments is very limited. While there are no defined factors that must be taken into account when appointing a chair or panel members, there are certain practical factors that are likely to be given consideration:

Considerations for choosing the right chair

- The experience and knowledge of potential candidates; can any gaps in experience be filled by the expertise of assessors, experts or panel members?
- Is there feedback from others as to their suitability?

[13] Laura Hughes, 'Grenfell row as Labour MP suggests "white, upper-middle class man" should not have been hired to lead inquiry' *The Telegraph* (2 July 2017) <www.telegraph.co.uk/news/2017/07/02/labour-mp-suggests-white-upper-middle-class-grenfell-judge-has/> (accessed 12 August 2020).

- Should other parties be formally consulted and the extent to which this could lead to delay?
- Does the candidate have the time (and willingness) to devote to what is usually a huge undertaking?
- Is the candidate able to take, and be seen to take, a fully detached view of the subject matter, ie not to predetermine the outcome?
- Is the candidate considered to be independent and politically neutral?
- Can the candidate cope with being in the public eye?
- Should the chair be a judicial appointment (see further below)?
- Does the candidate have experience of managing a team and a budget?
- Does the candidate have experience of dealing with the media and managing public relations?
- Does the candidate need to have a detailed understanding of the structure and workings of the Whitehall machine?
- And are all these elements essential, or can the chair be supported by experienced panel members and a well-equipped legal and administrative team?

Issue – Should the chair be a judicial appointment?

There has been some debate over the years as to whether or not appointing a serving or retired judge to chair an inquiry is always the right approach.

For the majority of inquiries, both statutory and non-statutory, a serving or former judge or a very senior barrister has been appointed as chair. For example, the Grenfell Tower Inquiry (retired Court of Appeal Judge, Sir Martin Moore-Bick), Undercover Policing Inquiry (retired High Court Judge, Sir John Mitting, who took over the role from retired Lord Justice Pitchford) and the Litvinenko Inquiry (retired High Court Judge, Sir Robert Owen).

One can understand why such appointments have been made. An inquiry involves collating, analysing and digesting huge volumes of evidence and distilling all of that evidence down into a series of conclusions and recommendations. An inquiry chair also has to deal daily with various legal issues, apply legislative provisions and make rulings on such issues, for example immunities from suit, anonymity applications, threats of judicial review and privilege issues. An inquiry chair is also responsible for ensuring the inquiry's work is conducted fairly and transparently and ensuring the principles of natural justice are upheld at all times. This would all be second nature to a judge or legally trained individual. Any lack of knowledge or experience in a particular field can be addressed by appointing suitably experienced panel members, assessors or experts to assist the chair.

Other inquiries have been well served by non-judicial or non-legal chairs. For example, Lord Bichard (a former senior civil servant) chaired the Soham Inquiry and the current chair of the Independent Inquiry into Child Sexual Abuse (Alexis Jay OBE) has a background in social care and academia. There is an argument that an inquiry could be just as well, if not better, served by a chair who has relevant expertise and experience in the subject matter of the inquiry, and who is supported by a strong legal team. Unlike judges or legally trained chairs, a 'lay' chair may also be more able to adopt a non-adversarial and inquisitorial approach.

The appointment of a judicial or non-judicial chair will depend on the inquiry in question, as well as, from a practical point of view, the candidates who are available and willing to make the huge commitment required.

Speed of the Appointment Process

Despite the choice of chair being critical to the success of the inquiry, the selection process and announcement of the chair has typically been carried out in alarming haste.

Quote

'Like most chairmen, I had the experience of being phoned up out of the blue and asked to decide within an hour whether I would like to chair the inquiry because the Minister was in a hurry to make an announcement ...'

Sir Robert Francis QC, Chair to the Mid Staffordshire NHS Foundation Trust Public Inquiry, giving evidence to the House of Lords Select Committee on the Inquiries Act 2005

> Sir John Chilcot, when asked by the Foreign Affairs Select Committee on 4 February 2015 how long he had to accept the invitation to chair the Iraq Inquiry:
>
> '*Ten minutes.*'
>
> '*I was phoned at about 8.30pm to be told that the Secretary of State was delighted that I had agreed to take on this inquiry, which I might say left me with little room to negotiate.*'
>
> Professor Sir Ian Kennedy QC, Chair to the Public Inquiry into Children's Heart Surgery at Bristol Royal Infirmary, in evidence to the House of Lords Select Committee on the Inquiries Act 2005

Section 6 of the Inquiries Act 2005 provides that, when convening a public inquiry, the minister must make a statement to Parliament to that effect, 'as soon as is reasonably practicable'. This statement must also specify who has been appointed as chair and whether the minister has, or proposes to appoint, any other members to the panel. In 2014, the Government agreed to amend section 6[14] so that the announcement of the inquiry and the name of the chair (and, where appropriate, panel members) need not necessarily be made within the same statement, conceding that there is much to be said for a process that is less rushed. Although not yet formalised, this change to procedure has already been adopted. In June and July 2017 respectively, the prime minister announced that a public inquiry would be held into the Grenfell Tower fire and the contaminated blood scandal. Neither statement included an announcement of the name of the chair. While this approach may relax timescales somewhat, mounting public pressure for action when a public inquiry is announced may still, on occasions, result in the selection process taking place over a very short period of time. In the case of the Infected Blood Inquiry, however, the announcement of the chair came some seven months after the original announcement of the inquiry.

Issues for the Chair on Appointment

Once a chair is appointed, time may be of the essence. There is often significant political pressure placed on the chair to get started and show that progress is being made. The campaign for an inquiry may have been ongoing for years; once an inquiry has been announced, swift progress will then be expected to avoid any loss of momentum.

[14] Although the amendments have yet to be formalised.

The key steps taken by the chair in the early stages may include:

- Drafting the terms of reference (if not already in place)
- Appointing inquiry team members: it is customary for a chair to appoint counsel to the inquiry and to be consulted on other appointments, such as secretary to the inquiry, solicitor to the inquiry, assessors and any other person engaged to provide administrative, legal or managerial assistance
- Consulting with the minister over the appointment of panel members, if any
- Understanding the budget and guidelines relating to the budget
- Team planning meetings and agreeing responsibilities of team members
- Detailed analysis of the terms of reference (see further below)
- Identifying IT requirements for document management and file management, the inquiry website, simultaneous transmission of proceedings, live transcription and broadcasting and other IT requirements; managing procurement
- Initiating the search for suitable venues (see chapter three); ideally it is desirable to have the office and hearing venues located together
- Considering whether further staff appointments are needed (eg technical support, media officer and support staff)
- Once the office venue has been located, overseeing office set-up: IT systems, telephone, email, PO box, furniture, stationery, building security, scanners
- Preparing inquiry protocols (ie the rules by which the inquiry's work will be governed) (see chapter five)
- Identifying likely core participants and interested parties and key groups of witnesses; meeting with key individuals and organisations to seek to open strong lines of communication and build rapport and trust at an early stage
- Arranging for all key individuals and bodies to be contacted and asked to preserve all documents and records that may be relevant to the inquiry's terms of reference
- Setting up any witness support that may be needed (see chapter ten)
- Further planning or progress meetings
- Seeking advice on any initial complex legal issues
- Once the office set up is complete, and protocols drafted and signed off, arranging a preliminary hearing to formally open the inquiry
- Preparing a draft internal timetable

Consultation and Focus on the Terms of Reference

The precise terms of reference of an inquiry are crucially important. The terms of reference are an inquiry's mandate. They define the breadth and complexity of the inquiry's work and are also often used by the chair to defend against any calls for the scope of the inquiry to be widened, or in some cases to justify the breadth of its work. The usual tension that arises is from campaign groups lobbying for broader terms of reference, although the inevitable consequence of setting broad terms of reference is that the inquiry will take much more time to complete its work and, as a result, it will cost a lot more.

The interpretation of the terms of reference is as important as the original wording. An inquiry and its stakeholders must be clear about exactly what the inquiry is empowered to investigate and this must remain consistent throughout, in order to keep timescales and budget on track. A number of inquiries have prepared a 'list of issues' document to assist with this.[15] A list of issues is often used to outline how the chair or panel have interpreted the scope of the terms of reference and will provide an indication of the issues that the inquiry will be focused on.

Section 5(6) of the Inquiries Act 2005 sets out what the terms of reference must include for statutory inquiries. Although the terms of reference of many inquiries include a requirement to make recommendations, this is not a requirement under the Act.

In the past, the minister has usually drafted the terms of reference, perhaps with input from the chair. By virtue of s 5(4) of the Act, before setting out or amending the terms of reference the minister must consult the chair.

> **Quote**
>
> *'Usually, the Chair's input is taken into account when designing an inquiry's terms of reference; it is desirable for this to happen before any are published. It is very difficult if the Chair does not know what lies behind the terms of reference, and what the implications are.'*
>
> Sir Robert Francis QC, Chair of the Mid Staffordshire NHS Foundation Trust Public Inquiry

In theory, there is time between the appointment of the chair and the announcement of the terms of reference for discussions and consultation to take place with the chair and with those most closely affected by the subject matter of the inquiry.

[15] For example, a list of issues has been used by the Grenfell Tower Inquiry, Undercover Policing Inquiry and Infected Blood Inquiry.

In practice, in the past, consultation with the chair has often taken place before the chair has had the opportunity to make more than a cursory consideration of very limited material because the minister has been under intense public and political pressure to announce the terms of reference quickly. While some inquiries, such as the Foot and Mouth Inquiry,[16] had a period of consultation with those closely affected by the subject matter of the inquiry, others, such as the Iraq Inquiry,[17] had no consultation at all. It could be argued that if the government has decided that it intends to set up an inquiry, decisions around the limits of that inquiry have already been made, even if a level of consultation takes place later.

That said, in recent years there has been a shift towards wider public consultation on an inquiry's terms of reference. The Grenfell Tower Inquiry[18] has seen both a period of consultation with the chair and with the public, as has the Infected Blood Inquiry. In both inquiries the consultation was open to the public, not only those most closely affected by the subject matter of the inquiry. Public consultation on the terms of reference is also something that is being seen with non-statutory independent inquiries, such as the Independent Inquiry into Telford Child Sexual Exploitation, established by Telford & Wrekin Council. Such an approach can provide for greater public support for an inquiry and its work because there has been an opportunity to influence its scope. It may be that this will set a precedent for wider consultation for future inquiries.

The importance of the terms of reference cannot be overstated. If they are unclear or too wide, the inquiry may end up delivering recommendations that do not address the essential issues, as well as significantly increasing the cost and duration of the inquiry. But if they are too narrow, the inquiry will not have the scope necessary to deal with all relevant issues. It may also appear that the government is attempting to deflect criticism or avoid difficult political issues by restricting the scope of the inquiry.

> **Quote**
>
> When speaking to the BBC, Lord Butler, who headed up the non-statutory inquiry into intelligence on weapons of mass destruction, stated that governments, when setting up inquiries of this sort:
>
> *'try to satisfy everybody ... They do not want to be seen to be restricting anything, which can, or does, lead to great problems.'*

[16] Inquiry into the Foot and Mouth epidemic of 2001: see http://webarchive.nationalarchives.gov.uk/20100702215127/http://archive.cabinetoffice.gov.uk/fmd/ (accessed 12 August 2020).

[17] The Iraq Inquiry: see http://www.iraqinquiry.org.uk/ (accessed 12 August 2020).

[18] The Grenfell Tower Inquiry: see https://www.grenfelltowerinquiry.org.uk/ (accessed 12 August 2020).

He concluded that, when pressing for a public inquiry with a wide remit, people need to be mindful of unforeseen consequences.

'The essential beginning of a public inquiry is to state what it is not about as importantly as what it is about.'

Professor Sir Ian Kennedy QC, in evidence to the House of Lords Select Committee on the Inquiries Act 2005

'Not fixing the Terms of Reference sufficiently precisely can have a severe knock on effect. It is absolutely key to get it right – both the drafting, and the interpretation as to what the Terms mean.'

Nicholas Griffin QC, QEB Hollis Whiteman

Counsel to the Inquiry

The vast majority of inquiries, both statutory and non-statutory, appoint counsel. Counsel is invariably a senior barrister, or barristers, who are appointed to provide legal advice to the chair and question witnesses. Counsel is often the first appointment to be made by the chair.

Quote

'... the reason why it is wise to have counsel to an inquiry is that if the chair starts asking all the questions, there is a real risk that at some point he or she is going to look parti pris. It is much better for the counsel to have that much distance from the chair.'

Sir Stephen Sedley QC, in evidence given to the House of Lords Select Committee on the Inquiries Act 2005

Appointment of Counsel

The Inquiry Rules 2006 define counsel to the inquiry as 'the qualified lawyer or lawyers, if any, appointed by the chairman to act as counsel'.[19] However, neither the Inquiry Rules 2006 nor the Inquiries Act 2005 prescribe how counsel should

[19] Inquiry Rules 2006, r 2.

be appointed, and there are no defined criteria to take into account when making such an appointment.

In practice this appointment is made by the chair, occasionally with recommendations having been put forward by the sponsoring department. Many chairs will appoint someone either with whom they are familiar (and therefore someone they know they can work with), or someone who is a leading barrister in the field of work relevant to the inquiry's subject matter.

Issue – Independence and choice of counsel

One contentious issue relates to the possible involvement of the minister in the choice of counsel. Many argue that, for reasons of independence, the chair and only the chair should appoint counsel to the inquiry. This recommendation was rejected by the Government in its response to the Report of the House of Lords Select Committee on the Inquiries Act 2005 on the basis that 'ministers will want to retain control of such issues which affect departmental budgets and the terms of reference of an inquiry'.[20] This raises concerns that this is another example of the potential for political interference in the independent public inquiry process.

That said, the government does have legal panels in place; appointments to these panels are regularly reviewed, with the quality of the panellists' work assessed and rates negotiated. Potentially, a minister could restrict a chair's choice to barristers on the relevant legal panel. As an inquiry is paid for by the public purse, costs control issues will come into play.

Quote

Sir Robert Francis QC, chair of the Mid Staffordshire NHS Foundation Trust Inquiry, agrees that the current approach works:

'I would be reluctant to restrain the Chair in relation to choice of Counsel. It is such a personal appointment. You are talking about a personal advisor. To have someone imposed would create an entirely different relationship. To prohibit a connection between the Chair and Counsel would be unfortunate.'

[20] Ministry of Justice, Government Response to the *Report of the House of Lords Select Committee on the Inquiries Act 2005* (Cm 8093, 2014).

Others have also stressed the importance of a good working relationship:

'It is important that the Chairman and Counsel work well together and there is mutual respect.'

Nicholas Griffin QC, QEB Hollis Whiteman

'One of the most important decisions the Chair/Panel makes is the selection of the lead Counsel to the Inquiry. If the choice is a good one and, perhaps more importantly, if the working relationship between them is a strong one, the hearings run more efficiently and more effectively.'

Rory Phillips QC, 3 Verulam Buildings

Role of Counsel

The role of counsel to an inquiry and the level of their workload depends heavily on the nature of the legal support provided, and the size of that team. However, set out below are the tasks that counsel will usually be responsible for during the course of an inquiry.

Checklist – Counsel to the Inquiry's role

- Advising the chair on legal issues (such as threats of judicial review, evidential issues, and applications for anonymity).
- Reviewing of evidence in advance of hearings and analysing the evidence.
- Formulating lists of issues for the hearings and questions for witnesses as the inquiry progresses.
- Advocacy and the examination of witnesses during the oral hearings, including delivering opening and closing statements and final submissions.
- Responding to applications received from core participants and interested parties, including proposed questions submitted and deciding on what is appropriate.
- Drafting copies of the chair's decisions or restriction notices, although the solicitor to the inquiry and their team may also take on this responsibility (see below).

- Liaising with the core participants or interested parties and their legal representatives on a daily basis at the hearings.
- Assisting with the warning letter process, including identifying proposed criticisms and advising on responses to such letters.
- Assisting the chair with the drafting of the report.

Appointment of the Solicitor to the Inquiry

The next appointment for the chair to consider is that of the solicitor to the inquiry and their team. In some circumstances, an inquiry will also appoint a named deputy solicitor.

For a statutory inquiry, the Inquiry Rules 2006 state that the 'solicitor to the inquiry' means the qualified lawyer (or other person certified by the Head of the Government Legal Service as suitable) appointed by the chairman to act as solicitor.[21] There are no other provisions or requirements related to the appointment of the solicitor to the inquiry.

As with the appointment of counsel to the inquiry, the appointment is at the chair's discretion. However, as counsel to the inquiry is often appointed first, counsel will usually be heavily involved in the appointment process for the solicitor to the inquiry, or a lawyer may be seconded into the role from the Government Legal Department. The solicitor to the inquiry and their team will have to work closely with counsel to the inquiry over many months and therefore it is important that they work well together. For example, the knowledge and information gained during evidence gathering (including the review of disclosure, taking evidence from witnesses and during the hearings) has to be continually shared between the two teams. Consistent information must be provided by both teams to core participants, interested parties and their legal teams, and IT systems must be shared and managed together.

Quote

'The personalities and skills of the Chair, Counsel and Solicitor are important. They need to think independently but to work together as a team. When that doesn't happen, inquiries become dysfunctional.'

Peter Skelton QC, One Crown Office Row

[21] Inquiry Rules 2006, r 2.

The legal team supporting the solicitor to the inquiry will usually be substantial in size, and the work they are undertaking (as set out below) will need to be constantly managed as the evidence develops and the work of the inquiry progresses. This team may be a team of junior barristers, a team of solicitors, or a combination of the two.

Checklist – Solicitor to the inquiry's role

- Assisting with and contributing to the set-up of the inquiry, including designing and managing the IT systems and the office and hearing room set up.
- Assisting the chair in drafting the inquiry's protocols and key documents.
- Establishing contact with key individuals and groups, and establishing working relationships.
- Gathering the evidence: documents and witness statements.
- Reviewing and analysing documents for relevance.
- Managing the statement-taking process, including locating witnesses, taking evidence and preparing statements (see chapter ten).
- Instructing experts (see chapter twelve).
- Liaising and corresponding on a daily basis with participants, including core participants, interested parties and their legal representatives, witnesses, experts and media representatives. Dealing with issues of disclosure, managing applications made, timetabling witnesses, dealing with any queries, and managing contact with all potential witnesses.
- Advising the chair on legal issues and research.
- Assisting the secretary to the inquiry in dealing with applications for costs and expenses.
- Preparing documents for counsel in advance of hearings and assisting counsel before and during oral hearings.
- Responding to applications received from core participants and interested parties.
- Managing and designing the rolling timetable of evidence, both for disclosure and oral hearings.
- Drafting copies of the chair's decisions or restriction notices (although counsel to the inquiry may take on this responsibility).
- Assisting the chair with the warning letter process.
- Assisting the chair with drafting the report.
- Assisting with publication of the report and the lock-in procedures.

- Advising on 'closing down' the inquiry, and managing the archiving process (see chapter fifteen).
- Taking responsibility for decision logs, risk logs and performing project management tasks.

Appointment of the Secretary to the Inquiry

Another key appointment is the secretary to the inquiry.

Rule 2 of the Inquiry Rules 2006 states that the 'secretary to the inquiry' means 'a person appointed by the chairman to carry out (with the assistance of any deputies that may be appointed) the administration and management of the inquiry'.

Although the 2006 Rules say that the secretary is appointed by the chair, often this appointment is made by the sponsoring department and will be a senior civil servant of the sponsoring department, seconded to the inquiry. The appointment is usually made right at the outset, shortly after the announcement of the inquiry.

Role of the Secretary to the Inquiry

The role of a secretary to the inquiry varies from inquiry to inquiry. It usually involves managing operational issues, but can also include administrative and management tasks. The scope of the secretary to the inquiry's role is determined at the chair's discretion; it often becomes more established as the inquiry progresses and is influenced by the size and structure of the solicitor to the inquiry's team.

There are instances when the role of the secretary to the inquiry and the solicitor to the inquiry's team can overlap. Often the solicitor to the inquiry's team is expected to take on some of the administrative and management functions of the inquiry, using staff at a suitable level of experience and qualification for the particular tasks. This is partly because it is difficult to separate administrative tasks from the legal processes of evidence gathering and analysis, witness management, and communication with core participants and interested parties. This potential 'overlap' of roles can mean that tasks fall between the gaps, and so the parameters of each role should be discussed and agreed at the outset.

Checklist – The secretary to the inquiry's role

- Acting as the point of liaison between the inquiry and the sponsoring department.
- Establishing an office and hearings venue for the inquiry's work including buildings, security, furniture, stationery, telephones and IT set up.

- Managing the inquiry's budget and expenditure.
- Dealing with applications for costs, expenses and funding, and managing that process.
- Having responsibility for security, health and safety issues and management of the buildings.
- Ensuring the inquiry has sufficient staff and resources to fulfil its terms of reference.
- Advising the chair, counsel to the inquiry and the solicitor to the inquiry and their team on civil service procedures or policies and any impacting legislation.
- Liaising with interested parties and witnesses in order to open strong lines of communication and to build rapport and trust.
- Ensuring the hearings are set up and staffed appropriately on a daily basis.
- Carrying out any other operational or administrative tasks that might be required.
- Contributing to the selection of appropriate expert witnesses by counsel to the inquiry's team and the solicitor to the inquiry's team.

Issue – Independence of the secretary to the inquiry

The secretary to an inquiry's role is to support the chair and the inquiry's work; but they are also the main contact between the sponsoring department and the inquiry. There can be tension between these two roles and, in some inquiries, a perception that this tension gives rise to a conflict of interests.

Quote

'The secretary is, I will say, in the unique position – it may be the chairman is in a similar position as well – of having responsibility to the chairman to deliver the inquiry but also to the Secretary of State as accounting officer, in effect. You have that twin role that you have to fulfil.'

Lee Hughes, an experienced Secretary to inquiries, in evidence to the House of Lords Select Committee on the Inquiries Act 2005

'Secretaries to inquiries are generally found from within the sponsoring department. This has the advantage that the appointee will bring to the inquiry an in-depth understanding of the workings of the department. The disadvantage is the danger of a public perception that the department is able to exercise covert influence on the inquiry. My experience of two inquiries, one non-statutory and one statutory, suggests to me that any such perception would be wholly ill founded: the ability of dedicated civil servants to undertake this sort of role while exercising rigorous independence is worthy of great admiration. However it has to be considered whether it would not be prudent where the sponsoring department is to be scrutinised by the inquiry for the secretary to be found from elsewhere. There is indeed no absolute reason why the secretary should be a civil servant at all, although I for one would regret the loss of professional understanding offered by the present arrangements.'

Sir Robert Francis QC, in evidence to the House of Lords Select Committee on the Inquiries Act 2005[22]

Due to this tension between the secretary to the inquiry's two roles, secretaries should generally not take on any responsibility or role in the compilation of evidence or other areas that might give rise to direct conflicts. Where they do, it can cause problems.[23]

The Inquiry Team: Additional Considerations

The following additional considerations apply to the entire inquiry team, ie the chair, panel members, counsel to the inquiry, the solicitor to the inquiry and their team, the secretary to the inquiry, and administrative staff.

Security Clearance

Prior to individual appointments being made, the chair and sponsoring department have to consider whether security clearance is required for those working

[22] Select Committee on the Inquiries Act 2002, 'Written and Corrected Oral Evidence', available at https://www.parliament.uk/documents/lords-committees/Inquiries-Act-2005/IA_Written_Oral_evidencevol.pdf (accessed 12 August 2020).

[23] This was seen during the Magnox Inquiry, when the inquiry was judicially reviewed in relation to the conduct of the Maxwellisation process. One of the issues challenged was the alleged improper delegation of the drafting of criticisms by inquiry team members, particularly the secretary to the inquiry, who operated on this dual role basis.

on the inquiry, depending on the nature of the inquiry and the material that is likely to be handled during its work. Security clearance authorises an individual to access a defined category, or categories, of sensitive information for a specified purpose, which would otherwise be forbidden. Security clearance applications therefore determine an individual's suitability to work on a particular inquiry that is handling sensitive material.

It is for the sponsoring department to determine what level of clearance is required and the internal process to follow in order to carry out the necessary checks.

The most common form of clearance is 'Security Check' ('SC' or 'SC Cleared'), which is required for people who have substantial access to 'SECRET', or occasional controlled access to 'TOP SECRET', material. However, some inquiries have required those working on the inquiry to be 'Developed Vetting' ('DV' or 'DV Cleared'), which is required for people with substantial unsupervised access to 'TOP SECRET' material.

The level of vetting is selected by reference to the particular role or set of responsibilities that an individual will have. The clearance will usually lapse at the conclusion of that role or responsibility, which will often be at the end of the inquiry. The security clearance process has to be considered at any early stage to avoid any impact on the inquiry's progress, as it can take some months to receive approval, particularly at the higher levels of clearance.

Confidentiality Undertakings

Once all key appointments have been made to the inquiry team, it is important that the inquiry obtains undertakings from each individual who is working for the inquiry, or who has access to its records. This can include any member of the solicitor to the inquiry's team reviewing documentary evidence, administrative assistants, counsel's clerk, and even those providing IT support or the cleaners for the premises where the inquiry is taking place. This process is usually coordinated by the solicitor to the inquiry's team, although, for some inquiries, it has been carried out by the secretary to the inquiry.

The undertakings are designed to protect the confidentiality of the inquiry's work and prevent any leaks of information.

Basic wording along the following lines is often used:

> I ACKNOWLEDGE that all material shown to and provided to me by the [inquiry name] ('the Inquiry') is confidential and, in consideration of the provision of that material to me, agree to take all necessary steps to preserve that confidentiality.
>
> I UNDERTAKE to the Inquiry not to disclose, publish or pass on to any third party the existence of or the content of any information contained within that material shown to me by the Inquiry.

Immunity from Suit

For statutory inquiries, during the operation of the inquiry, members of the inquiry team – that is, the chair, panel members, assessors,[24] counsel to the inquiry, the solicitor to the inquiry and their team, the secretary of the inquiry and any person engaged to provide assistance to an inquiry – will receive immunity from civil proceedings in respect of any act or omission relating to the inquiry's work.[25] The immunity does not exclude judicial review proceedings.[26]

The immunity relates to acts or omissions made in the execution of that person's duty, or in good faith in the purported execution of that duty, during the course of the inquiry.[27]

For the purposes of the law of defamation, absolute privilege is conferred on witnesses giving evidence to a statutory inquiry established under the Inquiries Act 2005, both in statements given in advance of the inquiry and during the oral hearings. It also applies to the statutory inquiry report and any interim report as well as reports of the proceedings before the inquiry, as would be the case if those proceedings were before a UK court.[28]

The same statutory immunity from suit, however, does not apply to those involved in non-statutory inquiries nor inquiries convened under statutes other than the 2005 Act.[29] For those inquiries, such as the Bloody Sunday Inquiry and the Rosemary Nelson Inquiry, immunity from suit was dealt with by way of indemnities being provided by the sponsoring department on an individual inquiry basis.

In terms of defamation, common law principles apply to inquiries that are not convened under the 2005 Act, depending on the nature of the particular inquiry. If an inquiry is deemed to be acting in a manner similar to a court, it may be argued that absolute privilege will apply in the same way as it would to proceedings before a court.[30] Evidence and submissions made to the inquiry will be protected by qualified privilege, although that is forfeited if malice can be proven against the maker of the statement.[31] Other principles, such as Parliamentary privilege, may also apply.

[24] See chapter twelve.

[25] Inquiries Act 2005, s 37(1).

[26] See chapter fourteen in relation to the justiciability of statutory and non-statutory inquiries.

[27] Inquiries Act 2005, s 37(2).

[28] Inquiries Act 2005, s 37(3).

[29] In practice, there are very few inquiries convened by a minister under statutes other than the Inquiries Act 2005: see chapter one.

[30] See the principles developed in Fry LJ in *Munster v Lamb* (1883) 11 QBD 588, 607 (CA); *Dawkins v Lord Rokeby* (1873) LR 8 QB 255 (Exch); and *Royal Aquarium and Summer and Winter Garden Society Ltd v Parkinson* [1892] 1 QB 431, 442 and the discussion in Jason Beer, James Dingemans and Richard Lissack (eds), *Public Inquiries* (Oxford University Press 2011), paras 7.29–7.32.

[31] *Harrocks v Lowe* [1975] AC 135, 149–50.

Specific Training

Once the inquiry team has been appointed, and before the inquiry's work starts in earnest, the chair of the inquiry[32] will consider what training and briefing is required for the inquiry team. In some cases, the inquiry team will include members who are very experienced in working on public inquiries and they may be engaged to deliver training to less experienced members, such as panel members.

Checklist – Internal training provided to the inquiry team

- A whole team briefing on the subject matter of the inquiry, the key background facts and the key individuals and organisations involved with the events being investigated.
- Topic-specific training, for example the relevant constitutional set up of the government structure being examined, or the organisational history of an NHS Trust, care system or military structure
- IT training on inquiry systems.
- Training on working with witnesses, core participants and interested parties.
- Training on working with the media.
- Interviewing skills training.
- Budgeting training.

The Role of the Sponsoring Department

When an inquiry is established, usually a specific government department will be appointed to be the main point of contact or 'lead' for that inquiry. Typically this will be the department with the closest links to the subject matter of the inquiry and will often be the department who first called for an inquiry to be established.

[32] Or, on occasions, also counsel to the inquiry and the solicitor to the inquiry and their teams.

Inquiry	Sponsoring department
The Baha Mousa Inquiry	Ministry of Defence
Mid Staffordshire NHS Foundation Trust Inquiry	Department of Health
Al-Sweady Inquiry	Ministry of Defence
The Azelle Rodney Inquiry	Ministry of Justice
Inquiry into Culture, Practices and Ethics of the Press (Leveson Inquiry)	The Department for Culture, Media and Sport and the Home Office
Litvinenko Inquiry	The Home Office
The Independent Inquiry into Child Sexual Abuse	The Home Office
Infected Blood Inquiry	Cabinet Office[a]

Note
[a] See 'Issue – Where the department with the closest links to the inquiry is itself under scrutiny' below.

The sponsoring department's initial role is to work with the relevant minister to set up the inquiry, for example assisting with steps taken to appoint the chair, allocate the budget, potentially identify a secretary to the inquiry and other staff, and then to support the inquiry throughout its work.

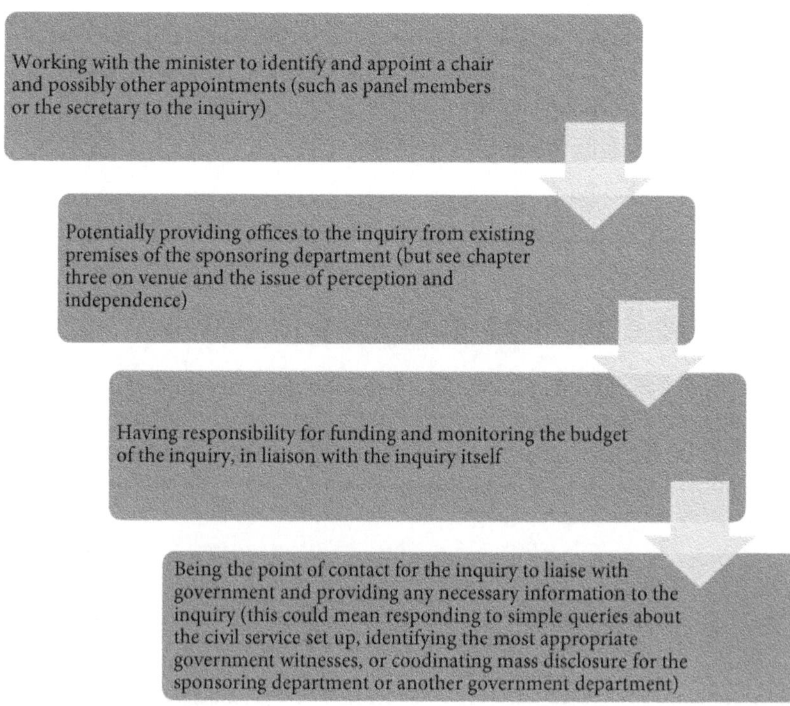

Once those first steps have been taken, the chair has been appointed and the terms of reference agreed, it is then for the inquiry chair to take the decisions about how the inquiry will operate and fulfil its terms of reference (of course within the confines of its powers).

The role of providing support to an inquiry can become blurred and may be called into question if:

- the sponsoring minister, or a member of the sponsoring department, seeks to control or dictate the course that the inquiry takes; and/or
- the sponsoring department finds itself in a position where it is also a party to the inquiry.

Inevitably, both scenarios present a potential conflict of interest problem and issues of perception of independence.

Issue – Sponsoring department and independent management and administration of the inquiry

Issues have occurred where a sponsoring department steers the inquiry's management and direction, rather than leaving this to the control and discretion of the chair.

The Independent Inquiry into Child Sexual Abuse

The Independent Inquiry into Child Sexual Abuse was plagued with problems at its outset, with two chairs resigning in the early stages due to perceived conflicts of interest. However, despite the inquiry seemingly starting afresh with the appointment of Dame Lowell Goddard in February 2015, and being newly constituted as a statutory inquiry in March 2015, the progress of the inquiry unravelled again in August 2016 with the resignation of Dame Goddard. Dame Goddard submitted a report to the House of Commons Home Affairs Committee in September 2016 setting out the reasons for her departure. One reason included:

'*... the Panel and I have had little or no input into either the composition of the senior management team or the recruitment of secretariat staff during the lifetime of the current Inquiry ...*

The administrative arrangements made by the Home Office as the inquiry's sponsor meant that in the recruitment of staff priority was given to civil servants and any non-civil service staff had to become civil servants unless they were employed on contract through the Solicitor to the Inquiry. In practical terms this meant that the skills and qualifications of many recruits did not fit the tasks which they were called upon to perform, as none of the secretariat or senior management team had previous experience of running an inquiry of this nature. Therefore they did not fully understand or appreciate its organisational and operational needs. Their approach has been bureaucratic and the Inquiry's progress has been impeded by a lack of adequate systems and personnel, leading to critical delays.

I felt as Chair handicapped by not being given a free hand to recruit staff of the type that I judged to be essential.'

The Scottish Child Abuse Inquiry

The Scottish Child Abuse Inquiry, set up in October 2015, has also been beset with issues over its independence and allegations of Government interference.

One of the inquiry's panel members, Professor Michael Lamb, resigned on 28 June 2016 stating in his resignation letter as follows:

'it has become increasingly clear over the last nine months that the Panel cannot act independently and that the Scottish Government intends to continue interfering in ways large and small, directly and indirectly. Continuing interference threatens to prevent the Inquiry from investigating thoroughly and taking robust evidence of the highest quality … Crucially, its fact-finding should not be constrained or micro-managed by one of the bodies whose actions or failures to act may ultimately be criticised.

Repeated threats to the Inquiry's independence have undermined the Panel's freedom to address the Terms of Reference and have doomed the Inquiry before the first witness has been heard. The Scottish Government has delayed or prevented the appointment of crucial members of staff for prolonged periods of time while its officials have questioned the decisions made by the supposedly independent Inquiry. As a result of this interference, the Inquiry has been forced to work without the key personnel and resources needed to ensure progress.'

Just a week later, on 4 July 2016, the chair of the inquiry, Susan O'Brien, resigned also citing reasons of government interference. In her letter of resignation, Susan O'Brien was highly critical of the government's attempt to control the inquiry and its work:

'Scottish Government officials have sought to micro-manage and control the Inquiry, and I have resisted this. What Professor Lamb did not say, but he knew, is that my position as the independent Chair of this Inquiry has been actively undermined by some Scottish Government officials over the past months. One even went so far as to threaten what he called "the nuclear option", by which we understood he meant my removal, in January 2016, during a dispute about funding for statement taking …

You have had ample warning of Prof Lamb's and my own concerns about the integrity of the Inquiry process and the need for its structural independence from Government, to ensure that it can consider all matters fearlessly and impartially, even when Government supported institutions might be in line for criticism ... The Inquiry's work has already been hampered by the approach of officials who seem to believe that they can control the Inquiry's decision making, particularly when it relates to proposed expenditure ... This means that the Inquiry cannot carry out its statutory function in a manner which is compatible with the Convention rights of the survivors. Its work will have no value unless it is the product of a truly independent approach to the issues which are articulated in its Terms of Reference ...

In short, I cannot reassure the public that this Inquiry will be conducted independently of Government. My trust that the Scottish Government will actually respect the independence of the Inquiry has gone.'

In both examples above, the true independence of the inquiries have been called into question. The public's expectation is that an inquiry will conduct an independent investigation, devoid of any Government influence or interference. Independence is clearly key to a successful inquiry.

Independence from the sponsoring department is even more important in circumstances where that same department is a core participant or interested party to the inquiry. This has been a common feature in inquiries, with government departments being core participants or interested parties as well as sponsoring departments, such as with the Mid Staffordshire Inquiry, Al-Sweady Inquiry, and the Baha Mousa Inquiry.

Quote

'... in cases where ministerial conduct of the performance of the sponsoring department is likely to come under scrutiny, considerable care needs to be taken over ministerial and departmental contacts. A clear and mutual understanding of the independence of the inquiry is essential.

As the inquiry process is intended to be transparent any briefing should probably be required to be a matter of public record ... It would also assist transparency if the chairman was in a position to be supported by an independent inquiry secretary even at this early stage.'

Sir Robert Francis QC, in evidence to the House of Lords Select Committee on the Inquiries Act 2005[33]

[33] Select Committee on the Inquiries Act 2002, 'Written and Corrected Oral Evidence' (n 22).

As a result of this crossover and potential conflict of interest, extreme care must be taken to ensure that the sponsoring department sets up two individual units to manage its contact with the inquiry: one unit to be the sponsor unit (eg dealing with costs, legal indemnities, arrangements for immunities from suit, arrangements for archiving material at the conclusion of the inquiry etc) and another to be a liaison unit.[34]

Even with such a divide or 'Chinese wall' in place, a sponsoring department has to take great care to ensure that its actions do not call into question the independence of the inquiry (and therefore damage the public's confidence in the effectiveness of the inquiry). Where the sponsoring department is also a core participant or interested party to the inquiry, there must also be an acute awareness that, in its capacity as a party to the inquiry, the sponsoring department is not immune from the consequences of the inquiry. The sponsoring department must assist the inquiry's work in the same way as any other core participant or interested party would do, rather than adopting a passive approach.

Issue – Where the department with the closest links to the inquiry is itself under scrutiny

Following the announcement of the public inquiry into the contaminated blood scandal during the 1970s and 1980s, there were vehement objections from victims and family members to the Department of Health having any involvement in the running of the inquiry, on the basis that the role and actions of the Department in that scandal would themselves be under scrutiny. It was subsequently announced that the Cabinet Office would be taking over the role of sponsoring department for what became the Infected Blood Inquiry.

This is a departure from previous practice and it remains to be seen if this will set a precedent for how such conflicts of interest may be dealt with in the future.

[34] As recommended in the Cabinet Office's draft Inquiries Guidance: Cabinet Office, *Inquiries Guidance* (n 9).

3

Location and Venue

Introduction

In contrast to the court system, there are no permanent venues for public inquiries. While some inquiries are held in court buildings, many are held in government or council buildings, converted offices or other public or privately owned premises. One of the early decisions that a chair of an inquiry has to make is choosing the location where any hearings will be held. The chair must also decide where the inquiry office will be based and where the inquiry will conduct its business. Until the location of the inquiry is agreed, and the premises set up, the inquiry's work cannot start in earnest.

Premises and location

The type of premises chosen, and the reasons behind the choice of location, vary from inquiry to inquiry:

- The Baha Mousa Inquiry, the Al-Sweady Inquiry, the Detainee Inquiry and the Iraq Inquiry (all military-related inquiries) were based in government-owned buildings in London.
- The Mid Staffordshire NHS Foundation Trust Inquiry was based in council offices in Stafford, close to the hospital concerned.
- The E-Coli Inquiry was held in a government-owned building close to the location of the e-coli outbreak.
- The Leveson Inquiry was based in the Royal Courts of Justice in London.
- The Independent Jersey Care Inquiry was located in a privately-owned building (there had been a decision not to use States of Jersey premises given that the subject matter of the inquiry included allegations of state cover up).
- The Grenfell Tower Inquiry moved location part way through its work. Many of those most affected by the fire originally wanted the inquiry to be held at Notting Hill Town Hall, but this was considered by the inquiry to be too small. The Inquiry was therefore first located at Holborn Bars in London, a business centre close to the Royal Courts

of Justice. However, after Phase 1 of the inquiry was completed, the inquiry moved to a venue closer to Paddington, in West London, for Phase 2 of its work. This followed representations from the bereaved, survivors and residents of Grenfell Tower, who wanted the inquiry to be located closer to the site of the Tower, in a place more convenient for travel and with better facilities.

- The Infected Blood Inquiry is holding its hearings at venues across major cities in the UK. For example, in Belfast, Edinburgh, Leeds, London and Cardiff, reflecting the Chair's commitment to ensure that those affected, from all over the country, should have the opportunity to be heard.

Geographical Location

The first question for an inquiry to determine is whether there is an obvious geographical location where the inquiry should be held.

Quote

'It might be necessary to have an inquiry closer to the location of an accident or incident. That might make it easier for witnesses to be there. It might be necessary for people on the panel to visit, as compared to having a location in central London. All that will vary depending on the circumstances.'

Shailesh Vara MP, in evidence given to the House of Lords Select Committee on the Inquiries Act 2005[1]

Unless there is a good reason not to,[2] inquiries into disasters are widely held in a location close to the scene of the events that are the subject matter of the inquiry, to facilitate attendance by survivors, victims and families of those affected. The public inquiry into the Manchester Arena terror attack and the Edinburgh Tram Inquiry are just two examples of inquiries that have based themselves close to the site of the events in question. Equally, one could argue that holding the inquiry close to the area that has been affected by the issues in question sets the right tone, rather than the inquiry basing itself in an 'ivory tower' headquarters in London.

[1] Select Committee on the Inquiries Act 2005, 'Written and Corrected Oral Evidence', available at http://www.parliament.uk/documents/lords-committees/Inquiries-Act-2005/IA_Written_Oral_evidencevol.pdf (accessed 12 August 2020).

[2] For example security considerations relating to the chair, witnesses and in particular those giving evidence anonymously.

On the other hand, if the inquiry is looking into questions of government conduct or policy-based issues, it is probably appropriate to hold hearings at a central location in London,[3] given the proximity to documents and the personnel of relevant government departments or other bodies. But again, if there is no particular pull towards the capital, premises outside London are likely to be much less expensive and therefore the inquiry may consider basing itself at a central location in a large city, such as Birmingham or Manchester, where travel links are good and premises are cheaper.

In some circumstances (if, for example, hearings are not required), and a number of locations are affected by the subject matter of the inquiry, the chair might even consider travelling to all cities and larger towns affected, to allow full participation. It will be important to consider whether this will be viable from the perspective of cost before making this decision. The Truth Project, which is part of the Independent Inquiry into Child Sexual Abuse, offers victims and survivors the opportunity to share their experiences confidentially with the inquiry. It has held sessions at various venues across the country. The Infected Blood Inquiry is also holding hearings at venues across the UK, to ensure full participation is possible for those most affected.

Whilst the issue of cost is very important when selecting a location for the inquiry's work, and the chair is required to avoid unnecessary costs when making decisions,[4] it is important that the location does not set the wrong tone for the inquiry and thereby lose public confidence.

Choosing the Right Type of Premises

In recent years, inquiries have sought to use cabinet office premises or government-owned buildings to house their work, in order to save costs. The buildings are not purpose built for an inquiry, but this may still, on the face of it, be an attractive option.

Some have suggested that the use of existing government buildings can bring with it the benefit of using associated supporting infrastructure, including IT systems, security vetting (eg swipe card access, protected entrances), press office, access to existing contracts at preferential rates (eg cleaning and catering contracts), access to resources such as graphic design and assistance with production of the final report, and access to finance systems.[5] Similarly, it may make good financial sense to make use of existing, purpose-built courtrooms.

For some inquiries, existing government offices or courtrooms are viable options. However, there are a number of potentially very significant issues when

[3] For example, the statutory Undercover Policing Inquiry.

[4] Inquiries Act 2005, s 17.

[5] See Michael Collins, supplemental written evidence to the Lords Select Committee on the Inquiries Act 2005 (n 1), para 8.

using courtrooms, or government buildings which, on occasions, may make the use of other types of premises, such as office buildings, more appropriate.

The first consideration is what a particular building represents. A courtroom is an adversarial environment, often associated with criminal trials, whereas an inquiry should be, and should be seen to be, inquisitorial in nature. A courtroom may make witnesses uncomfortable and less likely to give open and frank evidence for fear of assumed personal repercussions. A courtroom may also create an environment that feels intimidating, overly formal and closely associated with the exercise of power and the establishment. This will be particularly inappropriate if the focus of an inquiry is the scrutiny of the role and exercise of power by the establishment. Similarly, the use of government buildings may damage the perception of impartiality.

> **Quote**
>
> *'Incidentally, if I could just make one practical point, and it is very much a practical point, it was something that I learnt from Lord Scarman. I appeared in front of him in the Brixton inquiry in the early 1980s. In one of my discussions with him he said, "One of the important things you should do if you are doing a commission of inquiry is not sit in a courtroom. Try to find a public building that sends out a message to the public that this is an inquiry for them. It is not a piece of litigation". It is very important and I think he held all his inquiries in public buildings.'*
>
> Sir Louis Blom-Cooper QC, in evidence to the House of Lords Select Committee on the Inquiries Act 2005

The second consideration relates to its utility. The chair of an inquiry needs to think carefully about what is required from the premises.

- The needs of an inquiry will change as an inquiry progresses, for example, its requirements when carrying out document analysis and review are different to those once the oral hearings start.
- IT systems and other electronic facilities (including internet access) in the premises must be suitable for the needs of the inquiry.
- The premises must be adequately cabled, or capable of being so at little expense.
- There must be sufficient and secure document storage space.
- It may be that additional premises will be needed for a variety of purposes, such as holding meetings, carrying out witness interviews, providing prayer facilities and witness support services, or in order to allow participants to maintain anonymity.

- The premises should be located close to the area where the likely witnesses to the inquiry live. If not, additional travel costs will be incurred (and see additional considerations below).
- Where possible, the office facilities for the inquiry team should be located on the same premises as the hearing room. Before, during and after hearings, there is constant interaction between the various members of the inquiry team (eg counsel to the inquiry's team, the solicitor to the inquiry's team and the secretary to the inquiry) to ensure the smooth operation of the hearings and to share information as necessary. Being located in the same building makes that process much easier.

Government-owned buildings can be altered and arrangements made to meet the needs of an inquiry. However, all of these alterations and arrangements of course cost money. Using a government-owned building that would need major alterations to house the inquiry and its team may in fact be a false economy.

Summary – Choice of premises and location

- If possible, an inquiry should be located as close as possible to the geographical area in which those affected by the subject matter of the inquiry live.
- It should be convenient to reach by public transport.
- A courtroom environment should be avoided where possible
- Buildings or premises associated with a particular body or organisation that may be subject to scrutiny during the course of the inquiry, including government departments, should be avoided.
- The premises must have adequate facilities to meet the needs of the inquiry through the various stages of its work.
- Where possible, the office facilities for the inquiry team should be located in the same premises as the hearing room.

What to Expect from the Inquiry Premises

Inquiry premises vary considerably from one inquiry to another, depending on the size, nature and subject matter of the inquiry. Lists of the facilities that inquiries typically require in order to carry out their business are set out below.

It is not always possible to find ideal premises in the preferred geographical location. Some inquiries use designers and architects to reconfigure and redesign entire floors of buildings to meet the needs of an inquiry. Others may have to find alternative solutions to meet their needs.

An inquiry may provide all or only some of the facilities within the following lists.

The hearing room

- A large hearing room (with easy access to the office accommodation where the legal and secretarial teams will work) large enough to accommodate the anticipated number of inquiry personnel and visitors, including:
  - core participants (and any representatives permitted for each core participant);
  - members of the public;
  - members of the media;
  - panel members and assessors;
  - counsel to the inquiry team;
  - the solicitor to the inquiry, or a note taker on their behalf;
  - stenographer to transcribe the proceedings.
- A 'witness box' for witnesses who giving oral evidence that allows for screens to provide anonymity if necessary.
- A separate meeting room for the panel, where space allows. Alternatively the chair and panel members' offices might be used as space for meetings.
- A reception area large enough for witnesses or parties attending hearings for use on arrival and during break times
- Where inquiry witnesses are likely to be granted anonymity, private rooms and private entrances and exits will be required, away from the public areas. This is to avoid them being seen by the public at the inquiry premises and risk them being identified inadvertently (see below).
- Rooms adjacent to the hearing room for the core participants and their legal representatives to meet.
- Water and tea or coffee making facilities for witnesses and the public.
- Security arrangements for entry to the hearing room. (The inquiry team often has access to unredacted documents in the hearing room. When hearings are not running, the hearing room will usually be secured to prevent access to confidential and privileged material.)
- Hearing room equipped with a hearing loop and any other facilities required to make it accessible to disabled users.
- Hearing room located in premises close to public transport and car parking facilities.
- Video-link facilities.

Configuration of the hearing room

- The hearing room should provide an inquisitorial rather than adversarial feel; this may be achieved by, for example:
  - using a semi-circular layout;
  - positioning witnesses as the central focus of the room;
  - avoiding seating the chair and panel behind a high desk or bench (as would usually be the case in a courtroom).
- Seat friends, family (or other witness support) and the public in the eye-line of the witnesses.
- Carefully consider the positioning of core participants within the hearing room (eg avoid seating survivors and victims next to alleged perpetrators).
- Choose appropriate office equipment, furniture and IT facilities for the specific needs of the inquiry.
- Use of colours and symbols should be considered carefully as some might cause offence or create inadvertent associations.
- Provide an opportunity for witnesses to visit the hearing room in advance of giving evidence, to allow them to familiarise themselves with the set-up of the room.
- Provide public access to electronic screens displaying the inquiry documents.

Professor Sir Ian Kennedy provided a detailed explanation of the design and planning that went into the layout for the Bristol Royal Infirmary in his published lecture 'Public Inquiries: Experiences from the Bristol Public Inquiry' in J Carrier and others (eds), *Law, Medicine and Ethics: Essays in Honour of Lord Jakobovits* (Cancerkin 2007).

Office accommodation

The following office accommodation will be required:

- Separate offices for the chair and panel members.
- An office for counsel to the inquiry (and their team).
- Offices for the inquiry solicitor's team and supporting staff. Legal teams are often large; in some cases an inquiry may have to accommodate teams with in excess of 30 staff outside the hearing room environment.

- An office for the secretary to the inquiry (and their team).
- Other staff involved with an inquiry might include a media team, IT specialists, researchers and legal costs draftsman. In some cases, staff within these categories are not present at the inquiry's offices every day and therefore allocated desk space is not required.
- Spare offices for witness interviews, team meetings, and quiet work space for members of the inquiry solicitor's team if an open plan environment is used.
- Secure office accommodation and working areas, with security restrictions to ensure the public do not have access to confidential inquiry documents. Individual offices and desk drawers in open plan areas must be locked when not in use.
- Separate rooms for certain categories of core participants and witnesses (see below).
- A dedicated room for use by the media (see below).
- A secure document room and storage facilities.
- General office space to house printers, photocopiers, scanners, shredders, confidential waste bins, stationery, and general storage cupboards.
- A suitable kitchen or refreshment area and toilets.
- A family room for young children.
- Facilities for members of the inquiry team to use for secure storage, shredding and disposing of confidential material.

Separation of Certain Categories of Core Participants and Witnesses

Some inquiries provide rooms for core participants to use during breaks in the hearings. This can be useful for core participants who wish to prepare for hearings and for legal representatives who need to take instructions from their clients.

An inquiry may consider it necessary, because of the subject matter of the inquiry, for different categories of core participants to have separate rooms; for example survivors and families and those they may regard responsible for the matters under investigation. Keeping parties separated can avoid potential conflict and allow open discussions to take place without fear of offence or confrontation.

However, an inquiry's ability to offer separate rooms depends on the space available. During the Mid Staffordshire NHS Foundation Trust Inquiry, there were only two such rooms available: one for the victims' families and patient support groups and the second for all other core participants. During the Leveson Inquiry[6] a number of individual rooms were provided for the core participants to allow them to prepare for the hearings. The venue at which the Grenfell Tower Inquiry has been held during Phase 2 of its work includes a separate screening room to view the hearings, a quiet room and two conference rooms for the bereaved, survivors and residents and their legal representatives, and a general room with desks and chairs for all other core participants.

Where witnesses have been granted anonymity, an inquiry will usually put separate arrangements in place to ensure that their identities are not revealed. Again, the detail of those arrangements depends on the particular premises being used by the inquiry, but the key driver is to prevent witnesses from being seen by the public, media and core participants. For example, during the Independent Jersey Care Inquiry, a concealed entrance on a separate floor to the main entrance was used for witnesses who had been granted anonymity, so that they could enter and exit the building. A separate room (within the inquiry team's office accommodation, which was not accessible nor visible to the public) was used by those witnesses prior to the hearing and during breaks.

Facilities for the Press and Broadcast Media

In recent years, as the number of public inquiries has increased, so has the degree of media scrutiny. An inquiry can expect a media presence during at least part of the inquiry's proceedings, in particular at the commencement of the inquiry and when the report is published. In some cases, there will be a media presence throughout (eg during the Leveson Inquiry and the Independent Inquiry into Child Sexual Abuse).

An inquiry's work is clearly of public interest and, where a public inquiry's proceedings are held in public, in whole or in part, they should by their very nature be accessible to the public and media. Inquiries therefore need to make provision for members of the media during their hearings.

Such provision might include a dedicated media room, equipped with desks for working; plenty of power sockets for charging laptops and electronic devices; wifi access; and electronic screens displaying the live transmission of proceedings. (This also gives the advantage that a public gallery will then be just that, for the public, rather than all seats being occupied by members of the media.)

Many inquiries issue regular press releases and appoint dedicated media officers to assist with media inquiries. At the same time, however, it is important that the inquiry strikes a balance and ensures that the media is not provided with better facilities or assistance than the core participants (such as survivors and their families) or given preferential treatment. Some inquiries provide facilities for social media journalists.

[6] Held at the Royal Courts of Justice.

While making provision for the media, care must also be taken to manage its presence. Inquiries often deal with sensitive issues that are difficult for victims and families to deal with; often professional reputations will be at stake and witnesses may be nervous about giving evidence. Media intrusion can make this process more difficult and an inquiry should ensure that media access is appropriately managed. Some inquiries issue a specific protocol setting out the inquiry's expectations of the media; explaining who would be included in the definition of 'the media' (eg whether bloggers will fall within this definition); and the access that the media can expect to be granted by the inquiry (see further chapter five).

Venue Set-Up

Once suitable premises for the inquiry's work have been identified, the secretary to the inquiry and the solicitor to the inquiry will coordinate the set up of the premises. The requirements will depend on the nature and size of the inquiry, but below are a list of steps that are likely to be required to get the premises functioning:

- Register web domain name
- Establish email addresses using the same domain name as the website
- Set up PO Box number for post to be delivered
- Organise postage facilities. How will this be managed? A franking machine, or taken to the post office every day by support staff?
- Set up dedicated, freephone number
- Set up secure office phone lines and answer phone functionality. Do the team need mobile phones?
- Depending on the security requirements of the buildings, order staff the necessary key fobs / key cards
- Design a simple logo for the inquiry – avoiding any colours / symbols that have an association with any organisation involved in the inquiry or political party
- Order stationery
- Order or lease office furniture
- IT set up (see chapter four)

4

IT Systems

Introduction

IT systems are the lifeblood of an inquiry. For participants and the public, the inquiry's IT systems present the primary means by which information about the inquiry, transcripts of the oral hearings, copies of documentary evidence and the overall progress of the inquiry can be accessed and monitored. For the inquiry itself, putting into place user-friendly and easily accessible IT systems is vital to its smooth operation, and effective and transparent engagement with participants and the public.

This chapter looks at the range of systems an inquiry is likely to use, both from the perspective of an inquiry team setting up a public inquiry and also from the perspective of participants, their legal advisers and the public engaging with the inquiry. Those systems include:

- inquiry management systems, for managing day-to-day processes and communications;
- document management systems (sometimes known as evidence management systems) for storing and processing the vast quantity of documents received;
- hearing room systems, for visual presentation of evidence to the public and use by the chair or panel, counsel to the inquiry and core participants (or, in the case of non-statutory inquiries, interested parties) during hearings;
- transcription processes, for recording evidence during an inquiry's public hearings;
- inquiry websites – the public face of the inquiry;
- internal communication systems for members of the inquiry team; and
- long-term data storage systems.

The security of all of the above systems is crucial as all inquiries will process and store sensitive material and many will hold extremely sensitive, and possibly classified, data.

Cost and Effectiveness

While IT systems can be expensive, this is an area where real cost and efficiency savings can be made. In the absence of effective IT systems, an inordinate amount of time and costs may be incurred by the chair or panel, counsel to the inquiry, the inquiry's lawyers, core participants and their legal representatives in managing documentary evidence, inquiry processes and communications. For many inquiries, the sheer volume of material can make tasks such as document analysis and redaction simply unmanageable without the appropriate electronic systems in place. It is also important to remember that many inquiries, if not most, commence oral hearings whilst the evidence-gathering process is still under way. This means that the ability to act swiftly and efficiently on the receipt of material, and to upload the documents onto relevant systems in a managed way, is key to avoiding delays.

Quote

'IT costs can seem high but if you get the right IT system in, you save an awful lot of court time and that keeps the costs down.'

Lee Hughes, an experienced Secretary to inquiries, in evidence to the 2013–14 House of Lords Select Committee on the Inquiries Act 2005[1]

Checklist – An inquiry's IT systems

An inquiry's IT systems should have the ability to:

- Manage and record communications between the chair, counsel, core participants and witnesses.
- Record, store and permit processing, annotation, redaction and the secure sharing of evidence with core participants and their legal representatives.
- Assist with workflow management and chronologies.
- Create bundles to assist with evidence taking and hearing preparation and facilitation.
- Display documents and live evidence during the hearings.

[1] House of Lords Select Committee on the Inquiries Act 2005, 'Written and corrected oral evidence' (2013), available at www.parliament.uk/documents/lords-committees/Inquiries-Act-2005/IA_Written_Oral_evidencevol.pdf (accessed 12 August 2020).

The IT systems should be used to:

- Manage the inquiry's processes and securely store vast quantities of material.
- Manage the selective disclosure of evidence to core participants or categories of core participants.
- Manage the redaction or restriction of confidential material.
- Disseminate information about the inquiry's progress.
- Support the oral hearings.

IT systems may also be required to:

- Run reports on the progress of the inquiry and the evidence-gathering process.
- Assist with the scheduling of interviews and hearings.
- Coordinate this work with witness files and email accounts.
- Password protect documents and issue passwords to witnesses using an automated process.
- Create bundles of material for witness interviews.
- Create bundles of evidence for counsel's use during the hearings.
- Establish a separate platform for core participants, to which the inquiry can disclose documents.
- Enable the analysis of all oral, written and documentary evidence, for example by issue, work stream or module, witness, or date range, to allow the report-writing process to be as smooth as possible.

There are a number of providers that deliver the various systems that an inquiry might need, but it is important to note that off-the-shelf systems are not traditionally designed with the public inquiry process in mind. The systems that are available have generally been designed for use in litigation and arbitration and are adapted for public inquiry use. There are some providers that have significant experience of public inquiries and are able to assist in tailoring systems for the public inquiry process. These systems have the potential to offer much greater functionality, but do tend to be more costly. However, well designed and well managed IT systems can dramatically reduce cost and increase the efficiency of an inquiry. Conversely, ineffective systems can significantly impede an inquiry's work. Making do with existing off-the-shelf systems, simply because they have been used before or because they appear cheaper, can ultimately lead to tremendous inefficiencies during the inquiry process. These inefficiencies impact not only the inquiry itself, but also those core participants and interested parties who interact with these systems, often on a daily basis.

Quote

Cost vs value

'When evaluating technology solutions, a simple cost-based approach can be misleading. Cost has to be considered alongside the new and added-value that can be unlocked for the inquiry. For example, using an electronic bundle can provide direct cost savings compared to printing paper sets. But the significant added-value achievable through time savings – for example by navigating a fully hyperlinked electronic bundle – is not necessarily reflected in a purely cost-based consideration.'

Oliver McClintock, Chief Commercial Officer, Opus 2

Checklist – Benefits of effective IT systems

An effective IT system will give a number of benefits:

- Helps the chair to fulfil their obligation to ensure that the record of the inquiry is comprehensive and well-ordered, in accordance with r 18 of the Inquiry Rules 2006.
- Provides transparency and associated accountability for the inquiry's work and its findings.
- Ensures inquiry staff can efficiently access and use information as necessary.
- Allows the inquiry team (eg counsel to the inquiry and the solicitor to the inquiry, and their respective teams) to liaise and work jointly on the examination of material and to share preliminary comments or views in anticipation of public hearings.
- Supports compliance with relevant legislation and ensures audit trails are in place.
- Helps protect personal or sensitive information, ensuring that it is stored and processed securely, in accordance with data protection laws.

- Facilitates the efficient selection and transfer of the inquiry record at the conclusion of the inquiry.[2]
- Ensures easy and timely exchange of information for core participants and interested parties.
- Allows core participants and interested parties to access documents, and often live hearings, remotely.

The Inquiry's IT Systems

The IT systems selected should link together the various aspects of the inquiry, as illustrated in the diagram below.

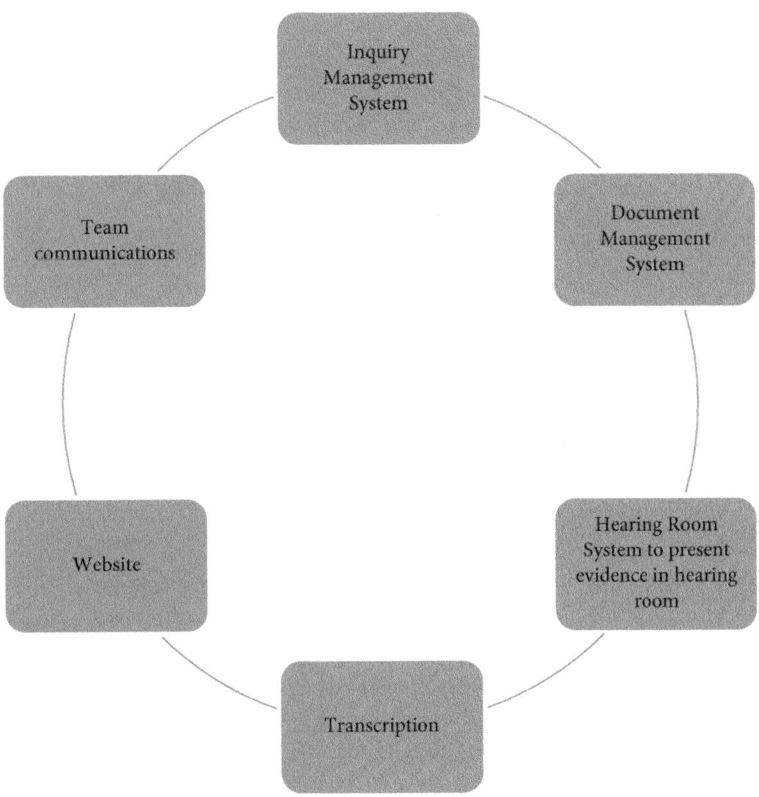

[2] At the end of the inquiry, the chair must transfer custody of the inquiry record to a department of Her Majesty's Government in the United Kingdom or to the appropriate public record office, as the Minister directs: Inquiry Rules 2006, r 18.

The Inquiry Management System

The inquiry will procure a day-to-day, inward-facing IT system, to provide a means of recording its communications with witnesses, core participants and other key individuals, such as experts. This system is not available to anyone outside the inquiry team. Often an inquiry will use the system to maintain separate folders for each key individual or witness, to record and store all communications with that individual such as letters, emails, notes of telephone calls and meetings, and to store documents such as draft witness statements. The system may also be used to enable the inquiry team to liaise and work jointly.

Most inquiries have significant engagement from the public, witnesses, core participants (and their legal advisers), as well as experts and the media. It is crucial to have reliable processes in place, and the necessary systems to support those processes, so that the entire inquiry team can access up-to-date information quickly and efficiently and record all interactions with those third parties. Otherwise an inquiry risks being exposed to criticism for being disorganised. An inquiry team may be made up of individuals working from different locations and with different ways of working, such as individuals from the government legal service, government departments, and the private sector including barristers' chambers and solicitors. These individuals need to have access to IT platforms on which all can converse and share work, to avoid siloed working and miscommunication. Team working is key to an inquiry team's success.

Checklist – Inquiry management system: likely challenges

- The system must be able to manage and record all of the inquiry's correspondence and communications, the inquiry team members' diaries and the various diaries that are used to administer the inquiry (such as interviewing schedules and hearing timetables).
- The volume of information managed is likely to be very large.
- The system must provide a full audit trail of correspondence, some of which may contain sensitive data. It is good practice for sensitive and personal data to be stored separately and securely from other non-inquiry related systems. Core participants, interested parties and witnesses will also want to be reassured that any personal data they are providing to the inquiry is stored separately and securely, to avoid any potential inadvertent access from outside the inquiry team.

- The system must permit simultaneous access from different locations, and by different individuals within the inquiry team, while ensuring the data is secure.
- Depending on the subject matter of an inquiry, correspondence and records of contact with witnesses may need to be held independently of any government systems (to ensure that the inquiry is, and is seen to be, operating independently of government).

Potential Features of Inquiry Management Systems

The inquiry management system may be able to cover a range of functions, as illustrated below.

Log and track all evidence	Monitor trends in evidence being collated	Manage all contact with people who are engaged with the inquiry
Provide diary and calendar system	Produce reports to monitor progress	Convert hard copy documents into electronic format so they are searchable
Index all information in a logical way so it is identifiable and retrievable	Manage confidential information appropriately	Store template letters to be efficient and consistent when corresponding with large numbers of witnesses

The Document Management System

Inquiries collect and analyse vast quantities of documents. The document management system is the inquiry's 'nerve centre'. It is the system within which all documents provided by all stakeholders, including core participants and witnesses to the inquiry are stored and analysed. It is also likely to be the system that core participants and interested parties, and their legal representatives, will use to access disclosure provided by the inquiry. A review platform will be set up for this purpose, as part of the document management system, which enables the inquiry to disclose relevant documents to core participants and interested parties. It is important to note that, while all the material is stored on this system and is accessible to the inquiry team, core participants and interested parties do not have wholesale access to the same system, or to all unredacted material received by the inquiry. Instead, separate 'workspaces' are usually set up for individual core participants and interested parties, through which the inquiry will disclose the material it considers to be relevant, usually with redactions applied.

An effective document management system must enable documents to be analysed by members of the inquiry team and to be tagged for relevant topics. The system must enable members of the inquiry team to work on documents concurrently. The system should also have the ability to disclose documents selectively to core participants or categories of core participants (see chapter six).

It is vital that the process is well managed, that the process of analysis is thorough and well ordered, and that the disclosure of relevant documents to core participants is timely and consistent, while protecting any sensitive data.

Quote

Effective document management

Inquiry into children's heart surgery at the Bristol Royal Infirmary:

'There were 980,000 documents. They were all scanned in; they were all given a particular number; counsel knew the number; and they were displayed on a screen. All that the counsel had to do was say, "Can I take you to document X, Y and Z?" and it came up on the screen. There was no searching for a box file in the corner. The view was that that saved between 25% and 30% of the time that would ordinarily have been spent in the inquiry, because of that immediacy.'

Professor Sir Ian Kennedy, Chair to the Public Inquiry into Children's Heart Surgery at the Bristol Royal Infirmary 1984–1995, in evidence to the 2013–14 House of Lords Select Committee on the Inquiries Act[3]

[3] House of Lords Select Committee on the Inquiries Act 2005, 'Written and corrected oral evidence' (2013), available at www.parliament.uk/documents/lords-committees/Inquiries-Act-2005/IA_Written_Oral_evidencevol.pdf (accessed 12 August 2020).

Quote

Delay caused by the lack of an effective document management system

Independent Inquiry into Child Sexual Abuse:

'The delays in proceeding to hold any substantive public hearings have regrettably resulted from the Inquiry's inability to obtain in any timely way the vital infrastructure necessary to prepare for and conduct public hearings. The lack of an Evidence Management System (EMS) fit for purpose has severely hampered the Inquiry's ability to manage the thousands (if not millions) of documents the Inquiry has been receiving, and the Solicitor to the Inquiry has consequently been unable to prepare the documents for public hearings.'

Hon. Dame Lowell Goddard, former Chair of the Independent Inquiry into Child Sexual Abuse, in her report to the House of Commons Home Affairs Select Committee dated September 2016, following her resignation[4]

Checklist – Document management system: likely challenges

An inquiry will usually receive, at a minimum, tens of thousands of documents; some inquiries have received many more. Effective electronic storage, management and review of that material is key to the efficient working of the inquiry. The document management system must provide support to the inquiry as follows:

- Enable the inquiry team to bring together the evidential picture (documents and witness evidence) and begin the inquiry hearings promptly.
- Enable the inquiry team to review the material for relevance, analyse it for key issues, identify its relevance to particular witnesses and identify evidential gaps, in preparation for witness interviews and for questioning of witnesses at any hearings. The analysis is usually carried out by the solicitor to the inquiry's team on a rolling basis, whereby they analyse the disclosure and apply certain 'tags' or categories to documents, for example 'relevant/not relevant', applying specific topics or themes, and

[4] Written evidence submitted by Lowell Goddard QC to the Home Affairs Select Committee September 2016, available at http://timtate.co.uk/wp-content/uploads/2016/10/Godard-letter-to-HA-Committee.pdf (available at 12 August 2020).

adding free text notes. An inquiry will usually design bespoke 'tags' to align with its term of reference. This analysis will remain internal to the inquiry team, and will not be provided to core participants and interested parties, even if the documents themselves are disclosed.

- Enable counsel to the inquiry and the solicitor to the inquiry, and their respective teams, to collaborate and share thoughts when reviewing material and to refer back to any notes marked on a document.
- Enable disclosure of material that is considered relevant to the terms of reference to core participants in an appropriate form, and manage more limited disclosure, perhaps to a single core participant only. Disclosure is often made in advance of hearings during which the documents may be considered.
- Enable redaction of the material on the system, so that information can be protected where necessary prior to being disclosed to core participants.
- Interact as seamlessly as possible with the system that will display the evidence in the hearing room.

Potential Features of a Document Management System

A document management system may include the following functions:

Retrieve material quickly and easily

Search with bespoke search terms relevant to the inquiry's subject matter

Use bespoke coding fields relevant to the inquiry's subject matter (eg documents relevant to specific witnesses or issues)

Redact material (key for data protection purposes and for classified material – see chapters eight and nine)

Group and categorise documents

Add working notes onto documents

Share selected documents with other third parties in a separate and secure workspace

Provide a secure, password-protected system

To avoid 'reinventing the wheel', ideally an inquiry team will speak to inquiry teams of earlier inquiries to find out what systems were used and ask what worked well and less well. However, given the speed of change in the IT industry, and the unique nature of each inquiry, technological solutions suitable for one inquiry will not necessarily be the most suitable solution for another (although they are often assumed to be so). Therefore, in addition to researching the technology used in earlier inquiries, each inquiry team will have to consider the situation afresh, to see what tools are available, what new technology solutions there are and consider what is best for the inquiry's work. The initial stage of scoping the IT needs of an inquiry is crucial.

Hearing Room Systems

Hearing room systems allow material to be displayed to those present at the hearing, including evidence referred to by counsel to the inquiry and put to witnesses during the hearing. Documents and evidence, which originate from the document management system, are usually displayed on a number of screens around the hearing room. This is so that evidence referred to can be reviewed by all core participants and interested parties, legal teams, the witness giving evidence, the chair or panel, counsel to the inquiry and the public gallery. This may include relevant witness statements, documents, voice recordings or video clips.

Hearing room systems are usually operated by a technician from the software company that is providing the system. This technician will be present during the hearings and follow instructions from counsel to the inquiry, or the chair or panel, as to which material to locate and display on the screens. Some hearing room systems also allow sections of documents to be highlighted live during the hearing to help illustrate the relevant material within the document that is being referred to.

The hearing room system must allow material to be transferred to it securely, swiftly and seamlessly from the document management system used by the inquiry, so that all relevant evidence can be presented at public hearings.

Interactions between a Document Management System and a Hearing Room System

Issues can often arise when seeking to transfer material onto a system that can display that material during the inquiry's hearings. The transfer poses inherent challenges, such as how to minimise delay when material is transferred from the document management system, particularly when considering the rolling basis of evidential disclosure and inquiry hearings. Receipt of material relevant to the hearing at the last minute is commonplace. Transfers need to take place while maintaining the integrity of the material, retaining file and folder structures and, crucially, ensuring the integrity of any applied redactions. For example, an inquiry must ensure that the transfer of documents between systems does not result in the redactions becoming 'editable' (see the checklist below). There are various solutions on the market that provide both document management functionality and the ability to display material during inquiry hearings in the manner required by an inquiry, but there can be challenges and limitations on their ability to transfer material from one system to the other seamlessly and instantly.

Generally speaking, document management systems currently on the market were originally designed for document review and disclosure in litigation cases. Similarly, the hearing room systems on the market are designed for court cases, not public inquiries. Inquiries need to take this into account when looking at the design of their document management system. Working with suppliers to tailor systems so that they are suitable for the needs of the inquiry, in order to avoid the common pitfalls that other inquiries have experienced, can save many hours of work and significant delays later on. There are now a number of suppliers who have credible experience of using their systems to support public inquiries.

Checklist – Hearing room system: likely challenges

- An inquiry should consider the requirements of its hearing system at the outset, long before the hearings are due to start, as its design and functionality will have to be considered alongside the design and layout of the inquiry's premises and facilities. (For example, it will be necessary to calculate the number of computer monitors needed for core participants and interested parties and their legal representatives and the number of larger screens needed for the hearing room and any overspill rooms, to ensure all participants can view the documents.)
- An inquiry will also consider the requirements of the hearing room system alongside its choice of document management system, since the two systems need to work together, and in a seamless manner, to avoid delays.
- In the past, the process of transferring a document, or set of documents, from the document management system to the hearing room system has been very slow (often at least 24 hours from the point of request for a transfer). This has caused delays to hearings, particularly

where counsel to the inquiry has needed to refer to a particular document at short notice. An inquiry needs to have a good understanding of the transfer process in order to manage its limitations and plan in advance, as well as needing a back-up system in place, such as the ability to display documents to the hearing room by placing them under a camera, should that be necessary. Although core participants and interested parties will already have access to the documents via the document management system (when these have been disclosed to them by the inquiry), it is important that the public have the ability to view documents being referred to during the hearings.

- Where an inquiry is dealing with documents containing personal and sensitive data and confidential material, it is often necessary for redaction to take place, obscuring that personal data and confidential information from unrestricted view (see chapters eight and nine). In the past, some inquiries have experienced issues when documents are transferred from one system to another. For example, the hearing room system may remove redactions that have previously been applied to documents in the document management system, or render the redactions 'editable', thereby potentially revealing personal and sensitive information. An inquiry must manage its systems carefully to avoid this happening, in order to protect personal data and confidential information, avoid any inadvertent breach of data protection obligations, and avoid having to repeat the redaction process at different stages, which takes time and costs money.

Possible Features of Hearing Room Systems

The hearing room system may provide the following functions:

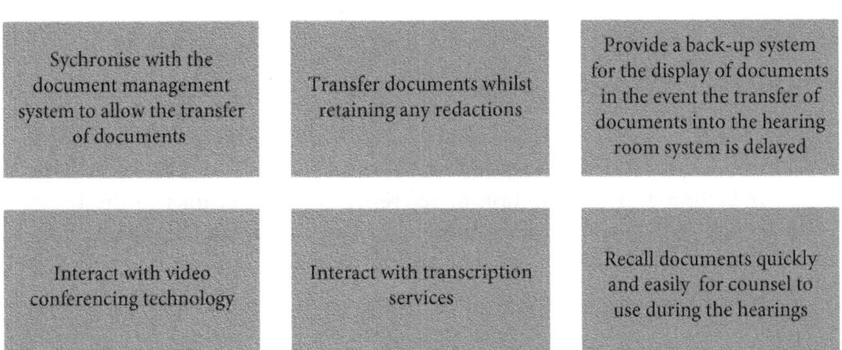

Transcription

A transcription system produces a written verbatim record of an inquiry's public hearings in a transcript form, which provides an essential written, public record of the proceedings. Inquiries almost always engage the services of external contractors to provide the transcription service. This service involves a stenographer being present in the hearing room, typing a transcript of the proceedings live during the hearing. The verbatim transcript is displayed as it is typed in real time during the hearing, with an edited version of the transcript with any errors corrected being made available soon after the conclusion of the hearing. Typically the final transcript will made available via the inquiry's website within approximately 24 hours of the hearing taking place, although the process is often much quicker than this, and it is sometimes made available within a matter of hours.

The transcripts can be read by those who cannot, or do not, attend the hearings. It can be referred to both during the course of the inquiry (eg to refer a witness to a particular extract of evidence) and at the conclusion of the hearings when the chair is writing their report. Usually core participants and interested parties, and their legal representatives, are provided with the ability to annotate their own confidential version of the live typed transcripts during the hearing by adding notes or applying tags to identify certain issues. This is a useful tool allowing instantaneous analysis of the evidence being heard. The annotated transcripts can then be downloaded from the system and used to share that analysis with others.

There are a range of transcription providers and varying levels of functionality available. For example, it is now possible to also have recordings of the hearings, making it possible to identify a particular section of the transcript and then play the recording of that part of the hearing. This can be particularly helpful for those not attending the hearings in person. Increasingly, inquiries may also live-stream hearings, which enables participants and the public to watch the hearings live without having to attend in person.

This formal record of evidence is key for public engagement, with many relying on the transcripts to stay abreast of the inquiry's work.

Checklist – Transcription: likely challenges

- Delays in transcripts being available to the public do occur. This is often due to practical steps that need to be taken prior to release, such as redaction and the addition of references and hyperlinks to the transcript. For example, a witness might refer to another individual by name; if that person has been granted anonymity their name would have to be redacted.

- An inquiry will usually publish a policy on transcribed evidence on its website, stating what will be uploaded and available to the public, where on the website it will be located, and when it will be uploaded. Sometimes only the transcript itself will be available; usually, however, all witness statements and corresponding exhibits of those witnesses giving evidence during the hearing will also be made available, usually on the day the witness gives evidence, with the statements being formally read into the record during the hearing. Some inquiries also publish all documents referred to during the hearing. The differing approach of inquiries depends on the sensitivity of the documents referred to and at what point the inquiry decides to place all these documents in the public domain.
- Where there are both public and private hearings during an inquiry, for example where some evidence is given anonymously or in private, the inquiry will notify participants and the public, usually via its website, to explain whether and in what form transcripts will be available. In the case of private hearings, transcripts will not be provided to core participants and interested parties, or the public, but they will still be produced for the benefit of the chair or panel.
- The inquiry team will liaise with the chair, any panel members and counsel to the inquiry over the publication of the transcript and the documents that should accompany it at the point of publication.

The Inquiry's Website

The inquiry's website is the public face of the inquiry; it is the point at which members of the public interact with the inquiry's work. A website is commonly used as a tool for setting out how the inquiry works (eg publishing inquiry protocols), sharing information (eg providing hearing timetables) and presenting key evidence. The website is also the primary record of an inquiry's work. At the conclusion of an inquiry and the publication of a report, often the whole website is retained and archived.

Considerations for the Inquiry when Setting Up its Website

The website needs to be user-friendly, using simple and clear language. It must be updated regularly and be able to store and maintain large quantities of material.

While the quantity of information stored on an inquiry's website at the outset may not be huge, that will very quickly change once evidence begins to be gathered and any oral hearings start. Transcripts, witness statements (often with large volumes of exhibits) and supporting documents will be uploaded on a daily basis. The capacity and flexibility of the website is therefore very important. At the design stage, the inquiry will need to consider the extent to which the website will be used, to ensure that the website created is fit for purpose. For those members of the public who are using the website to track an inquiry's progress, new material added to the website must be easily identifiable, otherwise additions get lost in a sea of material, which can become very frustrating for those seeking to keep abreast of new developments.

Key information, such as contact details, hearing timetables and the inquiry's protocols, must also be quick and easy to locate.

Checklist – An inquiry's website

A well-designed website should provide the following:

- A good platform for communication with the public, media and interested parties.
- The capacity to store large amounts of material.
- The ability to be regularly updated (at least once a day, at its peak), with large documents being uploaded quickly.
- Easy to use layout and clearly signposted locations of material.
- A search function and quick navigation links.
- Details of the terms of use, privacy policy and cookie policy for data processed on the website and by the inquiry more generally.

Suitable IT support should be provided to ensure the website is updated regularly and in accordance with any timescales prescribed in the inquiry's protocols.

The information contained on a website will vary from inquiry to inquiry. However, past inquiry websites have included information such as the following.

- Terms of reference for the inquiry and background to the inquiry
- Details of the inquiry team and their contact details
- Details of the chair, panel members, assesors and experts, if any
- Address, telephone and email details of the inquiry
- FAQs section on the inquiry's work and procedures
- Copy of the inquiry's protocols and policies, eg privacy policy
- Details of the venue and arrangements for hearings, if any
- Directions, orders and rulings made by the chair
- Hearing timetable
- List of core participants
- Daily transcripts from hearings
- Copies of winess statements and supporting documents
- Papers relevant to ancillary applications made
- Submissions
- Experts' reports
- Media releases and public notices
- Daily information updates
- Section detailing the inquiry's costs to date
- Proforma applications eg for expenses, applying for core participant status, applying to give evidence anonymously etc
- Contact forms, to allow visitors to the site to fill in and submit a query form
- Details of seminars / seminar report
- Details of witness support services
- Live feed to the hearings
- The report and any interim reports

Team Communications

The inquiry will also require a secure system for internal team communications, probably via a dedicated email system. The inquiry chair, panel, legal team and secretariat will all likely have their own personal and professional contact details, but it is important to create a structure and methods of communication that are specific to the work of the inquiry from the outset. Otherwise there will be inquiry-related material held on numerous different email accounts, which cannot easily be located; this may cause data protection issues and may create difficulties if material needs to be retrieved at a later date.

Checklist – Internal communication system: likely challenges

- The internal communication system must be secure and independent from other systems and servers.
- Members of the inquiry team must restrict themselves to using inquiry email addresses for inquiry business. They must not use alternative email addresses, such as counsel's chambers email or personal email, as this creates security implications and affects the inquiry's audit trail and eventual archiving.
- The internal communication system must have sufficient capacity to support and store the volume of internal communications required for the inquiry's work.
- It must allow for information to be extracted in response to data subject access requests.
- The stored communications may need to be extracted and archived at the conclusion of the inquiry (see chapter fourteen).

Other IT Issues to Consider

Virtual Hearings

The adoption of virtual hearings has been slow in the world of public inquiries, perhaps understandably given their 'public' nature and the general desire to be easily accessible and 'open' to all. However, the recent coronavirus pandemic has resulted in some inquiries reconsidering the option of virtual hearings, not least because of a desire to be able to move forwards with their timetable and ensure the prompt delivery of conclusions and recommendations. It will be interesting to see whether, in the post-pandemic world, there is a greater take up of virtual solutions, given the significant cost attributed to the often very large premises needed to accommodate the inquiry team, core participant legal teams and a public gallery.

Whether or not there are any significant changes in the future, the lockdown and social distancing restrictions imposed in response to the pandemic have illustrated the need to give careful consideration to the extent to which an inquiry could operate virtually, if needed, in all aspects of its work. The illustrations below demonstrate how technology has been adapted to manage the increased need for virtual hearings as a result of the pandemic, and how participants can be integrated into the hearings even if not present in person.

IT system for a public inquiry with live virtual hearings

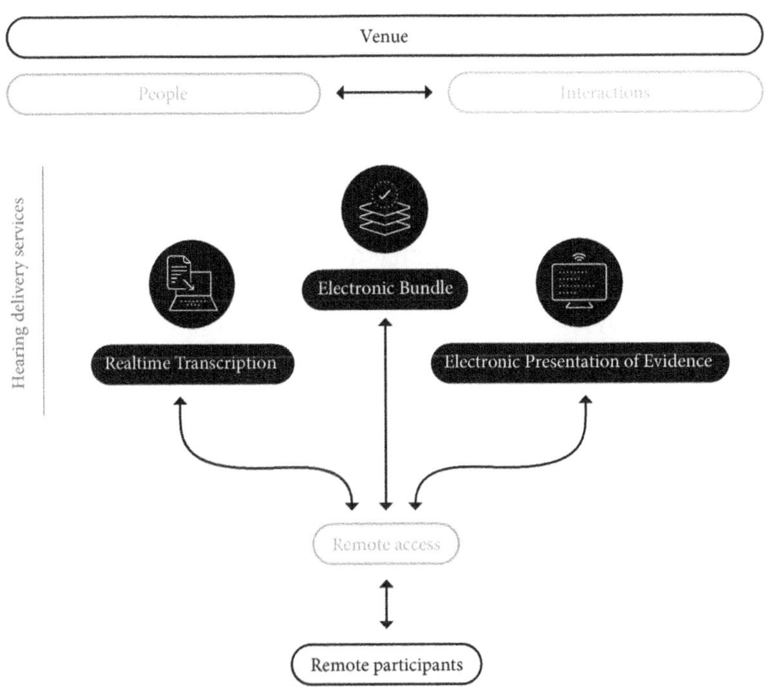

Source: Image provided by Opus 2 to illustrate generally available services that enable public inquiry hearings.

IT system for a public inquiry with live virtual hearings

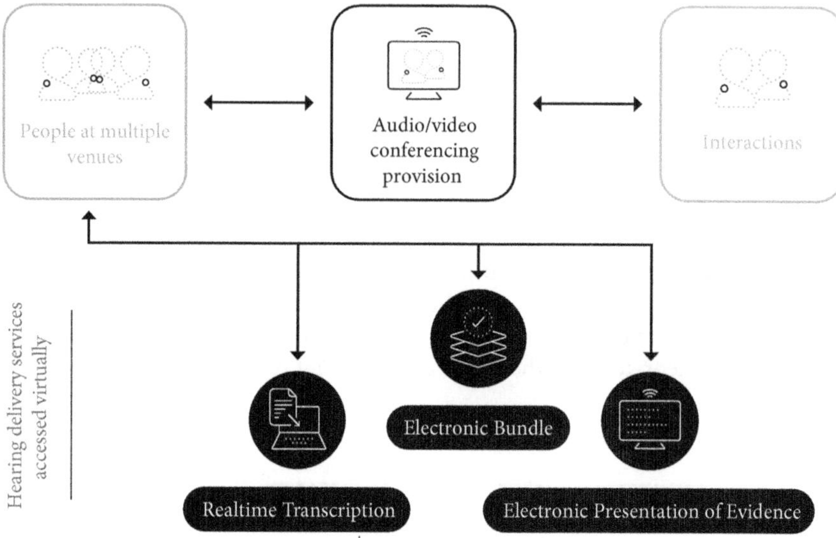

Source: Image provided by Opus 2 to illustrate generally available services that enable public inquiry hearings.

Data Security and Storage

Inquiries are usually tasked with examining very sensitive facts, sometimes involving classified material, and usually of public and media interest. An inquiry must take all reasonable steps to protect that data.

At the outset, careful consideration needs to be given to whether an inquiry is likely to be in receipt of classified material and, if so, how that material will be stored, both physically and electronically.

The data security of any inquiry is paramount and so obtaining specialist advice before the inquiry procures hardware or software is advisable. As the recent coronavirus pandemic has further demonstrated, secure remote access to inquiry systems is also vital.

The storage of data also becomes an important consideration at the conclusion of an inquiry's work. This is addressed in chapter fifteen.

Checklist – Data security and storage: likely challenges

Some of the challenges that will be faced by an inquiry regarding data security and storage are:

- The desire for members of the inquiry team to work remotely and the impact this has on the security of the systems.
- The need to receive large volumes of data.
- Suitable storage if any classified material is stored and processed.
- The need to transfer data between different systems and how this will be achieved efficiently and securely.
- At the end of the inquiry's work, the need to extract all of the data held by the inquiry on various systems so that it can be archived, keeping in mind that classified material may need to be treated differently.

Ongoing Technical Support

Given the reliance on IT systems, and the complexity of the systems that will be needed for the inquiry's work, ongoing technical support is vital to the smooth operation of the inquiry's systems. Many inquiries engage a number of different contractors to provide ongoing support to assist with IT issues and queries that arise during the course of the inquiry, for example website designers and technicians for uploading documents to the website. (It is rare to find one organisation with the IT capability to support all of the different systems used by an inquiry.)

Sending Documents to the Inquiry

Once the inquiry's IT systems have been designed and set up, the inquiry will put procedures in place for witnesses and core participants informing them how, and in what format, documents should be sent to the inquiry. Some inquiries, for example, specify that documents should be provided on a memory stick, by email or in hard copy; however, file sharing sites (sometimes referred to as secure transfer sites) and platforms are becoming increasingly common. If documents are to be provided electronically, the inquiry may specify a specific format required and the mode of transmission, for example whether documents are to be uploaded to a file sharing site or platform (which is the most common method used currently, given the volume of documents that is often involved), or simply sent as email attachments. These procedures are often published on the inquiry website and incorporated into the inquiry protocols.

By specifying the exact format for providing data, the inquiry will minimise any IT issues and delays that could be caused by software incompatibility problems, and the cost and time delays encountered when dealing with hard copy material.

As a core participant or interested party, it is important to ensure that, when sending material to an inquiry, it is made clear whether the material contains any sensitive, restricted or otherwise protected information and exactly what this consists of. It is also important to ensure that a confirmation receipt is provided by the inquiry for any material sent; if any original material or hard drives, for example, need to be returned, this should also be made clear.

If material is to be provided on a hard drive or in hard copy, this will need to be physically delivered to the inquiry's premises. Some inquiries specify what is acceptable in terms of postal or courier services, but careful consideration must be given to security.

From the inquiry's perspective, thought should be given to the transfer of material received, often in varying formats and of varying quality, onto the designated storage and review platform – ie the document management system. The transfer process, which may involve the uploading and downloading of material, can often take longer than anticipated. If all of the material is to be searchable, Optical Character Recognition (OCR) will need to be applied to documents at some point in the process. The work of many inquiries has quickly become impeded and delayed due to problems in the transfer of material. This is particularly the case when the investigation is into historic matters and there are vast quantities of hard copy material to be scanned and OCR applied.

5

Protocols, Rulings, Directions and Orders, and Engagement with the Media

Introduction

A statutory public inquiry is governed by legislation: the Inquiries Act 2005 and the Inquiry Rules 2006. However, there are very few provisions within the legislation that relate to the running of an inquiry. The chair is given a very broad discretion over how an inquiry should go about its business, with s 17(1) of the Inquiries Act 2005 providing that 'the procedure and conduct of an inquiry are to be such as the chairman of the inquiry may direct'. In doing so, the chair must act with fairness and also with regard to the need to avoid any unnecessary cost (whether to public funds or to witnesses or others) in accordance with s 17(3). The introduction of cost control is one of the major innovations of the 2005 Act, beyond its predecessor, the Tribunals of Inquiry (Evidence) Act 1921.

The legislation contains some provisions relating to procedure, such as the requirement to send a written request for evidence; the right for certain parties to make opening and closing statements; and the right to restrict public access to hearings in certain circumstances. The procedures set down in the legislation are, however, very limited in terms of detail. They provide no practical guidance as to how an inquiry should conduct itself and exercise its powers. Where the procedures do seek to give direction on certain issues, for example warning letters, they can create practical problems that were clearly not foreseen when the legislation was drafted.

A non-statutory inquiry can determine its own rules and procedures without reference to legislation, although it must design these around the principles of natural justice to avoid the inquiry being subject to judicial review. However, in practice many non-statutory inquiries base their procedures upon those used by statutory inquiries, as many of the issues they need to consider when setting up and running the inquiry are the same.

Protocols

In order to set out clearly how it will go about its business, an inquiry will usually prepare a suite of protocols. The protocols will set out how the inquiry will conduct itself on a daily basis and the procedures that it will follow, thereby providing a formal structure and point of reference for all those involved in the inquiry.

Inquiry protocols can also assist 'lay persons' who are involved in an inquiry by translating the rules and procedures already set down in legislation into more user-friendly language.

> **Quote**
>
> *'Every Inquiry needs a set of rules to govern its work, so that all participants understand how the Inquiry will function and what is expected of them'.*
>
> Frances Oldham QC, Chair to the Independent Jersey Care Inquiry[1]

Preparing and Publishing the Protocols

Protocols are usually prepared at the outset of an inquiry, before much of the inquiry's work is commenced, in order to help those involved in the inquiry understand, from the outset, how the inquiry will be conducted. They are therefore largely based on what the inquiry anticipates may develop, and how the inquiry would like to function, but before many procedures have actually been used in practice. A less common approach is for an inquiry to produce protocols as its work progresses, and produce a protocol for each stage of the inquiry's work (eg covering disclosure, the taking of witness statements and oral evidence). Protocols may be amended during the course of an inquiry's work to reflect any changes made to procedures, or to make useful additions, as the inquiry's work develops.

The solicitor to the inquiry generally drafts the protocols under the direction of the chair (see chapter two). Once finalised, protocols are usually published on the inquiry's website so that they are available to the public. Some inquiries formally introduce the protocols at a preliminary hearing before publishing them on their website shortly thereafter.

[1] http://www.jerseycareinquiry.org/Key%20Documents/AddressbyFrancesOldham.pdf (accessed 12 August 2020).

Issue – Precedent protocols

Many practitioners are concerned that each new inquiry seems to 'reinvent the wheel', by preparing inquiry protocols from scratch, rather than using what has gone before. However, using precedent protocols is not necessarily an easy answer. Public inquiries, their subject matters and the different issues at play, are all unique, and therefore one size will not fit all.

The practical implementation of the protocols is also very different. Simply because one inquiry used a set of protocols does not mean that they will be useful for the next inquiry. Feedback on what worked well, and what did not, is not shared or made public after the completion of an inquiry.

Examples of Inquiry Protocols

- Iraq Inquiry[2]
  - Witnesses Giving Evidence to the Inquiry
  - Hearing Evidence in Public and Identifying Witnesses
  - Sensitive Information
  - Documents and Other Written and Electronic Information
- Mid Staffordshire NHS Foundation Trust[3]
  - Assessors
  - Media and Accreditation
  - Procedures
  - Warning Letters
  - Legal Representation at Public Expense
- The Litvinenko Inquiry[4]
  - Measures to Prevent Disclosure of Sensitive Information during Open Hearings
  - Management of Sensitive Material
  - Applications for Anonymity and Other Protective Measures
  - Use of Live Text-Based Communications in the Hearing Rooms
  - Costs for Legal Representation at Public Expense

[2] A non-statutory inquiry (also known as the Chilcot Inquiry): see http://www.iraqinquiry.org.uk/the-inquiry/protocols/ (accessed 12 August 2020).

[3] Mid Staffordshire NHS Foundation Trust Inquiry: see http://webarchive.nationalarchives.gov.uk/20150407084240/http://www.midstaffspublicinquiry.com/key-documents (accessed 12 August 2020).

[4] The Litvinenko Inquiry: see http://webarchive.nationalarchives.gov.uk/20160613090338/https://www.litvinenkoinquiry.org/documents (accessed 12 August 2020).

- Undercover Policing Inquiry[5]
  - The 'Disclosure Protocol': the Provision of Documents and Other Information to the Inquiry by the Metropolitan Police Service
  - The 'Restriction Protocol': the Imposition of Restrictions to the Publication of Documents and Other Evidence Produced to the Inquiry by the Metropolitan Police Service
  - The Witness Statement Protocol
  - The Hearings Protocol

Common Issues to be Considered when Preparing Protocols

Inquiry protocols differ depending on the nature of the inquiry, their subject matter, the nature and number of core participants or interested parties, and the nature of the evidence that has to be gathered. A significant proportion of a protocol may be taken up by reciting relevant legislation, for example dealing with applications for core participant status and costs, or case law, for example dealing with applications for anonymity. There are, however common issues that most inquiries will consider when preparing their protocols, which include:

- gathering of evidence;
- core participants and legal representatives;
- conduct of the hearings;
- the media and communications;
- the treatment of evidence;
- costs.

The following checklists illustrate some of the issues that might be addressed by inquiry protocols.

Checklist – Gathering evidence

Issues that a protocol may address include:

- Setting out the types of information that will be sought from core participants as part of the evidence gathering phase of an inquiry, and how that information should be delivered, for example:
  - Will all documents be gathered, irrespective of their format (such as reports, emails, calendar entries, notes, drafts, voicemails, text messages)?

[5] See https://www.ucpi.org.uk/protocols/ (accessed 12 August 2020) (list complete at time of writing).

- Does the inquiry want documents submitted in electronic format only or are other formats permitted and, if so, what are the practical arrangements for delivery of that material?
- Will requests for documents be 'anything that is relevant to the terms of reference' or will requests for documents be limited by factors such as by date range, creator, custodian and geographical location?

- Explaining how information will be requested, for example using written requests for documents, taking written witness statements and hearing oral evidence. Alternatively a request for information may simply involve a general call for voluntary disclosure of evidence that is not addressed to a particular person. For statutory inquiries, written requests addressed to a particular person must comply with the notice requirements of r 9 of the Inquiry Rules 2006 and s 21 of the Inquiries Act 2005, which have consequences if not complied with. They may also include other requirements the chair considers relevant (see chapter ten).
- Explaining the obligation on participants to provide information, the inquiry's expectations for delivery of any material (eg timescales, how information should be provided and in what format) and potential sanctions if a request for information is not complied with, as set out in s 35 of the Inquiries Act 2005 (see chapter ten).
- Explaining the process that participants should follow to search for documents and provide them to the inquiry, for example any specific parameters of a search (eg what search terms should be used to filter material, what sources of documents should be searched) or how to agree specific parameters with the inquiry, and the process for requesting an extension to timescales for carrying out searches for documents.
- Setting out what systems and archives will be searched by the inquiry itself, if any.
- Explaining how witness evidence will be taken, for example who will prepare the witness statements; how the content of each witness statement will be approved by the witness and signed off; what will happen if there is a dispute as to what was said during the interview; what format the witness statement should take and how documents should be exhibited to the statement.
- Setting out details of any witness support arrangements that have been made.

- Explaining how information will be categorised by the inquiry once it has been received and the IT systems that will be used to review and categorise that information.
- Stating whether there will be different categories of relevance assigned to documents, such as 'highly relevant', 'relevant' and 'not relevant'.
- Explaining whether witness statements will be categorised differently to other documents.
- Explaining whether the inquiry will seek to refer to documents during its proceedings by reference to unique document reference numbers generated by the inquiry's IT systems.

Checklist – Core participants and legal representatives

Issues that a protocol may address include:

- Stating what category of person or entity may or will be afforded core participant or interested party status.
- Setting out the core participants' role in the inquiry and the inquiry's expectations of their conduct (eg that they will cooperate with requests for information and adhere to the chair's rulings, and that they are entitled to appear at hearings).
- Setting out the application process that a participant will need to follow to apply for core participant status.
- Stating the criteria that will be considered by the chair when making decisions on designating core participant or interested party status (including the requirements under r 5 of the Inquiry Rules 2006 and any other factors that the chair considers relevant (see chapter seven)).
- Stating whether there is a process for reconsidering applications.
- Explaining what provision there will be for core participant or interested party access to information (eg the IT systems to which they will be given access, what documents will be provided to them and under what timescales).
- Stating whether the inquiry will require core participants or interested parties to sign up to confidentiality undertakings, in order to protect the confidentiality of specific inquiry information and to provide protection from information leaks.

- Explaining how legal representatives will be designated by the inquiry (including the requirements under r 6 of the Inquiry Rules 2006) and the circumstances under which joint representation may be considered appropriate (including the requirements under r 7 of the Inquiry Rules 2006) and any other factors that the chair considers relevant (see chapter seven).

(See chapter six for further details about core participants.)

Checklist – The hearings

Issues that a protocol may address include:

- Explaining where and when the hearings will be held.
- Setting out the format of the hearings, such as sitting times, the order of the day, whether the inquiry is going to conduct its work in stages or phases, and whether opening and closing speeches will be permitted (including the requirements under r 11 of the Inquiry Rules 2006), and the use of preliminary hearings.
- Explaining the use and availability of transcripts of the hearings, such as how soon after oral evidence will they be available, and how they can be accessed and by whom.
- Explaining who may attend hearings, an explanation of the principle of the hearings being open to the public (including the provisions of s 18 of the Inquiries Act 2005) and in what circumstances closed hearings will be permitted (including the provisions of s 19 and any other factors that the chair considers relevant).
- Explaining what witnesses should expect when giving evidence, such as whether they will have to give an oath or affirm,[6] whether counsel to the inquiry will take them through their evidence,[7] whether only the inquiry chair or panel and counsel to the inquiry will ask questions or whether cross-examination will be permitted and, if so, under what circumstances.[8]

[6] Inquiries Act 2005, s 17.

[7] For most inquiries, counsel to the inquiry will be appointed and will question the witnesses. Where counsel to the inquiry is not appointed, the questioning may be carried out by the solicitor to the inquiry, chair or panel members (see chapter eleven).

[8] Taking into account the provisions of the Inquiry Rules 2006, r 6.

- If cross-examination during hearings is not permitted, setting out the process by which other participants can submit questions to counsel to the inquiry, for example how soon prior to a witness giving evidence should proposed questions be submitted, and what (if anything) can be done if a question submitted is not asked by counsel to the inquiry.
- Setting out other measures that the inquiry will provide to protect the well-being of witnesses, such as appointing a supporter for witnesses when giving evidence; arrangements for witnesses to enter the hearing building via an alternative entrance away from the public; allowing witnesses to give evidence via video-link, excluding cross-examination (if permitted in any event) and setting out how witnesses can request such measures; and the criteria that will be applied when considering such requests.
- Stating the expectations of conduct within the hearing room, such as the prohibition of recording and photography.
- Explaining seating arrangements.
- Stating whether electronic screens will be available to allow evidence to be viewed within the hearing room.
- Explaining the procedures for access to the hearings by witnesses and the media. This may include restrictions imposed by the inquiry on access during private hearings or restrictions on the use of mobile phones or other recording devices. There may also be restrictions on physical access, for example stating that there will be no access to the hearing room by the public, media or core participants outside actual hearings. (See also the media protocol checklist below for more details.)
- Explaining how timetabling will be arranged, such as setting out the general order in which categories of witnesses will be heard; explaining whether witnesses will be expected to give evidence only once, in phases (eg by way of case studies, as adopted by the Independent Inquiry into Child Sexual Abuse (IICSA)), or whether they are likely to be re-called if needed; and whether and when the timetable will be published.

(See chapter eleven for further details regarding the conduct of hearings.)

Checklist – Media and communications

Issues that a protocol may address include:

- Setting out the approach the inquiry will take to media access and whether there will be a process for accrediting members of the media.[9]
- Explaining the practical implications of gaining media accreditation, such as the use of a dedicated media office within the inquiry premises; access to dedicated media seating within the public seating area in the hearing room; and inclusion on a mailing list for press releases.
- Explaining that members of the media will have the same access to transcripts, witness statements and documents as members of the public, ie only the material published on the inquiry website.
- Setting out the process for accrediting members of the media including the application form; criteria applied; any limit to the number of applications per media agency; application timescales; how the outcome of the application will be communicated; and the circumstances under which accreditation could be removed.
- Setting out any restrictions, such as not approaching members of the public for interview on the inquiry premises; not speaking to witnesses who have been sworn in until the conclusion of their evidence; restrictions on filming, photography, recording and the use of electronic devices within the hearing room and elsewhere; and restrictions on publishing information or removing information from publication upon the inquiry's request.
- Setting out details of the inquiry's use of press releases and announcements; stating whether interviews with members of the inquiry team will be permitted; and providing contact details for press inquiries.

Checklist – The treatment of evidence

Issues that a protocol may address include:

- Setting out details of the extent to which evidence will be published by the inquiry and any circumstances under which it might be passed to

[9] See chapter eleven.

third parties (eg the police).[10] For example, whether all relevant material will be provided to the public; how material deemed irrelevant by the inquiry legal team will be treated; whether the inquiry will classify any documents as confidential or secret and, if so, who will have access to this material.

- Setting out details of the records management policy, explaining how information will be stored, accessed and classified.[11]
- Explaining the privileges and immunities that will apply to information provided to the inquiry,[12] including privilege against self-incrimination and public interest immunity (see chapter ten).
- Stating whether any undertakings conferring immunity have been provided by the Attorney-General or an employer (see chapter ten).
- Stating whether the inquiry will allow witnesses to apply for anonymity. If so:
  - what options may be available to witnesses, such as giving evidence from behind a screen, or at an alternative location, or having their name (and identifying details) redacted from any documents disseminated to participants that are published by the inquiry on its website, including transcripts of hearings;
  - the application process, timescales for application, the format of the application, and the criteria that will be applied by the inquiry when considering applications;
  - who will have access to the applications (ie given the application relates to anonymity, will core participants or interested parties also be able to view the applications in order to make submissions on them?)
  - how decisions on anonymity will be communicated and to whom.
- If a witness is granted anonymity, explaining how their information will be treated.

[10] Evidence may be passed to a third party, subject to appropriate confidentiality undertakings being given, where criticisms or allegations are raised, in order for that third party to be able to respond (see chapter thirteen).

[11] This is key when it comes to closing down the inquiry and dealing with any subsequent freedom of information requests.

[12] See Inquiries Act 2005, s 2 'No determination of liability', s 22 'Privileged Information etc', and s 23 'Risk of damage to the economy'.

- Setting out the process the inquiry will follow to restrict the disclosure or publication of evidence, or restrict attendance at a hearing, for example by holding closed hearings (see chapter eleven).
- An inquiry has the power to grant restrictions of its own accord, but it may also allow formal applications for restrictions on the use of evidence to be made. If so, the protocol may provide details of the application process, timescales for applications, the format of the application, the criteria that will be applied by the inquiry when considering the applications, who will determine the applications, and how decisions will be communicated and to whom.
- Setting out details of the inquiry's policy on redaction of information prior to publication or partial publication, including:
  - what information will be automatically redacted;
  - the systems to be used for redaction;
  - who will redact the information;
  - how any dispute about the extent of redactions will be managed;
  - which parties will have access to unredacted material (if any);
  - whether parties can apply for additional redactions to be made and, if so, the process for applying.
- Explaining the inquiry's approach to warning letters, whereby individuals and organisations are warned about criticism that may be inferred from evidence given during the inquiry proceedings[13] (ie for statutory inquiries, how the inquiry will manage the r 13 process and interpret the requirements of rr 13 to 15 of the Inquiry Rules 2006; for non-statutory inquiries, the equivalent process adopted to satisfy the requirements of natural justice). See chapter thirteen.
- Stating the approach that the inquiry will take to Freedom of Information requests and data protection (see further at chapter nine).

[13] Inquiry Rules 2006, r 13. Note that the warning letter provisions relate also to warnings about criticism or potential criticism in the inquiry proceedings and criticism in the inquiry report or any interim report, as well as criticism that may be inferred from evidence given during the inquiry proceedings (see chapter thirteen).

Checklist – Costs

Issues that a protocol may address include:

- Setting out the procedures for dealing with the funding of core participants, interested parties and witnesses, to include details of who will be eligible to apply; the criteria that will be considered to determine whether or not a funding award will be granted; the application process to be followed, including relevant timescales; and what information should be included in any application.
- In a similar way, setting out the procedures for dealing with awards for other related expenses, such as travel and accommodation costs if asked to attend the inquiry, and other financial losses, for example through loss of working time if self-employed.
- Any limits and qualifications that may apply to funding awards; for example providing an indication of work type or tasks that may be covered by a funding award providing details of any limits on hourly rates or an upper limit on expenses (eg maximum cost per day).
- Setting out the process of assessment that will followed in relation to legal costs and expenses that fall within a funding award; for example, whether and how work plans for legal costs should be prepared and the process by which they will be approved; what information work plans should contain (eg details of the team, including levels of seniority, estimated hours, hourly rates); and how travel costs will be calculated.
- An explanation of the billing procedures that will be followed.
- Setting out the process for reconsidering any applications, or challenges to the scope of work plans or payment of bills. See chapter seven for further details on funding and costs.

Checklist – Other matters also addressed

Other issues that a protocol may address include:

- Explaining the approach the inquiry will take in general: inquisitorial, fair and transparent.
- Setting out the contact details of the inquiry, a list of key personnel, and details of any complaints procedures.
- Providing a definitions or glossary document setting out the key terminology and acronyms that the inquiry may use during its work.

- Providing proforma application forms for the various applications that can be made by interested parties and witnesses.
- Setting out the roles and duties of assessors and experts, if used.
- Setting out the procedures for managing sensitive material.
- Setting out procedures on special measures for vulnerable witnesses.
- Setting out details of any available support to witnesses.

Issue – Less is more?

Each inquiry decides how many of the points in the above checklists it will incorporate into its own protocols and in what level of detail.

Some inquiries decide to include as much information as possible, to try to address every possible issue that may arise. However, it is usually very difficult at the time of protocol drafting to predict what the inquiry will encounter as it progresses. Inquiries are often at an early stage, with evidence yet to emerge, and unexpected witnesses may be identified and legislative changes and legal challenges may affect the inquiry's work along the way. As such, it can be very difficult at the outset to predict everything an inquiry will face.

Some inquiries therefore adopt a 'less is more' approach. The chair of an inquiry has the power to determine the inquiry's procedures throughout the duration of the inquiry (taking into account fairness and costs) irrespective of whether they are contained within written protocols. Therefore, some inquiries, for example the Mid Staffordshire NHS Foundation Trust Inquiry, choose to prepare the essential protocols for the inquiry's work early on in the inquiry, subsequently adapting and adding to those protocols as the inquiry's work progresses.

Internal Protocols and Working Practices

External-facing protocols set out for participants, witnesses, legal representatives and the public how the inquiry will go about its work and implement the terms of reference. Internal-facing protocols and working practices will, however, also be important to the operation of the inquiry. Some inquiries choose to document some of their internal working process to assist the inquiry team, particularly if a large team is involved. Internal protocols vary, depending on the nature of the inquiry and the working practices that the chair has chosen to put in place. Set out below are examples of internal protocols that have been adopted by inquiries.

Checklist – Example internal protocols

- Internal security and treatment of information. Issues covered may include:
  - 'clear desk' policies;
  - names of witnesses not to be included in emails;
  - using approved methods for sending documents such as via a secure electronic system;[14] double enveloping any documents sent by post;[15] using named courier companies and not using overnight delivery for documents sent by courier;[16]
  - procedures for handling and securing documents when travelling;
  - inquiry matters not to be discussed in public.
- The inquiry's house style for all documents, statements and correspondence.
- The internal process for dealing with document analysis, from the receipt and uploading of documents onto the document management system, through processing, to redaction and dissemination (see chapter four).
- Details of instructions and timescales for preparing witness statements, from the process adopted for witness interviews, the preparation of witness statements, approval, through to the receipt of the signed witness statements and uploading onto the inquiry's system (see chapter ten).
- Details of support that may be available to those adversely affected by transacting the inquiry's business, for example workload management or vicarious trauma support and training.
- Guidance on the analysis of disclosure; for example, depending on the document management system created by the inquiry, instructions on how documents are to be categorised and analysed on the system.

[14] Such as specifying that documents may only be sent via the inquiry's email system, where security and access to inboxes can be controlled by the inquiry, and not via other professional or personal email addresses, or by a secure file transfer site.

[15] To provide additional protection to the documents enclosed in the event of accidental damage or inadvertent opening.

[16] As there is likely to be limited security while documents are left in an overnight depot.

- Guidance on the approach to redacting documents.
- Guidance for team members on handling vulnerable witnesses.
- Guidance to team members on personal security.
- Guidance to team members on allowable expenses and relevant approvals.

Rulings, Directions and Orders: Terminology

An inquiry records its decisions in a number of ways, using terminology similar to that used by courts, for example 'directions', 'rulings' and 'orders'. For statutory inquiries, the Inquiries Act 2005 and the Inquiry Rules 2006 do not set out nor describe the form of documents that should be used to record the different types of decisions made by an inquiry. It is therefore for the chair to decide the approach to adopt for an individual inquiry, in accordance with the chair's power to direct the procedure and conduct of an inquiry as they see fit.

Although there is no specific legislative guidance on how to record inquiry decisions, s 19 of the Inquiries Act 2005 does use the terms 'order' and 'notice' in the context of decisions made to restrict public access to inquiry proceedings and information. The provision provides that restrictions may be imposed by the minister by way of a 'restriction notice', or the chair by way of a 'restriction order', where restrictions are required by law, or considered conducive to the inquiry fulfilling its terms of reference, or considered necessary in the public interest.[17] (Of inquiry rulings, directions and orders, restriction orders are the most common.)

Despite the lack of legislative guidance, a common practice has developed whereby inquiry chairs have adopted similar forms of documents to record inquiry decisions, for example:

- Rulings – frequently used to record a chair's decision on a specific issue, particularly in response to applications made by core participants or interested parties, or witnesses.
- Orders – with the exception of restriction orders (see above), orders are used as an official inquiry document to record decisions whereby the chair has ordered something to be done, or not to be done.
- Directions – may be used to set out the steps that a chair of an inquiry directs that a party or parties must carry out.

[17] Chapter eight addresses the use of restriction orders and restriction notices in more detail.

Whilst the above are forms of documents often adopted, some inquiries do take different approaches. For example, inquiries have used 'Decision' documents (Renewable Heat Inquiry), a 'Response' document (Grenfell Tower Inquiry) and a 'Notice of Determination' (Infected Blood Inquiry).

As with the form of the documents used, the content and format are again subject to the discretion of the chair. As to publication, most inquiries will disseminate such documents to core participants and interested parties and publish them, given the obligation on the chair to take reasonable steps to secure public access to the inquiry's proceedings, subject to any restriction order or notice.[18]

Non-statutory inquiries often adopt a similar approach to statutory inquiries and devise procedures to record and publish a chair's decisions in the way that best fits with the inquiry in question.

Engagement with the Media

The media has an important role to play with regard to a public inquiry. By creating public interest in an inquiry's work, it can encourage engagement. It also assists in making an inquiry transparent and open to public scrutiny and accountability.

However, a tension can arise between the amount and nature of the information sought by the media and how much information the inquiry can divulge without hampering its work. When engaging with the media, the issues facing an inquiry include the following:

- Often the subject matter of an inquiry is very sensitive and the inquiry needs to consider issues such as the protection of witnesses, commercial confidentiality and national security.
- An inquiry would not want to be seen to be inappropriately courting the media and overly sharing information, as this may deter witnesses, particularly vulnerable witnesses, from engaging.
- Care must be taken to ensure that the media is not being treated more favourably than core participants, interested parties or the public itself, for example by the inquiry providing more, or earlier, information to the media or granting them greater access to the hearings.[19]
- An inquiry must ensure that any information provided is not perceived as the inquiry pre-judging any of the issues it is investigating.
- Care must be taken to avoid the publication of any 'media summaries' that do not accurately reflect the nuanced state of evidence.

[18] Inquiries Act 2005, s 18.

[19] In part, to maintain trust between the inquiry and the participants and public and to avoid giving any impression, however erroneous, that the inquiry is more concerned with its public profile and coverage than fulfilling its terms of reference and addressing public concern.

Nevertheless, a public inquiry is just that, public, and a level of media interest is inevitable. Media coverage can also be beneficial for an inquiry, for example in reaching potential witnesses when the inquiry is seeking evidence. An inquiry therefore needs to consider the strategy it will take regarding engaging with the media throughout its work and ideally a media protocol should be put in place (see above).

Similarly, core participants and interested parties need to anticipate media interest in connection with their involvement in an inquiry and accept that there is a balance to be struck between engaging with the media and not being seen to be divulging sensitive material.

Some inquiries engage a public relations media team to advise the inquiry and engage with the media. A media team can also provide a useful barrier between the inquiry team and the media, to avoid members of the inquiry spending too much of their time dealing with media queries and relations. Appointing a dedicated media team can, however, also create friction. Media advisers' propensity may be to create news, whereas an inquiry's inclination will be more restrained.

A strategy needs to be drawn up at an early stage to determine how the inquiry, and indeed any core participants or interested parties, will respond to media interest, including whether they will act proactively or reactively. In order to provide clarity and effectively manage the relationship, the level of engagement and where the lines will be drawn need to be established at an early stage and all media outlets should be treated in the same manner. Determining who is considered to be 'the media', and introducing an accreditation process, is also helpful. This is discussed further in chapter eleven.

Where an inquiry holds public events, such as seminars, the inquiry should give thought to issuing media guidelines in advance. These guidelines might specify whether recordings or interviews will be permitted, whether details of discussions will be restricted, and how much access or reserved seating will be provided to the media. Whatever approach is taken, good relations with the media can pay dividends for the inquiry's work.

6

Core Participants

What is a Core Participant or an Interested Party?

Some individuals or organisations have a particularly close connection with the work of an inquiry and may be formally recognised by that inquiry and designated an enhanced status. They may have been instrumental in campaigning for the establishment of an inquiry. They may have played a significant role in the issues being investigated by the inquiry, or be likely to face significant criticism during the course of an inquiry's proceedings or in the report itself. They may have a significant interest in the process and outcome of the inquiry, and perhaps in trying to persuade the inquiry to reach a particular conclusion.

Where inquiries are convened under the Inquiries Act 2005, those individuals or organisations are known as 'core participants';[1] for non-statutory inquiries they are generally known as 'interested parties'.[2] This privileged status is the primary means for participants to gain direct access to the inquiry's work.

Core participant status bestows a number of privileges. These include the right to appoint a legal representative, who must be designated as their recognised legal representative, unless the chair orders there be joint representation.[3] Other privileges include the right to receive disclosure of documentation; make legal submissions and statements; suggest questions to be asked during oral hearings; and receive advance notice of the inquiry's report.

Core participants or interested parties may therefore assist and contribute at every stage of the inquiry's work, and the way in which they interact with the inquiry's work (positive or otherwise) can have a huge impact on the success of an inquiry. The constructive involvement and contribution of core participants or interested parties is key to achieving a well-run and ordered inquiry.

For statutory inquiries, the process and criteria for applying for core participant status is set down in legislation. For non-statutory inquiries, the chair is at liberty to determine their own procedure. Some non-statutory inquiries decide to adopt a similar approach to that of statutory inquiries and appoint interested

[1] Inquiry Rules 2006, r 6.
[2] Or, sometimes, 'full participants'.
[3] See sections on recognised legal representatives and joint representation below.

parties, permitting them to have legal representation at hearings (eg the Hutton Inquiry).[4] Others choose not to have any interested parties, nor to designate any similar privileged status; instead restricting the involvement of participants to submitting documents and information and providing evidence as witnesses (such as the Iraq Inquiry).[5]

Accordingly, this chapter focuses on the approach applied to statutory inquiries and the designation of core participants, although many of the processes and criteria described below will often be adopted by non-statutory inquiries when designating interested parties.

Who can be a Core Participant?

The chair of the inquiry will decide which individuals or organisations will be core participants at a public inquiry. The potential list of categories is extensive.

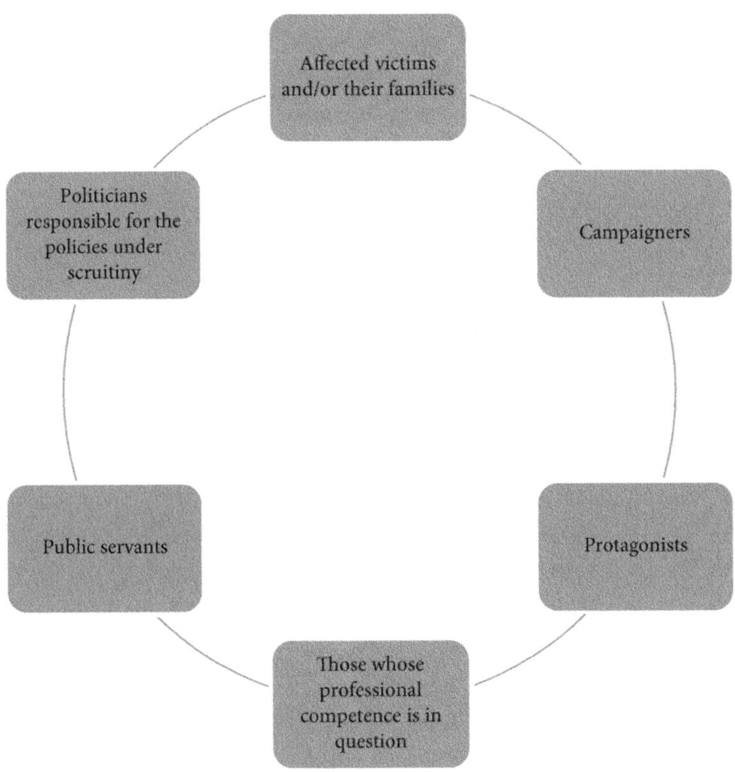

[4] Although more recent inquiries have not formally appointed interested parties in the same way.
[5] Also known as the Chilcot Inquiry, see http://www.iraqinquiry.org.uk/ (accessed 12 August 2020).

Applying for Core Participant Status

The Criteria

Under r 5(1) of the Inquiry Rules 2006, the chair of an inquiry may, on their own initiative, designate a person as a core participant, provided that person consents to being so designated. The scope of this provision also allows a person to make an application to the chair to be designated in such a way.

In assessing whether it is appropriate to award an individual or organisation core participant status, the chair must take account of the criteria set out in r 5(2) of the 2006 Rules, which considers whether:

(a) the person played, or may have played, a direct and significant role in relation to the matters to which the inquiry relates;
(b) the person has a significant interest in an important aspect of the matters to which the inquiry relates; or
(c) the person may be subject to explicit or significant criticism during the inquiry proceedings or in the report, or in any interim report.

The list of factors under r 5 are not exhaustive. The chair is at liberty to take into account other factors which they consider to be relevant to the specific inquiry when awarding core participant status.

Quote

During the Leveson Inquiry the chair, Lord Justice Leveson, made it clear that he was not limited to the factors set out in r 5:[6]

'In determining these applications [for core participant status], I am bound to consider the matters contained within rule 5(2), although this list is not exhaustive and it is also open to me to take into account any other relevant matters.'

A chair is not required to designate as a core participant every applicant who meets the criteria set out in r 5. No one has a right to be appointed as a core participant, and it is possible that even an applicant with relevant evidence to offer an inquiry, and who meets the test set out in r 5, may not be designated as such.

[6] In a ruling dated 14 September 2011.

Issue – How many is too many?

Awarding core participant status to every individual or organisation who applies and meets the criteria can be unmanageable. Having a large number of core participants may slow down the inquiry's progress and increase its workload. As a result, selection among qualifying applicants is often necessary in order to ensure efficient and cost-effective management of an inquiry. A chair must bear in mind the obligation under s 17(3) of the Inquiries Act 2005, to act with fairness and have regard to the need to avoid any unnecessary cost (whether to public funds, witnesses or others) when making any decision about designation. The more core participants and recognised legal representatives, the more likely it is that costs will substantially increase.

There are various ways in which an inquiry may approach designating core participant status to a selection of applicants who meet the criteria, thereby ensuring that all relevant individuals, organisations and interests are appropriately represented. An inquiry's approach will depend on the nature of the particular inquiry.

During the Penrose Inquiry,[7] the chair, the Rt Hon Lord Penrose, adopted an approach whereby core participant status was designated to patients and relatives of patients on a selective basis, with designations being awarded to:

- reflect the distinct interests of the applicants;
- ensure that no more core participants were designated than was necessary; and
- enable legal representatives to be 'adequately instructed' to represent the interests of the group as a whole; the designations took into account the issues relevant to the inquiry, thereby ensuring that the legal representatives could obtain adequate instructions from the designates on each of those issues.[8]

Another approach to ensure all interests are represented, but to keep the core participants to a manageable number, is the use of joint representation (see below).

[7] The Scottish Public Inquiry into Hepatitis C/HIV acquired infection from NHS treatment in Scotland with blood and blood products 2008–2015.

[8] As a Scottish inquiry, the Penrose Inquiry was subject to the Inquiries (Scotland) Rules 2007 (SSI 2007/560).

Quote

'In many inquiries the range of possible core participants could be very large. For example every victim and bereaved relative could in theory apply for separate core participant status, as could each person who might be subject to criticism, however trivial. If all were granted that status individually the inquiry could become unmanageable. It is here that the power to require joint representation becomes invaluable in that those who have common or similar interests can and probably should be required to be jointly represented.'

Sir Robert Francis QC, Chair of the Mid Staffordshire NHS Foundation Trust Public Inquiry, in evidence to the House of Lords Select Committee on the Inquiries Act 2005

This was also recognised by Sir Brian Langstaff, chair to the Infected Blood Inquiry, in his Statement of Intent on Core Participant Status published on 2 July 2018:[9]

'... the Inquiry I chair throws up challenges of scale which few other public inquiries have faced. Many thousands of people have been infected with Hepatitis C and HIV, and they and their families have been seriously affected as a result. There are also potentially significant numbers of people who are infected but do not yet know. The number of people who could potentially be designated as core participants is huge.

It would make for an unwieldy inquiry if every one of the several thousand people infected or affected were to be granted core participant status, and this could easily lead to the Inquiry being unmanageable and thereby defeat its purpose.

I must have regard to justice, which involves not merely getting to the right answers, but doing so with reasonable speed and without excessive cost. Justice is best served by taking decisions as to core participant status which facilitate the better management of the Inquiry as a whole.'

As chair to the Infected Blood Inquiry, Sir Brian Langstaff addressed this challenge by applying the following principles to his consideration of applications for core participant status:[10]

- Where individuals had openly and for some time campaigned for an inquiry, or where they had formed associations with others to discuss the issues and promote certain outcomes, thereby demonstrating an interest in the workings

[9] Infected Blood Inquiry, 'Chair's Statement of Intent on Core Participant Status', available at https://www.infectedbloodinquiry.org.uk/sites/default/files/documents/Chairs-Statement-of-Intent-on-Core-Participant-Status-1.pdf (accessed 12 August 2020).

[10] See n 9 above.

of the inquiry and its conclusions, those individuals should be granted core participant status.

- Where infected or affected individuals (which might include those that fall within the above point) had already instructed or authorised one of four specified law firms to act for them, those firms having played an active part in previous inquiries or associate litigation, and having accumulated knowledge, experience and expertise in respect of the issues the inquiry faced, those individuals should be granted core participant status.
- Other applications for core participant status would be determined by applying the factors set out in r 5(2) and taking into account in particular the extent to which individuals could show that their involvement as core participants would add further to achieving the aims of the inquiry, or other additional feature particular to an individual application.

Nevertheless, the number of core participants in the Infected Blood Inquiry is the highest seen in a public inquiry in the UK: in excess of 2,000 individuals and organisations.

The Core Participant Test Applied in Simple Terms

In practice, the test for designating core participant status becomes two-fold:

(1) does the applicant meet the qualifying criteria in rule 5(2) of the Inquiry Rules 2006; and, if so,
(2) does the chair consider that it would fair to designate core participant status to the applicant, having regard to the need to avoid any unnecessary cost,[11] in accordance with s 17(3) of the Inquiries Act 2005?

Every application is very specific to its own set of facts and whether or not an application is likely to succeed will depend entirely on the subject matter of the inquiry, the terms of reference and the approach taken by the chair.

Checklist – Additional factors a chair may consider when designating core participant status

- Would the individual or organisation assist the inquiry in fulfilling its terms of reference if they were actively involved in the inquiry's proceedings?

[11] Whether to public funds, or to witnesses or others.

- Could that individual's or organisation's assistance be equally well achieved by providing evidence to the inquiry as a witness, rather than a core participant?
- Might the applicant be subject to 'explicit' or 'significant' criticism? If so, would any criticism they may be exposed to be adequately addressed by 'the letter and the spirit' of the warning letter process in rr 13 to 16 of the Inquiry Rules 2006, thereby avoiding the need for core participant status to be granted?[12]
- Where there are many applicants and it is not proportionate, cost-effective or manageable to designate all applicants who meet the qualifying criteria, has a fair balance been reached to ensure that those the inquiry intends to designate adequately and proportionately represent the range of different interests that are relevant to the inquiry's terms of reference?
- Has a consistent and proportionate approach been taken to applications?
- What will be the impact on resources, for example the use of IT, licences and hearing room space? It is important to avoid the inquiry's work, and particularly the hearings, becoming unmanageable.

The Application Process

The Inquiry Rules 2006 do not prescribe when an application must be made and considered, nor what form it should take. Designation may take place at any stage. The interests of some individuals or organisations may only be discovered during the course of the inquiry's proceedings, resulting in designation being made at a relatively late stage. Many protocols do, however, put time limits on applications. Such times limits allow the inquiry to run efficiently and to a managed timetable, but this does not preclude an application from being made at any other time.

The application process, and approach to designations, varies from inquiry to inquiry. Some chairs invite individuals and organisations to put themselves forward and make an application for core participant status. Other chairs proactively make the determination themselves based on the papers before the inquiry.[13]

[12] As was decided by Lord Justice Leveson when considering the application for core participant status for module 1 of the Leveson Inquiry, brought by Rebekah Brookes: Ruling on Core Participants, 14 September 2011, para 29.

[13] Provided that person consents to being so designated.

Designation may not necessarily be for the whole period of the inquiry's work and the chair may specify a date, or phase of the inquiry, when the designation will end. Core participant status may also be limited in other ways, for example limiting access to certain documents or limiting participation to the process of giving oral evidence. For example, during the Azelle Rodney Inquiry,[14] the Association of Chief Police Officers and the Mayor's Office for Policing and Crime were awarded core participant status for the limited purpose of receiving the inquiry's report and executive summary prior to publication. The Independent Inquiry into Child Sexual Abuse, whose work is split into different investigations with each investigation being further split into various case studies, awarded individuals and organisations core participant status for those case studies which were relevant to them, rather than for an entire investigation.

What is consistent between inquiries is that those conducting the inquiry must ensure that the application process is clear, fair and that applications are considered at an appropriate time, or the inquiry will open itself up to potential judicial review challenges.

Checklist – Application process for core participant status

- The question of core participant status should be considered at the outset of an inquiry, with a common date set for any applications, to enable the inquiry to manage the timetable for such applications (although not precluding applications from being made at any other time). Ideally the application date will be during the early stages of the inquiry, after the chair, any panel members, and the legal and administrative teams have been appointed, and the procedures for the inquiry have been put in place, but before any evidence is gathered or proceedings commenced. The cooperation of core participants during the evidence gathering stage will be vital.
- When considering the applications for core participant status, the chair may also consider whether there are any other individuals or organisations who have not made an application, but the chair wishes to designate as a core participant (provided they consent to such designation).
- The chair will determine at the outset whether the inquiry will provide reasons for decisions on specific applications, whether those reasons will be made public, and whether the inquiry will allow challenges against designation decisions. If challenges are to be allowed, the process will be documented (see chapter five).

[14] June 2010 to July 2013.

- A proforma application may be provided to all applicants, identifying the criteria that the chair will use to consider any applications.
- The inquiry should review the position of core participants at regular intervals.
- The chair of the inquiry will determine how, and in what format, designation decisions will be published.

Challenging a Decision not to Designate Core Participant Status

An inquiry may decide to include, within its protocols, a process for challenging core participant designation decisions. Such a process should include the potential grounds that will be considered, specify who will consider it, explain the practical process for challenging (eg the format of the challenge and timescales for making it) and set out how an 'appellant' will be notified of the outcome. If, however, such a process for challenge does not exist, or if that internal process has been exhausted, the process by which an unsuccessful applicant may challenge a decision not to designate core participant status is judicial review, during which a judge will review the lawfulness of the decision. In practice, however, such applications are very rare.

During the Leveson Inquiry, a challenge was brought against Lord Justice Leveson's decision not to grant core participant status to Mrs Elaine Decoulos. The High Court rejected Mrs Decoulos' application for permission to apply to judicially review Lord Leveson's decision and, in doing so, Lord Justice Moses emphasised the fact that the decision to designate a person as core participant is at the discretion of the chair, stating:

> There is no obligation upon the Chairman of the Inquiry to make such a designation … the only basis upon which this court can interfere is on the basis of an error of law such as, for example, a breach of the requirement of fairness within the rules or a decision which is outwith the bounds of reasonable conclusion.[15]

Why be a Core Participant?

Core participants to a public inquiry may have a number of rights and privileges over and above those of non-core participant witnesses or the public, which

[15] *R (Decoulos) v The Leveson Inquiry and Secretary of State for Culture, Media and Sport* [2011] EWHC 3214 (Admin).

allow active involvement in the inquiry's proceedings and greater visibility of the inquiry's work. A core participant:

- has the right to appoint a legal representative, who must be designated as their recognised legal representative, unless the chair orders there be joint representation;[16]
- has prior access to the material collated by the inquiry after it is uploaded onto the inquiry's IT systems;
- is likely to receive advance notice of evidence before it is published (although, in practice, this 'advance notice' may only be a matter of hours or days);
- has the right to make an opening and closing submission;[17]
- has the right to apply for permission to ask questions of a witness giving oral evidence, and more generally has the right to propose questions for counsel to the inquiry to ask witnesses,[18] although in limited circumstances witnesses can also make a request to do so;[19]
- has the right to be granted access to the final inquiry report prior to publication (in practice, this might be only hours in advance) and may be given an opportunity to comment on the inquiry's draft report, or critical sections of it.[20]

The chair will determine how these rights and privileges are exercised by core participants in accordance with s 17(1) of the Inquiries Act 2005, which allows the chair to direct the procedure and conduct of an inquiry as they see fit.

Quote

Lord Justice Leveson stated that being awarded core participant status during the public inquiry into the culture, practices and ethics of the press would in fact bring only limited advantage:[21]

'... it is important to emphasise that I do not consider that, for the purposes of Part 1 of this Inquiry, there need be a significant "bright line" between those

[16] Inquiry Rules 2006, r 7. This applies to core participants and witnesses.
[17] Inquiry Rules 2006, r 11.
[18] Inquiry Rules 2006, r 10.
[19] Inquiry Rules 2006, r 10(3).
[20] Inquiry Rules 2006, r 17.
[21] In his ruling on 14 September 2011.

who are designated as core participants and those who are not. In particular, the teach-in, or briefing sessions ... the seminars and the evidence sessions will be fully transparent to the public. As much documentary material as can be made available will also be published on line. It is then open to anyone to submit evidence to the Inquiry, to attend the evidence sessions, and to suggest lines of questioning to counsel to the Inquiry. Further, although it is open to core participants to seek to cross examine witnesses, I anticipate that I will pay strict attention to Rule 10 of the Rules and significantly limit (if not refuse) such applications. Finally, if I consider that it would be of value, I may also permit persons or bodies other than core participants to make written closing submissions which I shall consider. It is against that background that I consider the applications that have been made.'

And, in evidence to the House of Lords Select Committee on the Inquiry's Act, LJ Leveson also stressed:

'[core participants] do not have a different level of credibility. They have a different level of involvement. By being a core participant, you get to see the statements in advance. You get to make representations about the statements. You get to ask Counsel to ask questions. You get to make submissions of law. You get to make closing submissions and in some cases you get to make opening submissions. It is a different level of involvement. It is absolutely no different level of credibility.'

There are disadvantages as well as advantages to acquiring core participant status. If a potential core participant is simply seeking to ensure that their voice is heard, and the evidence is made known to the inquiry, acquiring core participant status may not be the most cost effective or apposite way of achieving this.

For many, however, other factors come into play. These include putting themselves in a position, as far as possible, to be able to protect their reputation, manage press attention, respond to, or pre-empt, the inquiry's conclusions, divert or minimise criticism, or indeed seek to persuade the inquiry to reach a particular conclusion.

Keeping a low profile may be preferable for some, particularly when considering cost implications. Nevertheless, it can be a risky strategy to fail to keep abreast of the inquiry's work and the direction it is taking. During many inquiries, it is obvious which individuals or organisations are likely to face criticism; there may, however, be some individuals or organisations who have not foreseen the possibility that they might become subject to criticism by an inquiry and who have been taken by surprise.

Serious consideration should be given to the advantages and disadvantages of acquiring core participant status before an application is made, or consent given, to designation.

Advantages and Disadvantages

Advantages	Disadvantages
A core participant is likely to be better placed to anticipate and influence the direction of the inquiry as it progresses	Acquiring core participant status can increase the profile of the individual or organisation during the inquiry, increase scrutiny and the risk of criticism, and potentially attract wider negative publicity
A core participant is likely to have advance sight of the evidence, so will be better placed to anticipate, deflect and manage any criticism they may face	Involvement as a core participant will increase the costs incurred, which will be bourne by the core participant, if not being funded by the inquiry (see chapter seven)
A core participant is likely to be better placed to offer additional material to the inquiry, to facilitate their voice being heard	A core participant is expected to cooperate with any request from the inquiry for evidence or documentation and will be subject to criticism from the inquiry if cooperation is not timely
A core participant will be given a copy of the report prior to publication which will provide some time, albeit limited, to prepare a response and statement before its general release	Core participants are expected to assist the inquiry with its work and are usually expected to be present during the hearings when the evidence is pertinent to them, which can significantly increase the time and cost burden

Checklist – Some additional points to consider

Advance notice of evidence

As mentioned above, core participants are likely to receive advance notice of evidence before it is published. This includes both documentary evidence disclosed by other parties and, later, witness statements, before those witnesses give evidence during oral hearings and their statements are published on an inquiry's website. In reality, this advance notice might only be a matter of hours and therefore may not provide any significant advantage, but core participants will know the nature of the evidence that witnesses will give in advance of the oral hearings, and where they are laying blame.

Documents are, however, often released at very short notice and in some cases after relevant oral evidence has already been heard. This may be because the inquiry itself has received the evidence at very short notice, or simply because the volume of material being processed is such that time did not allow for long periods of advance notice to core participants.

Ideally, all of this material should be reviewed and considered by core participants, to feed into their strategy and influence how they approach the oral hearings (eg in proposing questions to be asked of witnesses during oral hearings under r 10 of the Inquiry Rules 2006 (see chapter eleven)). Core participants may not, however, have the time or resources to process all of the material. Even when core participants are eligible for funding for legal expenses, the funding may be capped, limiting the amount of hours they can spend on the process. In practice, core participants will have to prioritise and make choices about what documents realistically can be reviewed.

Opening and closing speeches

Rule 11 of the Inquiry Rules 2006 gives a core participant the right to make an opening and closing statement to the inquiry. This provides an opportunity for the core participants to engage actively in the inquiry process, and to seek to influence its direction as well as to set out their own positions. It also offers the core participants what is often a much sought-after opportunity to publicly express their views, concerns and frustrations and for their voices to be heard. The closing statement, in particular, allows core participants to reflect and comment on the evidence heard by the inquiry and provides an opportunity to propose recommendations that the inquiry might want to consider making. Opening and closing speeches can often be used for an inquiry as a useful source of analysis and evidence to draft the report.

Access to the report pre-publication

Rule 17 of the Inquiry Rules 2006 gives a core participant the right to be given a copy of the final version of the report, following delivery to the minister but prior to publication. Practice varies between inquiries. This might be as little as hours in advance of publication or might be 24 hours or more, depending on the approach adopted by the chairman. This is dealt with in more detail in chapter fourteen.

This gives the core participants some time to consider the conclusions of the inquiry, discuss the report with their legal advisers and prepare their eventual media response when the report is released to the public.

Greater opportunity to question witnesses

There is a presumption that only counsel to the inquiry (or the solicitor to the inquiry if counsel has not been appointed), the chair and panel members may ask questions of witnesses in oral hearings. Questioning by legal representatives of witnesses or core participants is restricted and may only be permitted at the discretion of the chair. This has become the standard approach since the Bloody Sunday Inquiry, during which all core participants had a right of cross examination under the Tribunals of Inquiry (Evidence) Act 1921, but the evidence proved lengthy and repetitive.

Legal representatives of witnesses who are not core participants may only apply to question their own witnesses or another witness where evidence relates directly to the witness on whose behalf the question is being asked. However, a legal representative of a core participant may apply to question any witness. Core participants also have the right to propose questions to be asked by counsel to the inquiry (see chapter eleven).

Submitting statements, 'corporate' statements and attending witness interviews

Core participants and their representatives may also find themselves involved in preparing, or assisting with preparing, witness evidence. Depending on how an inquiry approaches the taking of witness evidence,[22] a core participant may be asked to attend an interview at which the inquiry records the evidence, or a core participant may be asked to prepare witness statements itself. This could be a statement from an individual witness, or if the core participant is an organisation, it could be asked to assist with, or prepare, a 'corporate' statement, this being a statement that sets out the evidence from the organisation's perspective. Whatever the approach taken to preparing this type of evidence, core participants and their representatives should be mindful of the fact that witness statements should set out the evidence the inquiry needs, and not just what the core participant wants to say.

[22] See further at chapter ten.

Recognised Legal Representatives

While inquiries are not adversarial in nature, legal representation can play an important role in helping the inquiry to establish the facts and ensure that core participants (and witnesses) are treated fairly, and that the inquiry acts appropriately.

Whilst it is not obligatory for core participants or witnesses to be legally represented, r 6 of the Inquiry Rules 2006 permits core participants and witnesses to appoint a qualified lawyer to act on their behalf. If they choose to do so, the chair must designate that lawyer as their 'recognised legal representative' for the purposes of the inquiry. It is difficult to see how a core participant could engage fully with an inquiry without the benefit of a lawyer experienced in the field.

The role that a legal representative may play is at the discretion of the chair and, in the case of questioning during oral hearings, will also be subject to the procedures set out in r 10. A legal representative's role during a public inquiry is very different to that during civil or criminal proceedings. Legal representatives are generally not permitted to cross-examine witnesses and they can only suggest lines of questioning. Witnesses are generally questioned by counsel to the inquiry, inquiry chair or panel (see chapter eight).

Nevertheless, legal representatives have an important role to play, not only in protecting their clients and ensuring that their clients' interests are best served during the course of the inquiry, but also in contributing to the inquiry process itself.

Quote

'I believe that some legal expertise to understand the process and to be able to make submissions aids the conduct of the inquiry rather than thwarts it. When I wanted submissions on rule 13, the lawyers all understood what that meant and were all able to put in skeleton arguments and focused submissions. Litigants in person would not understand, and I have no doubt that it would have taken a great deal of time to unpick the points they wanted to make. I believe that having some lawyers there aids the process.'

Lord Justice Leveson, in evidence to the House of Lords Select Committee on the Inquiries Act 2005

Joint Representation

Under r 7 of the Inquiry Rules 2006, where the chair of a statutory inquiry considers that core participants have similar interests in the outcome of the inquiry, the facts they are likely to rely on during the inquiry are similar: and it would be fair to do so, the chair can make an order that they be jointly represented by a single recognised legal representative.

Where possible, the core participants must agree the designation of a qualified lawyer for that purpose. However, if no agreement is forthcoming within a reasonable period, the chair may designate an appropriate lawyer who, in the chair's opinion, has sufficient knowledge and experience to act in this capacity.

Joint representation enables an inquiry to proceed at a greater pace. For example, during oral hearings, a single legal representative can suggest questions on behalf of several core participant clients. It also reduces costs, both for the inquiry and for the relevant participants, where they are privately funding the representation, and there will be less space required in the hearing room and less training and fewer IT licences required for access to the inquiry's IT systems. As a result, inquiry chairs are more likely to be intent on implementing joint representation arrangements under r 7 if it is the public purse that is paying.

This rule has been used successfully by inquiries in the past; for example the following were jointly represented:

- Mid Staffordshire Inquiry: the Patients Association and AvMA (Action Against Medical Accidents), both charities that represent patient interests;
- Leveson Inquiry: victims of phone hacking and invasions of privacy by the media; and
- Vale of Leven Hospital Inquiry: Health Facilities Scotland and Health Protection Scotland were jointly represented, as were the patients and relatives.

Joint representation does of course introduce many challenges to those representing the two or more parties, such as:

- maintaining client confidentiality of each party;
- fairly apportioning costs of representation between its clients;
- navigating any conflict between the parties about the best strategy to adopt; and
- the fact that non-cooperation of one party could taint the reputation of the other party or parties with whom they are jointly represented.

Core participants' legal representatives must consider these issues at the outset and put in place clear agreements with each core participant, setting out the procedures that should be followed. This may include an explanation of how instructions will be taken, a communications policy for disseminating information to each party, an information sharing policy between the relevant core participants, and an escalation process for any conflicts.

Funding

As a core participant there is no automatic entitlement to public funding for legal expenses, which is at the discretion of the chair. However, where a chair has concluded that a party satisfies the criteria for core participant status, that party may be more likely than other participants to be successful when seeking an award for legal representation expenses, although ultimately the inquiry will only grant funding awards where a core participant has no alternative funds available. (See chapter seven on applications for funding.)

A Good Working Relationship: Core Participants and the Inquiry

Public inquiries work best by consensus. Establishing a good working relationship between an inquiry, its core participants and their legal representatives, benefits all concerned and is vital to the smooth and cost-effective operation of an inquiry. It requires cooperation and effort from both members of the inquiry team and from participants.

An uncooperative or difficult core participant has the potential to significantly impede an inquiry's proceedings, for example by providing an inquiry with unnecessary or irrelevant material, launching unmeritorious challenges against an inquiry's decisions, and delaying responses to an inquiry's requests for information. The risk to core participants in adopting an uncooperative or unhelpful approach is that it can give the impression that they have something to hide. An inquiry may then, even if unconsciously, approach evidence relating to the core participant with a more 'sceptical eye'.

Equally, dealing with an inquiry that lacks transparency or is inflexible can significantly restrict a legal representative's ability to advise and protect their client's interests. For example, if an inquiry lacks transparency about the evidence on which it is relying, a core participant may have to second guess the direction the evidence is taking the inquiry, or the basis for selection of relevant material or on which witnesses are to give oral evidence, which may result in additional and unnecessary work, thereby increasing costs. The only recourse available to core participants is judicial review, but that is also costly and requires permission of the court.

There may be accounts of difficult experiences during some inquiries, both from core participants and from members of the inquiry team. For example there may be complaints made that an inquiry was disorganised, or failed to communicate key information, or that a core participant was unhelpful, uncooperative or demanding, increasing the inquiry's already heavy workload. Either way, the responsibility lies with both core participants and members of the inquiry team to work to establish a good working relationship. The inquiry's legal team will often be the first substantial contact with the core participants and witnesses, and will therefore carry a heavy burden in that regard.

Checklist – Tips for establishing a good working relationship

The inquiry

- The inquiry team, particularly the legal team, must work to gain the support, cooperation and trust of all participants.
- The inquiry team, including counsel to the inquiry, the solicitor to the inquiry and their teams, should aim to communicate frequently and clearly with core participants and their legal representatives on progress, or lack thereof, with reasons. (It is, however, more difficult for the chair to build a similar relationship as this may create the perception of a lack of independence and influence from others.)
- The inquiry should adopt a flexible approach when warranted. For example, by agreeing to extensions of time for core participants to comply with requests for information, if there is good reason for the extension, and the delay would not materially impact the inquiry's work.
- The inquiry must be seen to remain impartial throughout and not appear to favour anyone or be on anyone's 'side'. All parties should always be treated in like manner.
- The inquiry should clearly document its procedures, and keep them regularly updated, so that all participants are clear about the inquiry's remit, functions and limitations. This will also help keep queries from core participants and their legal representatives to a minimum.
- The inquiry should be as open as possible and share what information and material it can with core participants; if material cannot be shared, the inquiry should explain why, where possible.
- For each core participant or group of core participants, the inquiry should appoint a member of the inquiry team to be their primary point of contact.
- The inquiry should provide core participants and legal representatives with as much notice as possible when, for example, disseminating witness statements in advance of oral testimony, or when providing a hearing timetable.

- Wherever possible, the inquiry should consult core participants, for example, on the terms of reference, the contents of the inquiry's protocols, or the set up of the IT systems.
- The inquiry team should ensure that the section of the IT systems to which core participants and their legal representatives have access are well-ordered, with logical folder structures, and with notifications to alert them when new documents are loaded onto the system. This will help the core participants and legal representatives to navigate the system, as well as limit the number of queries concerning documentation, thereby reducing the time and costs spent.
- During the inquiry, the inquiry team should reassure the core participants and their legal representatives that the inquiry is reading their submissions and evidence and is taking them into account.
- Whilst remaining impartial, it is particularly important for an inquiry to build a good relationship with victims, survivors and their families.

Quote

'Of course, some inquiries have huge numbers of victims and representatives and the task of liaising with them becomes enormously burdensome and complex. However, I believe that it is always worth devoting time and energy to this.'

Rory Phillips QC, 3 Verulam Buildings

Core Participants and Legal Representatives

- A core participant's role is to assist the inquiry, not merely to promote a particular point of view.

Core participants and their legal advisers should:

- Cooperate fully and assist the inquiry in fulfilling its terms of reference, whilst protecting their or their client's interests.
- Respond to requests for information promptly.
- Provide documents in a clear and ordered format and in accordance with any inquiry procedure.
- Comply with any inquiry procedures within the specified timescales or explain in advance why a timescale might not be met and when the procedure in

question will be complied with (this is particularly important because the inquiry will be handling a very large quantity of material under very tight deadlines).

- Communicate regularly with the inquiry; often a phone call is better than a long letter or email.
- Appreciate the weight of the inquiry team's workload and the calls on their time and assist where possible.
- If undertaking work for which the inquiry will in principle pay, ensure that there is prior approval both as to the content and extent of the work and subsequent expenditure.

7

Funding

Introduction

Public inquiries convened by ministers into matters of public concern, whether statutory or non-statutory, are funded by government through a central government department, the 'sponsoring department'. The sponsoring department is accountable to the government for the cost of the inquiry.[1]

For those participating in a public inquiry, the cost of legal representation, loss of time, or other expenses incurred in attending or otherwise being involved in an inquiry, can be substantial. However, there is no automatic entitlement to public funding.[2] Participants are usually self-funded if they are able to afford it. Funding awards are, however, made to some inquiry participants and the cost of those awards often constitute the most significant part of the total cost of an inquiry.[3] At the outset of an inquiry, the chair will set out clear procedures for dealing with the funding of core participants, interested parties and witnesses and the criteria that will be applied to determine who may receive funding. As explained in chapter five, this will usually involve the inquiry preparing and publishing a costs protocol.

Benefits of Receiving Funded Legal Representation

Participants who have received funding for legal representation have reported significant benefit from the legal representation received. Legal representation

[1] As explained in chapter one, inquiries are not restricted to those convened by ministers into matters of public concern. Inquiries can be convened by any person or body, whether they be public or private, to look at any issue which they consider requires investigation. Local authorities commission and fund their own inquiries, such as the Independent Inquiry into Child Sexual Exploitation in Rotherham and the Independent Trojan Horse Investigation in Birmingham. Local authorities are also accountable to the government for the cost of those inquiries.

[2] There have been exceptions to this, such as funding in the Grenfell Tower Inquiry, where the prime minister determined that three categories of individuals would automatically be granted funding for legal representation upon their involvement in the inquiry: (a) the families of the victims of the Grenfell Tower tragedy; (b) the survivors of the Grenfell Tower tragedy and their families; (c) local residents affected by the Grenfell Tower tragedy (see also below).

[3] Explanatory Notes to the Inquiries Act 2005, para 97.

may include advice on inquiry procedure and legal complexities; management of the huge quantity of documents and evidence required when preparing for the inquiry; support for preparing witness statements and the disclosure of relevant documents to the inquiry; advice on the protection of confidential information; and support in preparing suggested lines of questioning for counsel to the inquiry. Further, while a public inquiry cannot make findings of civil or criminal liability, liability may be inferred from what is said during an inquiry and reputations may be damaged or destroyed. As a result, many participants are keen to have legal representation to protect their interests and find the fact there is very limited public funding available frustrating.[4]

There is of course no obligation to seek access to public funds; any participant who can afford to do so, whether a witness, core participant or interested party, can seek legal advice in relation to an inquiry's work. The question being explored is whether, and to what extent, the cost of that legal advice might be met by public funds.

Quote

'Well, I certainly would not have been able to appear with anything like the confidence that I hope I did have had I not had available the benefit of legal advice in preparing for the inquiry and, indeed, at the time that I was giving evidence to the inquiry.'

Christopher Jeffries (who was falsely accused of murdering Jo Yeates and gave evidence to the Leveson Inquiry), in evidence to the House of Lords Select Committee on the Inquiries Act 2005[5]

'We had barristers and a legal team and without them we would never have been able to get at the truth. We would never have been able to prepare ourselves. The NHS is such a complex body, with the legislation, the Acts, we just would not have been able to manage without a legal team. I believe our legal team were a great asset to the public inquiry.'

Julie Bailey, Cure the NHS, a Core Participant to the Mid Staffordshire NHS Foundation Trust Public Inquiry, in evidence to the House of Lords Select Committee on the Inquiries Act 2005[6]

[4] See chapter six for further discussion on legal representation.

[5] Christopher Jefferies, oral evidence taken before the HL Select Committee (23 October 2013) Q251, http://www.parliament.uk/documents/lords-committees/Inquiries-Act-2005/IA_Written_Oral_evidencevol.pdf (accessed 12 August 2020).

[6] Julie Bailey, oral evidence taken before the HL Select Committee (n 5) Q168.

Other Expenses

Individuals and organisations involved with an inquiry may suffer other financial losses: through loss of time (eg if they are self-employed, but are required to spend time giving oral evidence to an inquiry) or by incurring other related expenses (such as travel and accommodation when attending the inquiry).

The Approach to Expenses of Participants to a Public Inquiry

Historically, the general position has been that those organisations which have sufficient funds to meet the cost of legal representation and other related expenses should not receive public funding. In response to a question in Parliament on 29 January 1990, the Attorney General stated:

> So far as the costs of legal representation of parties to any inquiry are concerned, where the Government have a discretion they always take careful account of the recommendations on costs of the tribunal or inquiry concerned. In general, the Government accept the need to pay out of public funds the reasonable costs of any necessary party to the inquiry who would be prejudiced in seeking representation were he in any doubt about funds becoming available. The Government do not accept that the costs of substantial bodies should be met from public funds unless there are special circumstances.[7]

In principle, this position has not changed since this statement was made. Prior to the Inquiries Act 2005 coming into force, it had been for the minister convening the inquiry to decide, in consultation with the chair, on matters of funding. The minister and chair would consider which parties and individuals participating in the inquiry were considered to have such a direct interest in the inquiry that they required representation, but might be unable to pay for representation and associated expenses themselves. The introduction of the 2005 Act and the Inquiry Rules 2006 has largely left that position unchanged.

For statutory inquiries, funding awards are made at the discretion of the chair, subject to such conditions or qualifications as may be determined by the minister[8] and the provisions within the Inquiries Act 2005 Act and Inquiry Rules 2006. Non-statutory inquiries often adopt a similar approach to funding, although the chair is not always given the authority to determine funding decisions[9] which may rest with the body funding the inquiry (eg the relevant local authority). Nevertheless, familiarity with the statutory position is useful, as similar provisions are often adopted.

[7] HC 29 January 1990, vol 166, col WA 26.

[8] Inquiries Act 2005, s 40.

[9] For non-statutory inquiries that have not been convened by a minister, funding decisions may rest with the funding body, for example where a local authority has convened an inquiry.

Who may Apply

Section 40 of the Inquiries Act 2005 and rr 19 to 34 of the Inquiry Rules 2006 contain provisions that allow a person to apply to a statutory inquiry for reasonable expenses incurred or to be incurred. This includes legal costs, compensation for loss of time, and other expenses incurred in attending, or otherwise in relation to, the inquiry.[10]

Applicants will only be eligible to apply for an award of costs if:

- they have been asked to attend the inquiry to give evidence or to produce any document or other thing, or
- in the opinion of the chair, they have such a particular interest in the proceedings or outcome of the inquiry as to justify such an award.[11]

Where an applicant has been granted core participant status, they are likely, though not guaranteed, to be eligible to apply for a funding award;[12] although this by no means guarantees that such an application will be successful. However, an organisation or individual does not need to have been awarded core participant status by the chair of the inquiry in order to make an application for funding.

Criteria

When determining whether or not a funding award should be granted, the chair of a statutory inquiry is required to take into account the following criteria:

(a) the financial resources of the applicant; and
(b) whether making an award is in the public interest[13]

as well as any other conditions or qualifications that the minister has determined should apply.[14]

Decisions will also be guided by the general principle that the chair will act fairly and with regard to the need to avoid any unnecessary cost (whether to public funds or to witnesses or others).[15]

[10] Inquiries Act 2005, s 40(1).
[11] Inquiries Act 2005, s 40(3).
[12] See chapter six and the criteria for designation as a core participant set out in the Inquiry Rules 2006, r 5(2).
[13] Inquiry Rules 2006, r 21(2).
[14] Inquiries Act 2005, s 40(4).
[15] Inquiries Act 2005, s 17(3).

Issue – The statutory criteria for funding awards are vague

The criteria that the chair is required to consider when determining applications for funding are relatively vague. Individuals and organisations seeking to make applications for funding awards may therefore find formulating applications a challenge.

The chair of an inquiry is, however, at liberty to determine the conduct and procedure of the inquiry as they see fit[16] and can therefore provide further detail as to how such applications will be considered. Increasingly, inquiries are doing this by publishing protocols that set out the procedure for making legal funding applications, which often set out additional criteria that the chair will consider when making the determination.

For example, wording similar to that set out below has appeared in a number of inquiries' protocols on legal representation at public expense:[17]

'the Chairman envisages that normally awards will be made only in cases where he decides that:

a. the applicant –
   i. has a direct link to, and evidence to provide in respect of, the matters set out in the Inquiry's terms of reference; and/or
   ii. has a significant interest in an important aspect of the matters set out in those terms of reference; and/or
   iii. may be subject to explicit or significant criticism during the Inquiry's proceedings or in the report, or in any interim report; and

b. the applicant would be prejudiced in seeking representation if there were to be any doubt about funds becoming available and there are no other means by which such representation can be funded; and

c. it is fair, necessary, reasonable and proportionate to make an award.'

Even if an inquiry does not publish a protocol, nor provide any further detail as to how applications for legal funding will be determined, it is useful to bear in mind the above criteria when applications for funding for legal representation are being prepared.[18]

Where applications are made for other expenses, such as compensation for loss of time or other costs incurred in attending or otherwise in

[16] Inquiries Act 2005, s 17(1).

[17] See for example the protocols for the Undercover Policy Inquiry, Grenfell Tower Inquiry, Al-Sweady Inquiry, and the Renewable Heat Incentive Inquiry.

[18] The process by which applications are to be made are set out under r 20 of the Inquiry Rules 2006.

connection with the inquiry, there is additional guidance as to what criteria should be addressed in any application made:

- in respect of compensation for loss of time, the inquiry must have regard to:
  - actual sums lost by the applicant as a result of attending the inquiry; or
  - if no such sums can be identified, such other amount as the solicitor to the inquiry considers proportionate and reasonable.[19]
- in respect of an award in respect of other expenses, the inquiry must have regard to whether the expenses:
  - were proportionately and reasonably incurred; and
  - are proportionate and reasonable in amount.[20]

Awards in respect of legal costs are often granted to survivors, families of victims and other core participants with limited funds. Recent examples of this include the Infected Blood Inquiry and the Grenfell Tower Inquiry, where the minister who convened the inquiry made the decision at the outset that survivors and families of victims would automatically receive an award, regardless of their financial means. The scope and terms of those awards was left to be determined by the chair.

There are circumstances where the granting of funding awards is, however, unlikely. For example where an applicant's interest in the inquiry is limited; where the applicant is an organisation which has sufficient funds to meet its own cost; or where the applicant is applying to be represented separately from another group of core participants who are jointly represented, have aligned interests and are already funded, and that group could adequately represent the applicant (see below on joint representation).

The Scope of Awards for Funding

Even where an award is granted, it is rare for that award to be open-ended and without limitation. Awards are usually limited to specific issues or tasks and are capped in terms of time and cost. The limits could be applied in a number of ways: for example hourly rates; limits on expenses that can be claimed, capped

[19] Inquiry Rules 2006, r 28(1).
[20] Inquiry Rules 2006, r 28(2).

by the relevant minister; no costs to be paid if not incurred in accordance with a workplan that is pre-agreed by the chair; or costs limited to certain tasks or costs incurred during certain modules or phases.

It is now quite common for an inquiry to conduct its business in modules or phases. An applicant, and the chair, will therefore need to bear in mind that the matter of costs and funding, and its application to a module or phase, will need be reconsidered at each stage, depending on an evaluation of the applicant's role and relevance to that stage.

> **Quote**
>
> *'Also in terms of awarding funding, I think sometimes people feel that you have to fund somebody for the whole duration of the inquiry, whereas often you can work out that those witnesses may criticise this person and therefore this person needs to be represented when they are giving evidence, and so forth. So you can parcel it up and give somebody limited funding for up to 10 hours of representation over a two-day period, and they can always apply to extend. If you have a stringent cost protocol which people sign up to before funding is awarded, then that does help and section 40 kicks in at that point as well.'*
>
> Judi Kemish, in evidence to the House of Lords Select Committee on the Inquiries Act 2005

Once an award has been granted, the chair is likely to specify conditions or limitations to that award, or conduct an assessment of costs already incurred. The two processes are as follows:

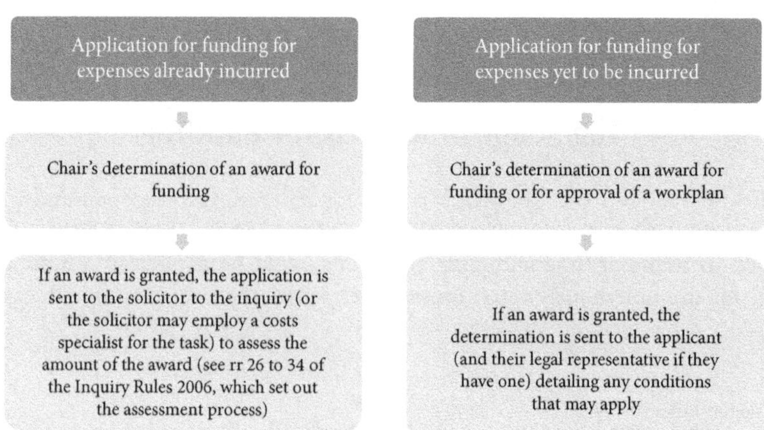

While the legislation does envisage these two processes for seeking approval for funding, legal advisers and clients should, where possible, avoid incurring costs without prior approval. It is likely an inquiry will be reluctant to grant funding that has been incurred outside of any agreed workplan unless there are exceptional circumstances.

Information that must be Included in an Application for Funding

Rule 20 of the Inquiry Rules 2006 sets out the information that must be contained in an application for funding for legal representation, to assist the chair in determining the nature and scope of the representation being sought, and what conditions would be appropriate.

> Where the application relates to amounts to be incurred in respect of legal representation, the application must state –
>
> (a) the nature and estimated duration of the work for which the award is sought;
> (b) the proposed hourly rates; and
> (c) any other amounts which the person anticipates claiming in relation to legal representation.

The inquiry may also have a protocol in place which specifies what, if any, other information should be included in an application for funding.

Checklist – Conditions on funding awards

An award for funding will almost always include a series of conditions. This is to control the costs incurred and set clear limits on what will be paid by the inquiry.

Conditions on funding for legal representation

Rule 22 of the Inquiry Rules 2006 provides that, where the chair has determined an award should be made in respect of legal representation, conditions including but not limited to the following must be set:

(a) the nature and scope of the work to be funded;
(b) the hourly rates which will be paid, which may be capped by the minister;[21]

[21] In some cases, the applied hourly rates caps have been the same as those used on other inquiries several years previously.

(c) any upper limit or limits on the sums or number of hours which will be paid;
(d) the frequency with which bills must be submitted to the chair; and
(e) the form in which bills must be submitted to the chair.

An inquiry may set additional conditions, which the chair thinks is appropriate. These may include, for example:

- travel and waiting time will not be paid;
- a limit on expenses incurred, perhaps with a daily maximum being set; these may be predetermined by the minister and may not cover the actual expenses incurred; and
- any changes to the nature and scope of the work for which funding has been provided must be agreed in advance before the cost is incurred.

Awards for compensation for loss of time or other amounts

Similarly, if a chair has determined an award should be made in respect of compensation for loss of time, or in respect of other expenses properly incurred in relation to the inquiry, rr 23 and 24 of the Inquiry Rules 2006 state that an inquiry is required to set the following conditions:

Compensation for loss of time:

(a) an upper limit or limits on the sums which will be paid;
(b) the form in which bills must be submitted to the chair; and
(c) the supply of such documentary evidence as the chair considers necessary.[22]

Awards for other amounts:

(a) an upper limit or limits on the sums which will be paid;
(b) a requirement that the applicant provide evidence that the expenditure has been incurred; and
(c) the form in which bills must be submitted to the chair.[23]

Alternative Sources of Funding

If a participant is not successful in an application for funding for legal representation from the inquiry, the options for alternative sources of funding are limited.

[22] Inquiry Rules 2006, r 23.
[23] Inquiry Rules 2006, r 24.

The few potential sources of funding that can be explored, depending on the circumstances of the applicant and the nature of the inquiry, are as follows:

- Participants may have insurance in place that might cover the cost of legal representation at the inquiry, particularly if they have been formally compelled by the inquiry to provide documents or to appear at an oral hearing. If the applicant is engaging in the inquiry's work on a voluntary basis, however, an insurance policy is unlikely to cover such circumstances.
- Where the participant is an individual, and their involvement in the inquiry has arisen as a result of their employment or under a contract for the provision of services, they might be able to seek funding from their employer or the company engaging their services.
- If a participant considers there is a significant public interest in them being involved in an inquiry's work (even if an application to the inquiry on this basis has been refused), they could consider crowd funding (ie seeking donations from the public via an online appeal). Crowd funding for legal representation is still a novel route to securing legal funding and it has yet to be used for the purposes of securing representation at a public inquiry. It has however been used in high profile cases of public interest, such as Gina Miller's Supreme Court challenge to formal notice of the UK's withdrawal from the European Union being given without prior legislation passed by Parliament[24] and Noel Conway's challenge to the ban on assisted suicide.[25] The cases that are most successful at securing crowd funding tend to be those involving highly publicised proceedings (and a public inquiry is likely to fall within this category) and where the individuals or organisations concerned are able to engage well with the public.
- Depending on the nature of the inquiry, there may be specialist interest groups that might consider making a donation to fund legal representation for participation in an inquiry.

Joint Representation

> **Quote**
>
> *'In the Hamill inquiry, all the police officers bar two were represented by one group of lawyers. So there was a QC, he was not there all the time; there was a junior counsel; a solicitor, and there may have been a paralegal for that team. They represented all the police officers bar one or two. Where there was*

[24] *R (Miller) v Secretary of State for Exiting the European Union* [2017] UKSC 5.
[25] *R (Conway) v Secretary of State for Justice* [2018] EWCA Civ 1431.

> *a significant conflict of interest, they had to be separately represented. You are the ones awarding the funding so you can lay down the conditions.'*
>
> Judi Kemish, solicitor to Robert Hamill Inquiry and Azelle Rodney Inquiry, in evidence to the House of Lords Select Committee on the Inquiries Act 2005

As explained in chapter six, under r 7 of the Inquiry Rules 2006, where the chair of a statutory inquiry considers that core participants have similar interests in the outcome of an inquiry, the facts they are likely to rely on during the inquiry are similar, and it would be fair to do so, the chair can make an order that the participants are to be jointly represented by a single recognised legal representative. A decision to impose such an order is often driven by the chair's desire to reduce the time and cost of the inquiry; joint representation enables an inquiry to proceed at a greater pace with the potential number of funded legal representatives being reduced.

Publication of Costs of an Inquiry

The National Audit Office reported that more than £200m was spent by government on 26 public inquiries (statutory and non-statutory inquiries) that concluded between 2005 and 2018.[26] Where an inquiry is convened under the Inquiries Act 2005, the sponsoring minister is required to publish the inquiry's total expenses within a reasonable time after the end of the inquiry.[27] The sponsoring minister is answerable to Parliament for the cost of an inquiry.

Over time, best practice has developed whereby inquiries regularly publish their expenses, usually on their website, as the inquiry progresses. The inquiry, however, must take care when publishing such information to ensure that unnecessary, confidential details of the work undertaken (eg witness names, locations, applications for anonymity) are not released to the public at the same time.

[26] National Audit Office, *Investigation into government-funded inquiries* (2018) HC 836 Session 2017–2019.

[27] Inquiries Act 2005, s 39(6).

8

Documentary Evidence

Introduction

One of the key stages of a public inquiry's investigation phase is the gathering, review and analysis of documents and the subsequent publication of documents on the inquiry's document management system for core participants and ultimately on its website if referenced in evidence. This is often the most time-consuming and costly phase of an inquiry's work, both for the inquiry itself and those engaged with its work. Frequently, inquiries receive tens of thousands of documents and, in some cases, more. The advancement of technology, and the use of IT systems, has assisted with handling the vast volume of disclosure (see chapter four), but the gathering and review of documentary evidence remains a huge task for an inquiry.

The provision of documents to an inquiry, and the review of documents disclosed to, and by, an inquiry, is also one of the key stages during which core participants and interested parties engage with an inquiry's work.

Written Request for Documentary Evidence

Once the inquiry's team has been appointed and a core support framework for the inquiry's work established (eg protocols drawn up and IT systems put in place), the inquiry's first step in its investigations is usually gathering relevant documents. This involves the inquiry solicitor sending a written request for documents to those individuals or organisations from whom the inquiry wishes to obtain material.[1] The letter usually explains the terms of reference of the inquiry, why the person or organisation is being contacted, and identifies what documents, or categories of documents, are being sought.

Often, early requests for documents ask 'for all documents that may be relevant to an inquiry's terms of reference'. Such requests usually involve the recipient having to conduct a series of electronic searches of its IT systems to identify documents that are, or may be, relevant. The formal request for documents is therefore

[1] 'Or any other thing'. Inquiry Rules 2006, r 9. Witness statements are dealt with separately to documents: see chapter ten.

often followed by discussions between the inquiry solicitor and the organisation or individual to which the request was made, to agree the parameters of such searches to ensure that all relevant documents are captured, and to establish what the inquiry's interpretation of its terms of reference may be, so as to better understand 'relevance'.

Statutory Provisions and the Power to Require Disclosure

One of the crucial distinguishing features between a statutory and non-statutory inquiry is that a statutory inquiry has the power to compel witnesses to produce evidence to the inquiry under s 21 of the Inquiries Act 2005 (see the detailed discussion in chapter ten). These powers include the power to require a person to:

- provide any documents in his custody or under his control that relate to a matter in question at the inquiry;[2] and
- attend at a specified place and time to produce the said documents.[3]

Such requests for documents are often described as 'Section 21 Notices'.

The request for evidence must be made in writing and the written notice must:

- explain the possible consequences of not complying;
- indicate what the recipient of the notice should do if he wishes to claim that
  - he is unable to comply with a notice under this section, or
  - it is not reasonable in all the circumstances to require him to comply.[4]

Any claim made by a recipient that they are unable to comply, or that it is not reasonable to require them to comply, will be determined by the chair, having regard to the public interest in the information in question being obtained by the inquiry and the likely importance of the information.[5] The chair may decide to revoke or vary a Section 21 Notice.[6]

Despite these powers, many statutory inquiries choose to make voluntary requests for documents in the first instance, only resorting to issuing a formal Section 21 Notice if an organisation or person refuses to provide, or is delaying its production of, the requested documents. Even where the powers granted by the Inquiries Act 2005 are not actually exercised, the fact that these powers exist can provide a powerful incentive for ensuring co-operation with the inquiry.

[2] Inquiries Act 2005, s 21(2)(b).
[3] Inquiries Act 2005, s 21(1)(b).
[4] Inquiries Act 2005, s 21(3).
[5] Inquiries Act 2005, s 21(5).
[6] Inquiries Act 2005, s 21(4).

Enforcement of a Section 21 Notice

Failure to comply with a notice requiring the production of documents under s 21 of the Inquiries Act 2005, without reasonable excuse, renders the recipient of the request guilty of an offence.

It is also an offence to distort, suppress or destroy documents that are the subject of a Section 21 Notice.[7]

A person who is guilty of such an offence is liable on summary conviction to a fine or imprisonment.

(Sections 35 and 36 of the Inquiries Act 2005.)

When Might an Inquiry Compel the Production of Documents?

There are generally three instances during a statutory inquiry when the inquiry may decide that it is necessary to exercise its powers of compulsion and serve a Section 21 Notice, as opposed to sending a voluntary request for information:

- *Where a person or an organisation is refusing to provide documents.*
- *Where a person or an organisation is slow in producing documents.* Serving a Section 21 Notice can focus the mind of those tasked with collating the documents and speed up compliance, for example by resulting in additional resources being dedicated to responding to the request, to avoid any delay impacting on an inquiry's own timetable.
- *Where a person or an organisation wishes to establish legal grounds to legitimise the processing, and disclosure to the inquiry, of personal data.* Organisations are often reluctant to disclose documents that contain personal data without a formal statutory request being made, for fear of breaching any data protection obligations (see chapter nine). Section 21 notices may therefore be invited by document providers. If, however, an inquiry can provide assurances about how the documents will be used, securely stored and handled, and the legal grounds for justifying disclosure, this may be sufficient to allay any fears about potential breaches of data protection legislation and a Section 21 Notice may not be required.

As discussed in chapter seven, ideally an inquiry will start to gather documentary evidence some months prior to any witnesses being interviewed and the commencement of any oral hearings. Often, therefore, requesting the production

[7] Subject to the provisions of the Inquiries Act 2005, s 35(4) where the person is required or authorised to do so by the inquiry or where the document is privileged.

of documents is the first evidence-gathering step an inquiry will take. Reviewing the documents at an early stage, after provision, reduces the likelihood of an inquiry needing to interview a witness more than once, or recall a witness to appear at a later hearing to deal with issues that were not known to be relevant when the witness was first interviewed or gave evidence, thereby increasing efficiency and reducing time and cost. Consequently, there will usually be a delay between the analysis of documents provided and the taking of witness statements (assuming that it is the inquiry team that will be preparing the witness statements, rather than the recognised legal representatives, or the witnesses themselves: see chapter ten).

Inquiries, however, are usually run on very tight timescales. There is often pressure for the inquiry's work to progress as quickly as possible so that the inquiry can report its findings and recommendations, coupled with the fact that the longer an inquiry takes, the more expensive it will be. As a result, while an early review of documents is preferable, in some cases it is not possible and the inquiry may have to review documents on a rolling basis, alongside the witness interviews (if prepared by the inquiry team) and oral hearings.

Where an inquiry is not in a position to send requests and gather documents immediately, it may contact all relevant individuals and organisations to ask them to preserve all documents that might be relevant to the inquiry's work, so that they can be produced at a later date, if and when required. Where core participants and interested parties are organisations, they should, in any event, consider issuing an internal instruction to all staff, telling them to preserve all material that could be relevant to the inquiry, to avoid any later criticism that documents were not properly preserved for the inquiry's purposes. If documents that are relevant to an inquiry's work are destroyed, even if in accordance with an organisation's standard document destruction policies that had not been put on hold, the inquiry may publicly criticise the organisation, and may draw adverse inferences from the fact that the organisation did not take appropriate steps to preserve the relevant documents.

Issue – Requests for documents: specific or general?

Requests for documents may be very specific, asking for particular documents or categories of documents, or narrowing the request to certain issues. They may also be very broad and general in nature, for example a request for 'any documents relevant to the inquiry's terms of reference'. For an inquiry, there are challenges with both approaches.

Very specific requests for documents pre-suppose that the inquiry has already identified the issues and topics that will be most important to its work. In practice, however, at an early stage of the inquiry's investigations, determining the key issues and topics can be very difficult and the inquiry must keep an open mind from the outset about what may be, or become, relevant.

A broad request for documents can, however, also present challenges. For recipients of such requests, the process of searching for and collating all documents relevant to an inquiry's terms of reference can be very time-consuming and costly, possibly resulting in tens of thousands of documents being disclosed. The inquiry must then review all of the documents, establish whether they are, in fact, relevant, and organise them in a logical manner so that the documents can be readily used and referred to by the inquiry. This too is very time-consuming and costly. The extent of the work undertaken by recipients of such requests, and the inquiry itself, can have a significant impact on the progress of the inquiry's work.

For example, during the Edinburgh Tram Inquiry, requests were made for 'all' documents relevant to the inquiry's terms of reference, which meant all contractual documents and documents relating to disputes and arbitrational adjudications spanning years were provided, by many parties, creating a massive volume of material and huge duplication.

To avoid this problem, an inquiry will often adopt a combination of both forms of request. Early on in an inquiry's work, an inquiry may make a general request for all documents that are relevant to the terms of reference, but with accompanying guidance as to the types of documents in which the inquiry has most interest, for example by identifying a specific period of time that is particularly relevant or certain topics. It may also exclude certain topics or, where requests to a number of individuals or organisation would result in the receipt of duplicates of documents, it may tailor the requests made to avoid this. This can then open up a discussion between the inquiry and a document provider about how the search for documents could be conducted and, for example, agreeing the search terms to be applied to a search of relevant IT systems. This ensures that a broad search is conducted for all relevant material, but with sensible parameters in place that have been pre-agreed with the inquiry. From a document provider's perspective, agreeing an approach to the search in advance reduces the risk that it will be criticised later on in the proceedings for failing to disclose something that was not captured by the pre-agreed search, but was identified as being relevant at a later date.

As an inquiry's work progresses, more specific requests for documents may be made, as the evidential picture is built up and the key topics and issues become clearer.

It is becoming increasingly common for inquiries to request that a disclosure statement is submitted alongside documents disclosed in response to a Section 21 Notice (or the voluntary equivalent). Disclosure statements require the provider to set out the methodology used to search for relevant documents and confirm that the search conducted was reasonable and thorough, providing the inquiry with an extra level of assurance that the obligations of the document provider have been met. An inquiry may also require the disclosure statement to contain a statement of truth confirming that the details provided are true, to the best of the individual's knowledge and belief. When signing on behalf of an organisation, the statement of truth should be signed off by someone holding a senior level position, for example at board level.

Non-Statutory Inquiries

Non-statutory inquiries do not have powers to compel individuals or organisations to provide documents. They are reliant on the cooperation of the individuals and organisations involved with the inquiry. In some cases, this does not cause issues, either because the documents requested are provided voluntarily or, for example, because evidence provided by other individuals or organisations, who were willing to cooperate, is considered sufficient to allow the chair to satisfy the inquiry's terms of reference and draw conclusions. In other cases however, the inability to compel individuals and organisations to provide documents can hinder an inquiry's progress and prevent it from obtaining evidence that could be key to its terms of reference.

Although non-statutory inquiries do not have powers of compulsion, a recipient of a request for documents who refuses to provide these documents runs the risk of this fact being made public in the inquiry report and of adverse inferences being drawn. A refusal to cooperate can have serious reputational, political and commercial implications and concern over these risks is usually sufficient to secure the compliance of witnesses and production of documents, in the absence of good reason not to. A recipient who is considering refusing to comply with a request to produce documents should also bear in mind that, by doing so, they will lose the opportunity to provide documents that may be helpful to their position; the absence of any documents at all may be more damaging in the long run.

Timelines

For both statutory and non-statutory inquiries, at the outset of the inquiry's work some chairs make public statements setting out the expectations of the inquiry for the timing of the production of documents, making it clear that deadlines should be met unless an extension is agreed in advance with the inquiry. For non-statutory inquiries, this can be a particularly useful step, in order to encourage cooperation and to make it clear that the public nature of the inquiry will mean that any non-cooperation will be made public (something which was done by Lord Hutton in the Hutton Inquiry, see below).

> **Quote**
>
> *'The Government has ... stated that it will provide me with the fullest cooperation and that it expects all other authorities and parties to do the same. I make it clear that it will be for me to decide as I think right within my terms of reference the matters which will be the subject of my investigation. I intend to sit in public in the near future to state how I intend to conduct the Inquiry and to consider the extent to which interested parties and bodies should be represented by counsel or solicitors ... It is also my intention to conduct the inquiry mostly in public.'*
>
> Hutton Inquiry, Statement by the Right Honourable Lord Hutton[8]

Withholding Documents

During statutory inquiries, potential document providers can refuse to provide documents on a number of legitimate grounds:

Privilege

Under s 22 of the Inquiries Act 2005, a person may not be required to produce a document if information within it is privileged.[9] This means that an individual or an organisation may refuse to provide documents that fall within a Section 21 Notice provided:

- the documents are covered by legal professional privilege;
- the documents might incriminate them or their spouse or civil partner; or
- the documents relate to things said or done in Parliament and are covered by parliamentary privilege.

Despite these provisions, in practice, the presence of privileged information within documents rarely results in documents in their entirety being withheld from an inquiry, for a number of reasons:

- document providers are often willing, and are encouraged by an inquiry, to waive privilege and release documents to assist the inquiry's work;
- an inquiry and document provider may agree that the inquiry will receive a document or documents on the basis of guarantees of strict confidentiality and

[8] Hutton Inquiry, 'Investigation into the circumstances surrounding the death of Dr David Kelly: statement by the Right Honourable Lord Hutton', Press notice, 21 July 2003.

[9] Inquiries Act 2005, s 22(1).

for the sole purpose of reviewing the document or documents for relevance, while privilege is preserved; where a document is provided on this basis, the document provider will not subsequently be precluded from claiming legal professional privilege in respect of all or part of that document;

- although inquiries usually require documents to be disclosed in an unredacted form, if documents contain information over which privilege is being claimed, an inquiry may be willing to accept documents with privileged information having been redacted prior to disclosure.

Whether a document provider is prepared to waive privilege will depend on the circumstances of the inquiry and the nature of the documents requested. They cannot be forced to waive privilege nor can their decision to do so be expedited.

Where there has been a significant passage of time since the creation of the documents over which privilege is being claimed, inquiry chairs have expressed an expectation that privilege would not be used as a reason to withhold documents, for example during the Independent Jersey Care Inquiry and Infected Blood Inquiry (see below). In the case of both inquiries, a number of document providers agreed to waive legal professional privilege and disclosed the documents sought by the inquiry. (In such circumstances, document providers should bear in mind the fact that the passage of time, and dissemination of advice more widely, may be so significant that it may result in privilege having been lost in any event.)

Quote

'Organisations may consider that some of the documents or information they hold are potentially covered by legal professional privilege (LPP). The right to assert LPP, which exists in civil proceedings, is preserved in the context of public inquiries by s.22(1) of the Inquiries Act 2005. That being said, this Inquiry is tasked with investigating matters spanning a period of over 50 years, and given the passage of time LPP and confidentiality issues will in many cases have been eroded. With this in mind, and having regard both to the commitment made in Parliament and to the fact that issues of candour, openness and cover-up form part of the areas for investigation by the Inquiry, I expect all government departments, public organisations and others providing documents and information to the Inquiry to give careful consideration to waiving LPP where this issue arises. Indeed, those that do not will be conspicuous for that reason.'

Sir Brian Langstaff, Chair to the Infected Blood Inquiry, Statement on disclosure and legal professional privilege[10]

[10] https://www.infectedbloodinquiry.org.uk/sites/default/files/Chair%E2%80%99s-Statement-of-Intent-on-Disclosure-and-Legal-Professional-Privilege.pdf (accessed 12 August 2020).

Public Interest Immunity

A document provider may withhold documents from an inquiry, on the grounds of public interest immunity or 'PII', meaning that the documents are immune from disclosure for reasons of public interest. The 2005 Act expressly provides that public interest immunity applies in relation to statutory inquiries in the same way as it does to civil proceedings.[11]

A recipient of a request for documents who seeks to withhold documents on this basis is required to demonstrate that disclosure of the information would cause a real risk of serious prejudice to an important public interest (such as risk to national security) and that this outweighs the public interest in open justice.[12] It is then for the chair, and panel if appointed, to determine the balance of interests and whether the information should be disclosed to the inquiry and disclosed publicly and, if so, on what terms (eg in a redacted form).

As with legally privileged documents, it may be possible for the inquiry and the document provider to reach an agreement whereby the documents are disclosed to the inquiry on a strictly confidential basis and then disclosed publicly with necessary redactions applied.

Risk of Damage to the Economy

If a request for documents gives rise to a risk of damage to the economy, an application may be made on behalf of the Crown, the Financial Services Authority or the Bank of England to prevent disclosure on that basis. It is for the chair, and any panel if appointed, to determine the application by assessing whether the public interest in the information being revealed outweighs the public interest in avoiding a risk of damage to the economy. When carrying out such an exercise, the chair must not reveal the information, or allow it to be revealed, to anyone other than the inquiry panel.[13]

Breach of EU Law

The Inquiries Act 2005 also provides that if disclosing a certain document or class of documents would be incompatible with a Community obligation (ie anything arising from EU treaties, directives or regulations) then the document, or class of documents, are exempt from disclosure to the inquiry.[14]

[11] Inquiries Act 2005, s 22(2).
[12] *R v H* [2004] UKHL 3, [2004] 2 AC 134.
[13] Inquiries Act 2005, s 23.
[14] Inquiries Act 2005, s 22(1)(b), as amended post-Brexit.

Classified Material

Depending on the subject matter and the issues being explored, some inquiries will require the disclosure and use of classified information. The Government Security Classifications Policy, issued by the cabinet office, classifies government information to ensure that access is appropriately controlled and restricted, to prevent inadvertent or intentional disclosure of information to non-authorised individuals. Information may be categorised into 'official', 'secret' and 'top secret'.[15]

OFFICIAL	SECRET	TOP SECRET
The majority of information that is created or processed by the public sector. This includes routine business operations and services, some of which could have damaging consequences if lost, stolen or published in the media, but are not subject to a heightened threat profile.	Very sensitive information that justifies heightened protective measures to defend against determined and highly capable threat actors. For example, where compromise could seriously damage military capabilities, international relations or the investigation of serious organised crime.	HMG's most sensitive information requiring the highest levels of protection from the most serious threats. For example, where compromise could cause widespread loss of life or else threaten the security or economic wellbeing of the country or friendly nations.

Anyone working with government information is personally responsible for safeguarding that information in line with the policy. Depending on its subject matter, an inquiry may find itself in a position where material that is classified as 'secret' or 'top secret' is relevant to its terms of reference. However, obtaining disclosure of this information can be difficult.

Those in possession of such documents may include the security services, police forces and government departments and agencies. There is an obvious tension between the document provider's need to restrict access to secret material and the inquiry's need to discover and openly investigate all evidence relevant to its terms of reference. To address these tensions, inquiries may agree protocols and protective measures with the document providers, to ensure that the security of information is maintained and any access granted is limited and controlled, while also allowing the inquiry to use the information to further its terms of reference. Some of the issues that will be considered are set out below.

[15] Available at https://assets.publishing.service.gov.uk/government/uploads/system/uploads/attachment_data/file/709003/May-2018_Government-Security-Classifications.pdf (accessed 12 August 2020).

Checklist – Obtaining and handling classified material

- The inquiry and the government (usually via contacts within the inquiry's sponsoring department) will generally agree a documents protocol on handling any classified information provided to the inquiry, naming the Cabinet Secretary as final arbiter in discussions about disclosure.
- A classified documents protocol will set out a clear process for redacting and agreeing redactions for classified material, which is likely to be more onerous than the inquiry's standard redactions protocol (see below). A common approach is to require agreed categories of redactions to be applied on a document-by-document basis and then by bundle, for example bundles containing a particular type or category of evidence. This is to make sure that there are no triangulation issues (ie that there is no classified information that, although redacted in one document, could still be revealed as a result of other documents containing potentially identifying material being pieced together). No classified information should be released to the public until all material has been gathered, redacted and the redactions approved.
- The inquiry and the government will agree how information within the material can be used in the inquiry's hearing, and relied on in its final report, ensuring fairness to all parties.
- There may also be an agreement that only certain members of the inquiry team can access the material, for example those with security clearance to the requisite level.

Opposing a Section 21 Notice Requiring the Production of Documents

A recipient of a Section 21 Notice to produce documents may seek to oppose the request by claiming that:

(a) they are unable to comply with the request, because the documents are no longer in their possession or they have been destroyed (eg in accordance with an organisation's relevant document destruction policy or inadvertently); or
(b) it is not reasonable in all the circumstances to be required to comply, for example the request appears to be excessively broad and is arguably beyond the scope of the inquiry's terms of reference.[16]

[16] Inquiries Act 2005, s 21(4) for statutory inquiries.

Such claims are determined by the chair of the inquiry, as repeated below. Where it is argued that it is not reasonable in all the circumstances to be required to comply, the chair must consider the public interest in the information in question being obtained by the inquiry, having regard to the likely importance of the information.[17]

When making a claim of this type, consideration should be given to the following:

- *Is the request (and the extent of it) necessary and fair?* If the relevance of some of the documents requested is unclear, an explanation may be sought from the inquiry about how the documents in question are relevant to the inquiry's terms of reference. Similarly, an inquiry may make a very broad request for documents, rather than requesting specific documents, for example asking that certain searches be conducted of IT systems using key word searches. If a recipient of a Section 21 Notice believes that the proposed search is too broad, they can seek an explanation from the inquiry as to why the proposed search is likely to produce documents that are relevant to its terms of reference.
- *Has the need to avoid unnecessary cost been considered by the inquiry when formulating the request?* Under s 17 of the Inquiries Act 2005, when making any decision, the chair is required to have regard to the need to avoid unnecessary costs at all times; that includes not only the cost to the inquiry, but also unnecessary cost to those participating in the inquiry. It may be possible to argue that a request would result in significant cost and time being spent searching for potentially relevant material which is not essential to the inquiry's terms of reference, and therefore the request is not reasonable.
- *Are the documents requested in the possession of the recipient of the request or under their control?* If they are not, an explanation will have to be given as to why they are not, and who may now possess or control those documents. If the documents have been destroyed, an explanation will need to be provided as to why. This may be, for example, in accordance with a document destruction policy.

A claim to oppose a Section 21 Notice will be determined by the chair of the inquiry and the request or Section 21 Notice may be revoked or varied as a result. It is, however, unusual for such an application to be successful. An inquiry chair has a broad discretion when determining what might be relevant to an inquiry's terms of reference.

Claims have been made to vary and revoke Section 21 Notices where concerns have been raised in respect of: the protection of personal data, anonymity, wider

[17] Inquiries Act 2005, s 21(4).

disclosure and infringements of Article 8 of the European Convention on Human Rights, and the right to a private life.[18] Claims such as these are, however, often refused on the basis that the inquiry's policies and procedures on disclosure, redaction and data protection will mitigate any such concerns.

Admissibility

A public inquiry is not bound by the rules of evidence in the same way as adversarial civil and criminal proceedings; it is not restricted by the limitations of hearsay evidence, nor is an inquiry required to satisfy a particular burden of proof.

The chair of a statutory inquiry has a very broad discretion on how to approach the procedure and conduct of an inquiry,[19] and that includes its approach to the admissibility of evidence.

Similarly, there is no requirement for a non-statutory inquiry to adopt any specific rules of procedure. They are not bound by any statute nor any particular set of rules and therefore they are also at liberty to determine the inquiry's approach to admissibility of evidence. The only requirement, as with statutory inquiries, is to conduct the inquiry fairly and reasonably, and thereby reduce the potential for judicial review challenges.

Issue – Burden of proof and the 'flexible and variable approach'

Public inquiries are free to determine their own rules for establishing any standard of proof to be applied when considering evidence. The approach often adopted has become known as the 'flexible and variable approach'. The reasoning behind this approach was set out clearly by Sir Thayne Forbes, chair of the Al-Sweady Inquiry, in *The Report of the Al-Sweady Inquiry*,[20] with chapter five of that report specifically addressing the standard of proof applied:

'In making findings as to relevant facts, a Public Inquiry is in a very different position from a court of law. In both criminal and civil courts of law, findings are made in relation to specific allegations, where all parties are entitled to call evidence in support of their case. Importantly, the decisions in such cases also lead to findings of criminal or civil liability on the part of one or more of

[18] For example, Infected Blood Inquiry: Determination under section 21(4) in respect of an application by the Medical Defence Union dated 6 December 2018.

[19] Inquiries Act 2005, s 17(1).

[20] Sir Thayne Forbes, *The Report of the Al-Sweady Inquiry*, vol 1 (HC 818-1, HMSO 2014).

the parties, with an appropriate sanction/order being imposed by the Court on the party or parties as a result. By contrast, a Public Inquiry is tasked with establishing the facts as to what has happened, rather than making a decision upon competing cases …'

'… In my opinion, a certain amount of flexibility is needed with regard to the standard of proof that I should apply in this Inquiry, given that the entire emphasis of the Inquiry is on achieving an appropriate determination of the facts and in making recommendations. I can discern no good reason for my being limited to one set standard of proof, the application of which would not allow the sort of flexibility in standard that will be required to enable me to make appropriate determinations of fact in respect of the many and widely varying factual issues which I am called upon to decide in this Inquiry. In reaching that conclusion, I have been greatly assisted by a consideration of the approach taken to the same question in two previous major Public Inquiries, namely the Baha Mousa Inquiry and the Shipman Inquiry. In each of those Inquiries, the Chairman also decided to adopt a flexible approach to the standard of proof …'

'… The chairman of that Inquiry [Baha Mouse Inquiry], Sir William Gage, adopted what he referred to as a "flexible and variable" approach to the standard of proof. In this way he made provision for findings to be made to both the civil and criminal standard of proof. Sir William Gage also allowed for appropriate comment, where he felt unable to make any finding of fact as such …'

'… The "flexible and variable" approach to the standard of proof taken by Sir William Gage in the Baha Mousa Inquiry was one that he had adapted from that which had been adopted in the earlier Shipman Inquiry. The approach taken by the Chairman of that Inquiry, Dame Janet Smith, was not to apply an across-the-board standard of proof to her findings, but instead to make findings indicating which standard of proof had been met. In my view the "flexible and variable" approach is an entirely appropriate one that allows for appropriate findings of fact to be made with varying degrees of certainty. I have therefore also decided to adopt a "flexible and variable" approach to the findings of fact made in this Report. This has enabled me to make findings, to whatever degree of certainty I have felt able, on each of the issues that I have determined. In this way I have made findings of fact to both the civil and criminal standards of proof.'[21]

This approach has been adopted by a number of inquiries since, including the Undercover Policing Inquiry, the Litvinenko Inquiry, and the Anthony Grainger Inquiry.

[21] (17 December 2014) HC 818-I paras 1.165 to 1.171.

Advance Disclosure by the Inquiry

As explained in chapter six, one of the advantages of obtaining core participant status in a statutory inquiry is that core participants are usually provided with advance access to evidence (both documentary evidence disclosed by other parties and, later, witness statements) before it is referred to during oral hearings and made public.

Although there is no obligation on a chair to grant core participants advance access to evidence, this commonly happens in practice for reasons of fairness; core participants are awarded such status because they either have a significant interest, played a direct and significant role or may be subject to significant criticism in relation to the events and/or issues being investigated by the inquiry. Advance access to documentary material and witness evidence means that core participants will be better placed to anticipate, respond to, or manage any criticism that they may face during the course of an inquiry.

The way that this usually works in practice is as follows:

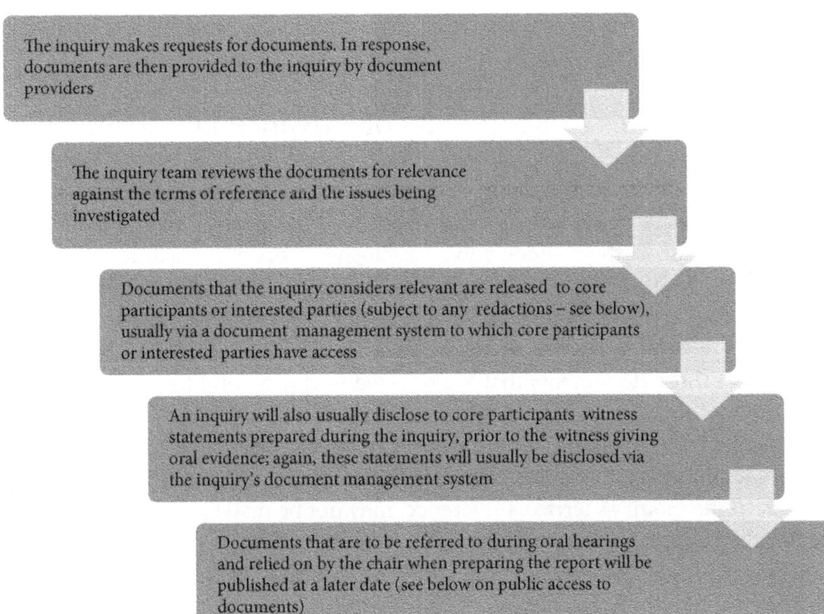

Recipients of advance disclosure must ensure that the documents disclosed to them remain confidential until full publication takes place. Steps taken by an inquiry, and precautions adhered to by the recipients of advance disclosure, for example signing confidentiality undertakings, are discussed below.

As mentioned above, advance disclosure is usually made via the inquiry's document management system (see chapter four). Each document on that system will be given a unique reference number, which allows it to be cross-referenced to other relevant material, allowing core participants and interested parties to prepare evidence in a managed way, to support their position and prepare for oral hearings, for example by proposing r 10 questions to be asked of witnesses during oral hearings (see chapter eleven).

In some circumstances, documents are released at very short notice, restricting the opportunity for core participants and interested parties to review the documents as part of their preparation; in some cases documents are not released until after relevant oral evidence has already been heard. This may be because the inquiry itself has not received the evidence until late in the day, or because the volume of material being processed is such that time does not allow for long periods of advance notice to be given.

Core participants may also not have the time or resources to process all of the material. Even when core participants are eligible for funding for legal expenses, the funding may be capped, limiting the amount of hours they can spend on the process. In practice, core participants will have to prioritise and make choices about what documents realistically can be reviewed, based on what is proportionate in the circumstances.

Advantages to Recipients of Advance Disclosure

As mentioned above, core participants and interested parties are likely to receive advance disclosure of documents disclosed by other parties and, later, witness statements, prior to their wider public disclosure. This may include documents that are due to be referred to during oral hearings. They are also often given access to other relevant documents that may not ultimately be disclosed publicly. An inquiry will often receive many thousands of documents during the course of its work. Those documents that are referred to during oral hearings,[22] and are relied on by the chair and panel when preparing the final report, will usually be made available to the public (see the section below on public access to documents). There will, however, be a proportion of documents disclosed that, although relevant to the inquiry's terms of reference, may not be made public if they are not specifically referred to or relied upon.

This advance disclosure may confer a number of advantages to core participants and interested parties by providing:

- Advance notice of the key issues on which the inquiry will be focusing, which:
  - assists with preparation in advance of oral hearings, including formulating suggested questions to be submitted to counsel to the inquiry, for putting to witnesses during oral hearings and familiarisation with the likely evidence to be heard;

[22] Including witness evidence that is read into the record.

- allows for an inquiry's likely conclusions to be anticipated;
- allows for remedial steps or improvements to be identified and implemented in advance of anticipated conclusions, thereby reducing the impact of any criticisms that may be made; and
- facilitates preparation for reputation management activities, in advance of wider publication of the documents.

• The opportunity to identify evidence that supports the core participant's or interested party's position and to seek to have it adduced formally into evidence and thereby made public.

As explained above, documents that are referred to during oral hearings, and documents relied on by the chair and panel when preparing the final report, are usually made available to the public. However, some disclosed documents, although relevant, may not be made public if they are not specifically referred to or relied upon. Where core participants or interested parties consider certain documents to be helpful to their position, they may seek to ensure that those documents are placed on the record.

This can be achieved in a number of ways:

• when preparing witness statements, referring to those documents by way of exhibits;
• when formulating suggested questions for counsel to the inquiry to put to witnesses, referring to those documents in the hope that the material will be referred to in oral evidence and thereby published with the other evidence at the conclusion of that day's hearing; or
• making an application to the inquiry asking for the evidence to be formally and publicly put on the record.

If an inquiry has released documents to core participants and interested parties on the basis that they are relevant, it is more difficult for an inquiry to subsequently justify withholding those documents from full public disclosure.

Confidentiality and Advance Disclosure

It is likely to be of great importance to core participants and interested parties involved with an inquiry's work that the inquiry ensures that documents that are the subject of advance disclosure remain confidential until decisions have been made about what will or will not ultimately be made publicly available and formal publication has taken place (see below). Core participants and interested parties often provide sensitive information and confidential documents to an inquiry and it is important that they feel confident that such material will be treated with care, both by the inquiry itself and those individuals and organisations that receive advance disclosure.

A common process adopted by inquiries is to require signed confidentiality undertakings from all individuals who may receive confidential information and material from the inquiry. Where a core participant is an organisation, these individuals might include, for example, all employees within that organisation who are involved with the inquiry and may receive inquiry material, every individual who is part of the core participant's legal team, and all administrative staff who may have access to the material. An inquiry should keep a record of all signed undertakings and ensure that no access to any IT systems or documents is granted until a signed undertaking has been received from the relevant individual.

When core participants or interested parties are asked to sign undertakings, the implications of doing so should be clearly explained. Where necessary, steps should be taken to ensure that they understand the nature of the undertaking and the ways in which the material should be protected from inadvertent disclosure.

Other steps can also be taken by an inquiry when sharing information in order to protect the confidential nature of material disclosed and to reassure core participants and interested parties. These additional steps may include:

- Sharing particularly sensitive information on a selective basis, by requiring applications from those who wish to access the information, obliging them to justify their request and explain on what basis the information may be relevant to them, or the party they represent.
- Sharing particularly sensitive information on a more secure basis, for example on encrypted memory sticks, which require separate undertakings to be signed and have specific instructions for secure storage of the information, rather than releasing the information using the standard IT systems used for disclosure.
- Protectively marking information when disclosed. This may include marking every copy of a document released with a different version number. As a result, if a document is ever leaked, the inquiry will be able to identify the source.
- Only allowing very sensitive information to be viewed at a secure location, where electronic devices are not permitted.

The necessity for such additional steps will depend on the subject matter of the inquiry and the nature of the information in question.

However, even if the above steps are taken, breaches and leaks do occur and it is usually difficult for an inquiry to easily identify the source. For example, the Phase 1 Report of the Grenfell Tower Inquiry was leaked to the press while under a short period of embargo from publication, despite the fact that those receiving a copy of the report were asked to sign additional confidentiality agreements covering the embargo period.

The only powers of enforcement at the inquiry's disposal to address such leaks are those set down in s 36 of the Inquiries Act 2005, which provides that if a person fails to comply with, or acts in breach of, a restriction notice or a restriction order, the chair (or the relevant minister at the end of an inquiry) can refer the matter to the appropriate court, which can then make such order by way of enforcement, as if the matter had arisen in civil proceedings. That will, of course, however only apply to information or documents that are subject to such a restriction notice or order.

Rule 17 of the Inquiry Rules 2006 also provides that the content of an inquiry's report is to be treated, until the report has been published by the chair, as subject to an obligation of confidence owed by each person who has received a copy of the report; that obligation being owed to the chair. Therefore, a breach of this confidence could give rise to an actionable claim for breach of confidence. Disclosure of other material made available under confidentiality arrangements could also, in theory, give rise to an actionable breach of confidence, or breach of an individual's privacy rights if the material contains personal data. However, bringing such proceedings takes time and money and can disrupt the work of an inquiry. Depending on the source of the leak, it may also be unattractive for an inquiry to bring such proceedings if there is the potential for reputational damage (eg if proceedings are brought against a victim or survivor).

Public Access to Documents

For statutory inquiries, s 18 of the Inquiries Act 2005 provides that, subject to any restrictions imposed by a restriction notice or restriction order under s 19 of that Act (see below), the chair must take such steps as they consider reasonable to secure that members of the public (including reporters) are able to obtain or to view documents given, produced or provided to the inquiry.[23]

The fact that the obligation is not absolute, but 'to take such steps as he or she considers reasonable', means that the chair of an inquiry will not usually disclose all documents provided. For example, most inquiry chairs will not disclose documents that are received but are not then considered relevant to the terms of reference. The chair's decision will also be influenced by the need to ensure fairness, the scope and scale of the inquiry, and cost.[24]

Section 18 does not specify how or when the documents should be made available to the public. In practice, most inquiries adopt the following approach:

- An inquiry will consider all documents provided to it by material providers for relevance to the inquiry's terms of reference. Those documents that are to be relied on by the chair in reaching conclusions and preparing the final report will be made public, usually by formally placing these documents on the inquiry record, either by exhibiting them to statements or expert reports, referring to them during oral questioning of witnesses, or reading them into the record.
- In respect of documents produced by an inquiry, where the documents produced contain a record of relevant evidence, for example a witness statement

[23] Inquiries Act 2005, s 18(1)(b) and 18(3).
[24] Including obligations under the Inquiries Act 2005, s 17(3).

or an expert's report, these will be made available to the public, again via the oral hearing process.

- Documents are usually published on the inquiry's website shortly after the oral hearing during which they are first placed formally on the record.

Non-statutory inquiries often follow a similar approach. Where inquiries do not hold oral hearings, there is, however, no comparable process whereby documents or witness statements are made public.

Redaction

Public inquiries, whether statutory or non-statutory, when investigating matters of public concern are often required to examine and investigate sensitive issues. For example, inquiries established over the past few years have included subject matters such as child abuse, child sexual exploitation, the Grenfell Tower fire where many lives were lost, and the contaminated blood scandal. Inquiries in Northern Ireland such as the Bloody Sunday Inquiry, the Rosemary Nelson Inquiry, the Billy Wright Inquiry and the Robert Hamill Inquiry have dealt with issues of state security, policing methodologies and knowledge, and the identities of parliamentarians and police and army informants. Some inquiries have to manage private medical records. As a result, public inquiries often receive and process very sensitive material and that material needs to be carefully protected. Breaches of security could lead to lives being lost.

Chapter nine addresses the data protection issues that can arise during an inquiry and how those issues can be addressed. Often one of the solutions is to protect personal data by way of redaction, and this process is commonly used by inquiries. However, it is difficult, time-consuming and costly, particularly if documents relevant to the inquiry contain a lot of very sensitive information that the inquiry has determined is not to be disclosed during the inquiry process.

Redaction may also be necessary where documents contain classified material (see above).

Issue – Redaction policy

Many public inquiries put formal redaction policies in place, which set out the inquiry's approach to the redaction of information prior to publication. Such policies might:

- State what information will be automatically redacted, if any.
- Make clear that all personal data will be redacted, save for that which is necessary for assisting the inquiry's understanding.

- Set out the systems to be used for redaction, for example what IT program will be used and the levels of security clearance required by those managing the material.
- State the process that will be used for agreeing and applying redactions.
- Identify who will redact the information and in what form documents should be disclosed (ie the original documents for redaction by the inquiry, documents marked up with proposed redactions by the document providers, or documents disclosed with redactions already in place).
- Explain how any dispute about the extent of redactions will be managed.
- Identify which parties will have access to unredacted material (if any).
- State whether participants can apply for additional redactions to be made and, if so, the process for applying.

An inquiry could ask document providers to disclose documents that have already been redacted, in order to avoid an inquiry incurring the time and cost of undertaking this task itself. However, this approach is problematic, as the inquiry has no way of determining whether the redactions have been applied correctly. An alternative is for the inquiry to ask document providers to mark up provisional redactions (for example by highlighting in yellow the information to be redacted). This reduces the time and cost spent by the inquiry team in carrying out the task, although they will still need to review the provisional redactions and apply them (ie 'blank out' the information) – but it provides the inquiry with visibility of the redacted material. This approach does however also present its own problems. For example:

- document providers may each interpret and apply an inquiry's redaction policy differently;
- documents providers are not in possession of all the material that is disclosed to an inquiry which, when read in conjunction with the documents being disclosed, could reveal an individual's identity or personal information and should therefore be redacted (also known as 'jigsaw-identification' redaction); and
- decisions around redaction can be quite complex and subjective; an inquiry has its own data protection obligations, which cannot be delegated, and it must ensure that its obligations are met.

It is therefore imperative that, if an inquiry goes down the route of asking document providers to provide proposed redactions rather than undertaking the redactions itself, those documents are still checked carefully to ensure all redactions have been picked up, including all 'jigsaw-identification' redactions.

The way an inquiry deals with redaction of documents that are the subject of advance disclosure and publication is generally as follows:

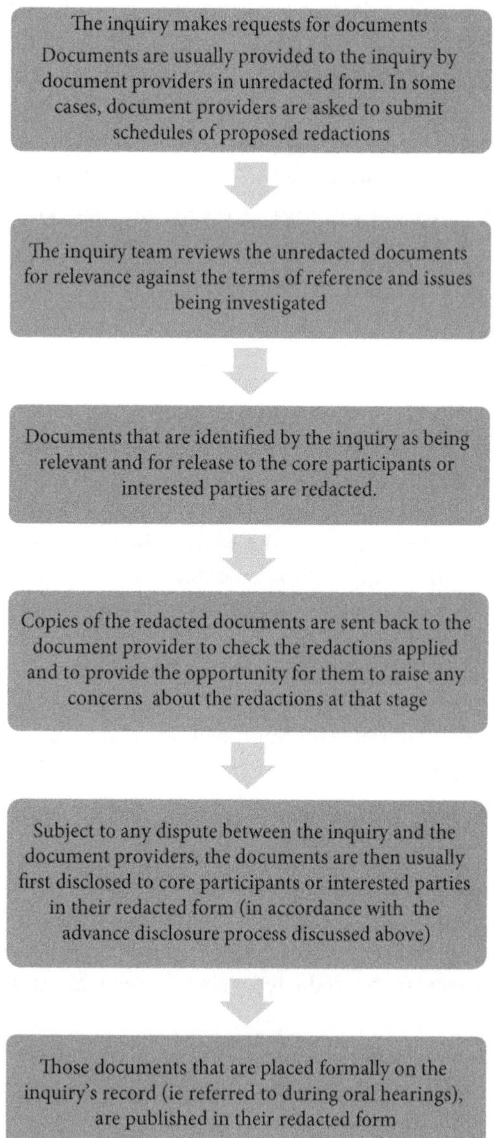

Issue – Redaction of identities

One of the issues that can often arise in respect of redactions is the question of the extent to which an individual's identity needs to be revealed. Document providers often feel strongly that it is not necessary to reveal an individual's identity where the role they played in the circumstances under investigation was minor, or where they consider the individual's identity to be irrelevant to the matters under investigation. An individual's identity may, however, be important to an inquiry, particularly where it allows the inquiry to draw links with other information and to draw conclusions. The issue of redaction can become the subject of dispute between the document provider and the inquiry.

An alternative to personal identities being disclosed in such circumstances is the use of ciphers. An individual may be allocated a cipher, such as a particular number or letter, so that information relating to the individual can be linked to related information, while protecting their personal information. Particular care is needed, however, when ciphers are used to conceal an individual's identity. Replacing names with ciphers alone is often not enough, as documents may contain other identifying information about an individual. If redactions and ciphering are not carried out with care, it can result in an individual's cipher itself becoming known, along with the individual's identity. It is a complex and time-consuming process.

Restriction Orders and Restriction Notices

Restriction orders and notices are considered in chapter eleven in connection with restricting public access and attendance at hearings. Restriction orders and notices may also be used to restrict public access (including the media's access) to documents given, produced or provided to the inquiry by restricting what is placed in the public domain.[25] Restriction orders can be made by a chair of an inquiry of their own volition,[26] or a chair may also permit formal applications for restrictions to be made by participants. A minister may also restrict the publication of documents, by issuing a restriction notice to the chair.[27]

Such restrictions are only permitted:

- as required by statute, EU law or rule of law (eg documents which attract legal professional privilege, which is not waived); or

[25] Inquiries Act 2005, s 19(1).
[26] Inquiries Act 2005, s 19(2)(b).
[27] Inquiries Act 2005, s 19(2)(a).

- as the minister or chair considers to be conducive to the inquiry fulfilling its terms of reference or to be necessary in the public interest, but having regard to:
  - the extent to which any restriction on attendance or disclosure might inhibit 'the allaying of public concern';
  - the risk of harm or damage that could be avoided or reduced, including death, injury, national security, damage to the economic interests of the UK, and commercially sensitive materials;
  - any conditions of confidentiality subject to which a person received the documents that have been given to the inquiry; or
  - the extent to which not imposing a restriction would be likely to cause delay, impair the efficiency or effectiveness of an inquiry or otherwise result in additional cost.[28]

A chair may decide to issue a number of restriction orders at the outset of an inquiry. For example, where an inquiry concerns allegations of sexual abuse, the chair may issue a restriction order at the outset to prevent publication of the identity of any victims or survivors. Equally, restriction orders may be issued by a chair as the inquiry's work progresses, on an ad hoc basis. For example, a restriction order may be issued where confidential information is inadvertently referred to by a witness during a public hearing; the restriction order will prevent anyone present at the hearing (including the media) from further publishing that information.

Issue – Sharing anonymised information with those against whom allegations are made

An additional issue that an inquiry and its participants must consider is how any anonymised information will be shared with those against whom allegations are made.

For example, an inquiry may agree that Child A can give evidence anonymously; Child A then makes allegations against Perpetrator B. If Perpetrator B does not know who Child A is (as their identity has been protected) they will thereby be restricted as to how they can respond to, or rebut, the allegations made.

This raises concerns around fairness. This is a common problem and the appropriate solution will depend on the circumstances of the particular inquiry.

- It may be that Perpetrator B is told Child A's identity under confidentiality terms, although Child A will need to be notified that this was the case.

[28] Inquiries Act 2005, s 19(3) and (4).

- Alternatively, Child A may decide they do not want the information shared in this way. As a result, the inquiry cannot use this evidence when making findings and criticisms, and must manage how the evidence, or parts of it, will then be used. For example, the inquiry would not be able to use the evidence to make any specific findings of fact or make criticisms in relation to Perpetrator B, but, depending on the inquiry's terms of reference, the evidence may still be valuable in contributing to the inquiry's wider, general findings.

Foreseeing these potential problems at the outset of an inquiry is essential, so that the necessary mechanisms and procedures (particularly the terms of an inquiry's privacy policy) are put in place from the beginning.

9

Data Protection

Introduction

The operation of data protection legislation in conjunction with the Inquiries Act 2005 creates significant practical and legal issues for public inquiries, for those engaged by inquiries to assist in their work and for participants. The General Data Protection Regulation (GDPR)[1] and Data Protection Act 2018 (DPA 2018) set out significant obligations regarding the management of personal data and accountability for how personal data is managed. An inquiry, and those processing personal data in connection with an inquiry's work, must ensure that procedures are designed in a manner that will meet those statutory obligations.[2]

The impact of the statutory requirements should not be underestimated. Set out below are some of the key issues that an inquiry, and those involved with an inquiry's work, must bear in mind. However, determining an appropriate approach to applying the principles and meeting the statutory requirements will depend on the inquiry in question, including the set-up of the inquiry (for example statutory or non-statutory); the nature of the data being processed; the reasons for processing, storing and sharing the data; and the particular procedures in place. It may be useful to obtain specialist advice and this should always be considered.

Issue – Practical examples of situations where data protection issues arise

- A police authority may be served with a Section 21 Notice[3] by the chair of an inquiry, requiring the authority to provide a list of police informants.[4]
- A social services department may provide an inquiry with a list of children who, on a particular date, were categorised as 'at risk'.

[1] Regulation (EU) 2016/679 (GDPR).

[2] The extent to which the application of the GDPR will change post-Brexit remains to be seen.

[3] See chapter eight.

[4] In addition to data protection issues, the inquiry must also consider issues arising under Art 2 of the European Convention on Human Rights, the 'right to life'.

- The employer of a person suspected of abuse may be asked by an inquiry to provide their employment record, even though that person has never been arrested.
- An NHS Trust may be asked to disclose medical records by a non-statutory inquiry which does not have the power to compel the production of documents.
- A witness may provide names and contact details of other individuals who may have relevant evidence to provide an inquiry, but without those individuals being aware of the fact, without them having consented to their details being stored, and without them having been notified of the inquiry's privacy policy.

Key terms under the data protection legislation

- **Personal data**

Personal data is data that relates to an identified or identifiable natural person who can be identified:

(i) from that data; or
(ii) from that data and using 'all means reasonably likely to be used'.[5]

Even if the data held does not itself identify an individual, it would still be considered personal data if, when coupled with other data (even if that other data is not held by the same organisation or person) an individual could be identified.

- **Special categories of personal data and criminal convictions and offences data**

There are special categories of personal data listed under Art 9 of the GDPR, which consist of information relating to:

(i) the racial or ethnic origin of the individual;
(ii) the individual's political opinions;
(iii) the individual's religious or philosophical beliefs;
(iv) whether the individual is a member of a trade union;
(v) the individual's genetic and biometric data;
(vi) the individual's physical or mental health; or
(vii) the individual's sexual life or sexual orientation.[6]

[5] GDPR, Art 4(1).
[6] GDPR, Art 9(1).

This 'special category data' (also known as 'sensitive personal data') is subject to additional protection under the GDPR.

In addition, Art 10 of the GDPR provides additional protection to personal data relating to criminal convictions and offences, or related security measures.

- **Data subject**

A data subject is an individual who is identified or identifiable, directly or indirectly, from the personal data.

- **Data controllers and data processors**

A data controller is the natural or legal person, public authority, agency or other body who, alone or jointly with others, determines the purposes and means of the processing of personal data;[7] in other words, they decide why and how data should be processed. Each data controller is required to implement appropriate technical and organisational measures to ensure, and to be able to demonstrate, that the processing of personal data complies with the legislation.[8]

A data processor is any natural or legal person, public authority, agency or other body who is responsible for processing personal data on behalf of a controller.[9]

Public Inquiries, Individuals and Organisations as Data Controllers

During its lifetime, an inquiry will receive, create, process, amend, share, publish and store many thousands of documents, in both hard copy and electronic form, including audio and video files and photographs. Given the purpose of an inquiry is to investigate a matter of public concern, these documents often contain personal data and special category data as defined in the legislation, such as medical records, contact details, photographs of individuals, police files, documents containing political opinions, and information revealing abuse suffered by an individual. Proper handling of this information is a significant issue that an inquiry must address from the outset, in order to satisfy its legal obligations under the GDPR and the DPA 2018 and to maintain the integrity of its work.

[7] GDPR, Art 4(7).
[8] Data Protection Act 2018, s 56.
[9] GDPR, Art 4(8).

Failure to comply with the GDPR and the DPA 2018 risks enforcement action, which may include criminal prosecution, as well as compensation claims from individuals. An inquiry that fails in its obligations may also suffer reputational damage. The inquiry must therefore ensure that it structures and manages its collection, processing, storage, sharing and deletion of personal data carefully, and that all necessary arrangements are in place from the outset. Inquiry participants will also want to ensure that the inquiry treats personal data appropriately and in accordance with its legal obligations.

In addition to the inquiry itself, other individuals and organisations involved in an inquiry's work may also be processing data as a data controller under the definition of the legislation and will therefore be obliged to comply with relevant legislation as a data controller. For example, solicitors to an inquiry or a witness support service could themselves be a data controller under the data protection legislation, rather than being simply a data processor (see definitions above).

The fact that an individual or organisation provides a data processing service to another, such as a public inquiry, does not necessarily mean that the former is acting as a data processor. They might be a data controller in their own right, depending on the degree of control they exercise over the processing operation. If, for example, an individual or organisation is asked to carry out a particular task for a public inquiry, but is free to determine how much data is gathered and in what form, the likelihood is that both that individual or organisation and the public inquiry will be data controllers.

Set out below are the issues that often pose the greatest challenge to a public inquiry and participants.

Issues

Registering with the ICO as a data controller

- Under the data protection legislation, where a person or organisation is in control of the purposes for which, and the manner in which, data is processed, they are required to register with the Information Commissioner's Office (ICO) as a data controller and to pay a fee[10] (unless they are exempt).[11] Failure to do so constitutes a civil wrong and a fine of up to £4,350 can be levied. The fees are used to fund the ICO's

[10] The Data Protection (Charges and Information) Regulations 2018 (SI 2018/480) require every organisation or sole trader that processes personal information to pay a data protection fee to the ICO.

[11] There are a number of different exemptions that apply. For example, from 1 April 2019, the Data Protection (Charges and Information) (Amendment) Regulations 2019 (SI 2019/478) exempted the processing of personal data by members of the House of Lords, elected representatives and prospective representatives. The ICO's self-assessment process describes the possible exemptions.

data protection work, and enable it to keep a record of those controlling the processing of personal data.[12]

- A public inquiry controls the way in which data is processed by gathering, analysing and publishing evidence. As such, it will fall within the definition of a data controller.
- Similarly, individuals and organisations involved in an inquiry's work and processing data as a data controller under the definition of the legislation must also be registered with the ICO.

Principles for Processing Personal Data

Data controllers and data processors are required to adopt seven key principles when processing personal data.[13] The principles state that personal data shall be:

- processed lawfully, fairly and in a transparent manner ('lawfulness, fairness and transparency');
- collected for specified, explicit and legitimate purposes and not further processed in a manner that is incompatible with those purposes ('purpose limitation');
- adequate, relevant and limited to what is necessary in relation to the purposes for which data is processed ('data minimisation');
- accurate and, where necessary, kept up to date ('accuracy');
- kept in a form which permits identification of data subjects for no longer than is necessary for the purposes for which the personal data are processed ('storage limitation');
- processed in a manner that ensures appropriate security and protection of the personal data ('integrity and confidentiality'); and
- the controller shall be responsible for, and must be able to demonstrate compliance with, the principles ('accountability').[14]

[12] Whereas fines are passed directly to the government.
[13] GDPR, Art 5(1) and (2).
[14] GDPR, Art 5.

Lawful Basis for Processing Data

An inquiry, like any other person or organisation, must have a valid lawful basis in order to process personal data in accordance with the 'lawfulness, fairness and transparency' principle. There are six available lawful bases for processing personal data.[15] The ones that are most likely to apply to an inquiry, or those participating in an inquiry, are:

- **Consent:** the individual has given consent to the processing of their personal data for one or more specific purposes.[16] There are, however, challenges with processing personal data by consent, which are discussed further below.
- **Compliance with a legal obligation:** the processing is necessary to comply with a legal obligation to which the controller is subject.[17] This may apply in particular to inquiry participants and witnesses who are required to disclose data to an inquiry[18] by way of a Section 21 Notice being served by the inquiry, requiring them to provide evidence or documents (see chapter eight).
- **Public task:** the processing is necessary to perform a task in the public interest or in the exercise of an official function. The task or function must have clear legal authority. For public inquiries, this basis is the one most likely to apply, with the legal authority being the legislation, or executive prerogative, under which the inquiry is convened. An inquiry must ensure that the purpose of the processing is within the scope of its terms of reference.[19]
- **Legitimate interests:** the processing is necessary for the purposes of the legitimate interests pursued by the inquiry or the legitimate interests of a third party, except where such interests are overridden by the interests or fundamental rights and freedoms of the individual data subject which require protection of personal data, in particular where the data subject is a child. The use of 'legitimate interests' as a legal basis for processing, and how to assess this, is discussed further below.[20]

[15] GDPR, Art 6.
[16] GDPR, Art 6(1)(a).
[17] GDPR, Art 6(1)(c).
[18] Disclosure of data is one type of 'processing'.
[19] GDPR Art 6(1)(e). For non-statutory public inquiries, authority will be based on the ministerial prerogative or the few examples of legislation other than the Inquiries Act 2005 under which they may be convened.
[20] GDPR, Art 6(1)(f).

Issue – Processing special category data and data relating to criminal convictions and offences

In addition to considering the principles and lawful basis for processing data:

- Where an inquiry is processing special category data,[21] such as data revealing racial or ethnic origin or data concerning health, the inquiry must also satisfy one or more of the 10 conditions set out in Art 9 of the GDPR.[22]
- Where an inquiry is processing personal data relating to criminal convictions and offences or related security measures, the inquiry must also comply with the additional safeguards in Art 10 of the GDPR.
- Where the type of processing is likely to be high risk to a person or persons' rights and freedoms, which may well be the case when processing special category data and criminal conviction data, an inquiry must carry out a data protection impact assessment (DPIA) designed to help systematically analyse, identify and minimise the data protection risks of its work.[23]

The Legitimate Interest Assessment (LIA) and Public Inquiries

The data protection legislation does not set out a list of what is considered a 'legitimate interest'. If an inquiry wishes to rely on 'legitimate interest' as a legal basis for processing data, it should consider carrying out an LIA. Whilst there is no obligation under the GDPR to do so, the 'legitimate interest' legal basis can apply to a wide range of circumstances, and an LIA provides a tool to demonstrate the justification for relying on 'legitimate interest' in the specific set of circumstances and enables a data controller to demonstrate compliance with the above principles.[24]

The approach involves following a three-part test of purpose, necessity and balancing.[25]

[21] See the 'key terms' section above.

[22] GDPR, Art 9. There are 10 possible conditions that could apply.

[23] GDPR, Art 35. The ICO provides guidance at https://ico.org.uk/for-organisations/guide-to-data-protection/guide-to-the-general-data-protection-regulation-gdpr/data-protection-impact-assessments-dpias/what-is-a-dpia/ (accessed 12 August 2020).

[24] Under the GDPR, Art 5(2), the data controller must be able to demonstrate compliance with the principles.

[25] More detailed guidance is provided by the ICO at https://ico.org.uk/for-organisations/guide-to-data-protection/guide-to-the-general-data-protection-regulation-gdpr/legitimate-interests/how-do-we-apply-legitimate-interests-in-practice/ (accessed 12 August 2020).

The Purpose Test

- The purpose test is to test whether there is a legitimate interest behind the processing of personal data.[26] Legitimate interests can include an inquiry's legitimate interests, the interests of any third party and the legitimate interests of the public in general, including wider benefits to society.
- To assist in identifying legitimate interests, the inquiry should consider what it is trying to achieve from the processing, who benefits from the processing (eg the wider public), how they benefit, and how important those benefits are.
- An inquiry must be open about its reasons and the purpose for obtaining personal data. It is therefore essential that an inquiry produces and publishes a data protection protocol or policy that sets out the inquiry's purpose for processing data, and its approach to handling and processing personal data, so that all parties are aware of how personal data will be used (see below).

The Necessity Test

- The necessity test is used to test whether the processing is actually necessary for the purpose identified in the purpose test.
- An inquiry must ensure that all requests for documents containing personal data are necessary, and within the terms of reference, or the interest is no longer legitimate. The request must be a targeted and proportionate way of achieving the inquiry's purposes and fulfilling its terms of reference.
- A request will not satisfy this requirement if there is a reasonable and less intrusive way to achieve the same end. In such cases, an inquiry would not be able to rely on the basis of legitimate interest and must rely on an alternate lawful basis for processing data (see above).
- An inquiry cannot simply apply a blanket approach to its data processing. It must consider the necessity of processing data on a case-by-case basis, for each request and each type of personal data.

The Balancing Test

- The balancing test considers the balance between the legitimate interests in processing the data and the interests of individuals to which the personal data relates.

[26] GDPR, Art 6(1)(f).

- The inquiry must be able to justify the reasons for its requests and to explain the prejudice likely to be caused if the information is not obtained.
- For a public inquiry, the balancing exercise is likely to involve balancing issues such as the wider benefits to society of conducting an inquiry in as transparent a manner as possible, and achieving its terms of references, against the interests and fundamental rights and freedoms of the relevant individual (including those guaranteed by Art 8 of the European Convention on Human Rights and Arts 7 and 8 of the EU Charter of Fundamental Rights).
- An inquiry must consider the nature of the personal data, the reasonable expectations of the individual and the likely impact of the data processing on the individual, together with any measures and safeguards that may be put in place to mitigate that impact.
- If an individual would not reasonably expect the processing, or if it would cause serious impact, their interests may override the legitimate interests of the inquiry. However, even where there is a high risk of a serious impact, an inquiry may be able to demonstrate compelling legitimate interests that would satisfy the balance test. It is important for an inquiry to record all decisions taken in this respect.[27]
- Where an inquiry is not sure about the outcome of the balancing test, it should consider relying on another lawful basis for processing the data. Legitimate interests will often not be the most appropriate basis for processing that is unexpected or high risk.

Where an individual or organisation involved in an inquiry's work is also processing data as a data controller under the definition of the legislation, they should also carry out an LIA.

Checklist – Data protection protocol or policy

In order to be open and transparent about its management of personal data, an inquiry should produce a data protection protocol or policy that:

- Explains the lawful basis for processing data, making it clear from the outset why the inquiry is collecting personal data and how it intends to process it.
- Specifies the type of data that will be processed (eg special category data) and the exemptions that apply to justify the processing.
- Sets out the rights of data subjects to access their personal data.

[27] See more detailed guidance from the ICO at https://ico.org.uk/for-organisations/guide-to-data-protection/guide-to-the-general-data-protection-regulation-gdpr/lawful-basis-for-processing/legitimate-interests/ (accessed 12 August 2020).

- Explains how the inquiry will receive, record and store evidence, and the circumstances in which data may be disclosed to third parties.
- Explains the measures in place to ensure that the data stored is secure and accurate.
- Explains for how long the data will be stored and what will happen to the data at the conclusion of the inquiry.
- Includes details of the data controller's data protection officer.[28] (The data protection officer is a mandatory role under Art 37 of the GDPR, with the appointed individual being responsible for ensuring compliance with the GDPR.)

Once the relevant policies and procedures are in place, an inquiry will still need to grapple with data issues throughout the course of its work, which may arise in a variety of circumstances. Examples could include:

- In response to a Section 21 request for documents, a police authority provides, amongst other things, a list of police informants. In addition to data protection issues, other considerations may arise under Art 2 of the European Convention on Human Rights and additional steps may need to be taken to protect the identities of the informants.
- A department of social services provides an inquiry with a list of children who on a particular date were categorised as 'at risk'.

Organisations Engaged by a Public Inquiry as Data Processors

As a result of the GDPR, in addition to data controllers, data processors[29] are also regulated and are open to direct action by regulators or persons whose personal data is being processed (known as 'data subjects'). Data processors must comply with a number of obligations under the legislation and cannot simply rely on a data controller's compliance. As a result, organisations who are engaged by an inquiry to process data on its behalf, for example IT providers or solicitors to an inquiry, must be familiar with, and comply with, their own data protection obligations.

[28] The DPA 2018, s 69, states that a data controller must designate a data protection officer. The specific tasks to be carried out by the data protection officer are set out in s 71 of the Act.

[29] Any person (other than an employee of the data controller) who processes the data on behalf of the data controller: see GDPR, Art 4(8).

These obligations include:

- implementing appropriate technical and organisational measures to ensure a level of security appropriate to the risks arising from the processing of personal data;[30]
- notifying their relevant controller of any data breach without undue delay;[31]
- maintaining a record of all categories of processing activities carried out on behalf of a controller;[32] and
- in certain circumstances, appointing a data protection officer;[33] for example where a data processor is a public authority or body, and there is data processing on a large scale. (This includes where the core activities of the processing involve large amounts of special category data or data relating to criminal convictions and offences, which may well be the case for an inquiry, depending on the nature of its subject matter.)

Failure to meet those obligations or acting outside the data controller's instructions may result in:

- liability for damages following civil court proceedings; and/or
- a fine or other penalties.

Data controllers, including public inquiries, may only appoint processors who provide sufficient guarantees to implement appropriate technical and organisational measures to ensure that data will be processed in accordance with the legislation and ensure the protection of the rights of the data subjects concerned. There must be a written contract between the data controller and data processor. The contract must set out the subject matter and duration of the processing, its nature and purposes, and the obligations, responsibilities and liabilities of both parties.[34]

Issue – Public inquiry participants: requests for documents, and obligations and exemptions under the DPA 2018 and the GDPR

Not only are public inquiries and those engaged to assist an inquiry in its work subject to the provisions of the GDPR and the DPA 2018, public inquiry participants that process data that they hold as part of their participation in a public inquiry must also comply with the provisions of the data protection legislation (for example government departments or core participants' legal representatives).

[30] DPA 2018, s 66(1).
[31] DPA 2018, s 67(9).
[32] DPA 2018, s 61(3).
[33] GDPR, Art 67.
[34] GDPR, Art 28.

'Processing data' includes disclosing it to a public inquiry. This can create challenges where an inquiry requests the production of information.

When responding to requests for data from an inquiry, understandably, participants are anxious not to breach the provisions of the GDPR and the DPA 2018 and thereby risk regulatory action. Participants may be able to rely on the exemptions from the GDPR set out in the DPA 2018 and exceptions within the GDPR itself, which mean that, in some circumstances, a participant may not have to comply with all the usual obligations under the GDPR, and may be able to disclose data without fear of breaching its obligations.

Exemption – information required to be disclosed by law

Schedule 2, Part I, para 5(2) of the DPA 2018 states:

'The listed GDPR provisions do not apply to personal data where disclosure of the data is required by an enactment, a rule of law or an order of a court or tribunal, to the extent that the application of those provisions would prevent the controller from making the disclosure.'

For statutory inquiries, the recipient of an inquiry's request for information could ask the inquiry to compel the production of the information formally, using a Section 21 Notice (see chapter eight).[35] The disclosure of any personal data disclosed as a result would thereby be required by an 'order of a … tribunal'; the exemption would apply and the recipient would avoid being exposed to potential breaches of the data protection legislation and the consequences that would follow.

A participant, however, may not want to be compelled to provide evidence or documents by formal notice, as this might impact negatively on their public perception and reputation. In this situation, when providing information voluntarily they must ensure that in doing so they are not in breach of their data protection obligations.

Non-statutory inquiries do not have the power to compel participants to provide information. Participants cannot therefore rely on this exemption. When providing information to a non-statutory inquiry, participants must ensure that they do not breach their data protection obligations and that they can justify the disclosure of any personal data. This may involve entering into a data sharing agreement with the inquiry or ensuring that justified legal bases for processing the data exist.

[35] Inquiries Act 2005, s 21.

Non-statutory inquiries and their participants may also be able to rely on other provisions to justify the disclosure of personal data.[36] The availability of alternative provisions will, however, be very fact-specific and will depend on the subject matter, nature and set up of the inquiry.

Anonymisation

An inquiry should always consider the extent to which information requested from a participant needs to include personal data in order to enable the inquiry to fulfil its terms of reference: in other words, is the personal data really necessary? If an inquiry determines that it does not need the personal data contained within a requested document, the document could be anonymised and all personal data or special category data removed before it is passed to the inquiry, thus avoiding any potential breach of the data protection legislation.[37]

This approach, however, presents its own practical challenges:

- Particular care must be taken by the recipient of the request when anonymising the data. An inquiry may well hold, or may obtain in the future, other information which, when read together with the recipient's information, could result in it linking the disclosed data to identifiable individuals. This would amount to a disclosure of personal data and may be unlawful.
- The anonymisation of all personal data may result in questions being raised about the transparency of an inquiry's work and whether it is truly public in nature.
- Anonymising the data can take a considerable amount of time and incur significant cost, depending on the volume of documents, and could therefore delay an inquiry's work further.

Consent

Another option to avoid the challenges posed by the data protection legislation is for the recipient of the inquiry's request for information to obtain consent for disclosure from each individual whose personal data and special category data is contained within the material held. This would avoid the need for an inquiry to serve a formal notice requiring the production of evidence and documents and would address concerns that the disclosing

[36] For example, s 10(5) of the Children Act 2004 requires certain organisations to cooperate with their relevant local authority in the making of arrangements to improve the well-being of children in the authority's area. This provision could be used by a local authority to issue an instruction that these organisations should provide relevant information to an inquiry, where the inquiry's purpose was to help improve the well-being of children.

[37] See chapter eight on redaction.

party may have around breaches of data protection legislation. However, there are practical challenges associated with obtaining consent:

- Consent can be withdrawn by an individual at any time and, in such circumstances, their data will no longer be available to the inquiry. Depending on the circumstances, this can be potentially very disruptive to an inquiry's work; for example, where an individual is unhappy with the approach an inquiry is taking in relation to a particular issue and accordingly withdraws consent for the use of their personal data. Where the inquiry is a statutory inquiry, it would still have the option to serve a Section 21 Notice and compel the production of evidence, but this could delay the progress of the inquiry.
- Consent must be both explicit and clear and must specify, in a high level of detail, how the information may be used. This is particularly important where the material in question contains special category data.

The consent should:

- identify exactly what information the individual consents to being used;
- detail exactly how the information may be used by the inquiry, ie the named individuals who may review the information, what the information may be used for, where it will be stored, how it will be accessed thereafter and for what specific tasks; and
- state if and when, and in what form, the information may then be published.

This is very difficult to achieve. Inquisitorial inquiries inevitably follow the evidence as it unfolds and do not pre-judge the inquiry's outcome or the direction investigations will take. Therefore, there are very few circumstances where obtaining explicit and clear consent will be possible.

For a core participant, interested party or a witness to an inquiry, the protection of data is one of the key issues that must be considered. Even if there are potential exemptions available to allow disclosure of documents to an inquiry that contain personal data, careful thought must be given to whether this would offer sufficient protection.

For statutory inquiries, core participants or others disclosing material to an inquiry must always consider asking the inquiry to formally compel the production of documents by way of a Section 21 Notice. Whilst that might give rise to concern about potential perceptions of non-cooperation, and the associated risk of reputational damage, that approach might be preferable to risking a breach of the data protection legislation or other actions, such as breach of confidence claims, that may follow if documents are disclosed without compulsion.

Freedom of Information

The Freedom of Information Act 2000 (FOIA 2000) provides for the disclosure of information held by public authorities or by persons providing services for them. In the UK, neither a statutory public inquiry held under the Inquiries Act 2005 nor a non-statutory inquiry is a 'public authority' for the purposes of the FOIA 2000[38] and therefore they are not susceptible to Freedom of Information Act requests during their lifetime.[39]

Despite this fact, there are still a number of FOIA issues that can arise and affect a public inquiry's work. In particular, this is because 'public authorities'[40] such as government departments, local government, the NHS, armed forces, police, BBC, the General Medical Council, the HM Chief Inspector of Prisons and many more, may participate in, or become involved in, public inquiries and, as a result, may have inquiry documents in their possession. Certain exemptions to disclosure may apply, depending on whether an inquiry is a statutory or non-statutory inquiry (see below).

Requests made of a Public Authority and Exemptions

Where a 'public authority' participates in an inquiry, for example as the sponsoring department of the inquiry or as a core participant, and that public authority receives a FOIA request for information, the starting point under s 1(1) of the FOIA 2000 is that the person making the request for information is entitled to:

(a) be informed in writing by the public authority whether it holds information of the description specified in the request; and
(b) if that is the case, to have that information communicated to them.

This must be done promptly and in any event generally not later than the twentieth working day following the date of receipt of the request.[41]

However, the public authority may withhold information or part of the information, for example by redaction, if an exemption applies. Where an exemption is absolute, the public authority may automatically withhold information. However, where an exemption is qualified, before deciding whether to withhold information, the public authority must consider the public interest arguments. This is a balancing exercise between the competing interests; the public authority must disclose the information unless the public interest in maintaining the

[38] FOIA 2000, s 3 and Sch 1.
[39] See chapter fifteen for freedom of information requests for inquiry records after its conclusion.
[40] As defined under the FOIA 2000 and listed in Sch 1.
[41] FOIA 2000, s 10.

exemption outweighs the public interest in disclosure.[42] Most exemptions are 'qualified', and there is only a limited number of 'absolute' exemptions.

If a public authority refuses a request for information, it must provide the applicant with a written notice stating that fact and specifying the exemption in question and why the exemption applies.[43] This must be done within the time set for responding to the request under s 1(1) of the FOIA 2000.

Checklist – Possible exemptions under the Freedom of Information Act 2000 in the context of a public inquiry

Below is a list of exemptions that may apply to prevent the disclosure of information under a FOIA request, in the context of an inquiry.

This is not an exhaustive list. The application of exemptions is very fact-specific and dependent on the circumstances concerned, including the nature of the particular inquiry, the request made, the information requested, and the public authority that is in receipt of the request.

Information in inquiry documents – s 32(2) of the FOIA 2000

- Section 32(2) is an absolute exemption and provides that information held by a public authority will be exempt from FOIA requests if it is held only by virtue of being contained in:
  (a) a document placed in the custody of a person conducting a statutory inquiry, for the purposes of the inquiry; or
  (b) a document created by a person conducting a statutory inquiry for the purposes of the inquiry.[44]
- The s 32(2) exemption does not apply in the context of non-statutory inquiries. (Section 32(4) of the FOIA defines 'inquiry' as 'any inquiry or hearing held under any provision contained in, or made under, an enactment'.)[45]
- Documents disclosed to an inquiry will be covered by the exemption. Equally, any correspondence created by an inquiry and sent to the relevant public authority, which is held by that authority only for the purposes of the inquiry, will be exempt from the FOIA 2000 under this rule.[46]

[42] FOIA 2000, s 2.
[43] FOIA 2000, s 17.
[44] FOIA 2000, s 32(a) and (b).
[45] This definition does apply to the limited number of inquiries that are convened under the very few statutory provisions other than the Inquiries Act 2005, under which an inquiry may be convened (see chapter one).
[46] Note, however, internal correspondence within the public authority about the inquiry would not be caught by the exemption.

- At the conclusion of an inquiry, documents are typically passed onto, and stored by, a public authority such as a government department or the National Archives. If and when such documents are archived in this way, the exemption under s 32(2) of the FOIA 2000 no longer applies.[47] Therefore, information requested under a FOIA request may, at that stage, be subject to disclosure (subject to any other exemptions that might apply).[48] An inquiry's privacy policy should set out details of what information will be archived, where, for how long, and what will happen to personal data that is not archived, ie whether it will be destroyed or returned. If there are concerns about protecting information, a participant may request that, at the conclusion of the inquiry, all information is returned, or destroyed.
- There are ambiguities around the extent of the application of the exemption under s 32(2) of the FOIA 2000 and how one should interpret the meaning of 'any document placed in the custody of a person conducting an inquiry'. One interpretation is any document sent to and held by the inquiry, which would include correspondence sent to the inquiry. However, guidance from the Ministry of Justice[49] suggests that 'placed in the custody of an inquiry' will primarily include 'evidence which is filed by parties to the inquiry' (such as witness statements and disclosure), rather than all documentation given to the inquiry.[50] It is therefore unclear how far the exemption can extend to any material held by a public body that is related to an inquiry's work.

The fact that the definition of 'inquiry' under s 32(4) of the FOIA 2000 does not include non-statutory inquiries means that information held by public authorities participating in, or otherwise involved in, non-statutory inquiries may be the subject of FOIA requests.

Prejudice to effective conduct of public affairs – s 36(2)(c) of the FOIA 2000

- Section 36(2)(c) of the FOIA 2000 provides that information will be exempt if, in the reasonable opinion of a qualified person, disclosure of the information would otherwise prejudice, or would be likely otherwise to prejudice, the effective conduct of public affairs.

[47] Inquiries Act 2005, ss 18(3) and 20(6).

[48] See chapter fifteen on freedom of information requests at the end of an inquiry.

[49] See https://webarchive.nationalarchives.gov.uk/20150603223404/https://www.justice.gov.uk/downloads/information-access-rights/foi/foi-exemption-s32.pdf (accessed 12 August 2020).

[50] However, the Ministry of Justice's guidance document is focused generally on applications involving adversarial proceedings, rather than an inquisitorial public inquiry.

- Under s 36(5)(a) of the FOIA 2000, where information is held by a government department, the qualified person includes the minister in charge of the department. The relevant minister must consider the circumstances of the particular case, and exercise their discretion to decide whether the exemption applies before it can be relied on to refuse a request for information.
- Prejudice to the effective conduct of public affairs includes an adverse effect on the public authority's ability to offer an effective public service or to meet its wider objectives or purpose. The effect does not have to be on the public authority in question; it could be an effect on other bodies or the wider public sector. It may also refer to the disruptive effects of disclosure, for example the diversion of resources in managing the effect of disclosure.[51] Prejudice may also arise, for example, if the request for information concerns an important ongoing issue on which there needs to be a free and frank exchange of views or provision of advice, which would be prejudiced by disclosure of the information.

Personal Information – s 40 of the FOIA 2000

- Section 40 of the FOIA 2000 provides that information is also exempt if its disclosure would result in the relevant public authority breaching their obligations under the DPA 2018 and the GDPR (see above). For example, the information sought might include special category data, such as an individual's medical details, and if the public authority were to disclose the information containing that third party special category data, it would be in breach of its DPA obligations.
- A further example is a document identifying members of staff. Whilst names of officials should normally be provided on request, if there is reason to think that disclosure of that information would put someone at risk (for instance confirming the work address of a member of staff who may be the subject of targeted harassment), that information may be exempt from disclosure.

Cost – s 12 of the FOIA 2000

- The FOIA 2000 recognises that FOIA requests are a demand on the resources of a public authority. A public authority may give notice in writing that a fee will be charged for complying with the request[52]

[51] *Ian Edward McIntyre v Information Commissioner and the Ministry of Defence* EA/2007/0068, 4 February 2008.

[52] FOIA 2000, s 9(1).

and the public authority is not obliged to comply with the request for information unless the fee is paid within the period of three months.[53] Section 12 of the FOIA 2000 states that a public authority can refuse a request if it estimates the cost of compliance would exceed the fees limit set by the Freedom of Information and Data Protection (Appropriate Limit and Fees) Regulations 2004.[54] Currently, the cost limit for complying with a request is set at £600 for public authorities listed in Schedule 1 to the FOIA 2000, such as government departments, local government, the NHS and the police, and £450 in the case of any other public authority.[55] The public authority is only required to estimate whether or not the limit would be exceeded. However, that estimate must be reasonable and must comply with requirements of the 2004 Regulations.

- If the public authority wishes to use s 12 of the FOIA 2000 (the cost limit) as the ground for refusing the request, it must send a written refusal notice.[56] This must state that complying with the request would exceed the appropriate cost limit, but must also confirm whether or not it holds the information requested. The refusal notice must also give the author of the request reasonable advice and assistance in order to refine their request, including an explanation of why the limit would be exceeded and what information, if any, may be available within the limits.

Issue – Potential FOIA issues for the inquiry

Where an inquiry does not have control over FOIA requests

While a public inquiry itself is not subject to the FOIA during its lifetime, the fact that public bodies participate in or are involved in an inquiry, not least as an inquiry's sponsoring department, means that the public bodies themselves are highly likely to hold documents relevant to the inquiry's work. Such documents may include correspondence with the inquiry,

[53] FOIA 2000, s 9(2).

[54] Freedom of Information and Data Protection (Appropriate Limit and Fees) Regulations 2004 (SI 2004/3244).

[55] Freedom of Information and Data Protection (Appropriate Limit and Fees) Regulations 2004 (SI 2004/3244), reg 3.

[56] FOIA 2000, s 17.

documents that have been disclosed as evidence, and draft witness statements. At the conclusion of the inquiry they may also be holding archived material from the public inquiry. These public bodies will be susceptible to FOIA requests. While there are a number of potential exemptions to prevent disclosure (as set out above), the inquiry itself does not have control over the public bodies' responses to FOIA requests.

The ICO's best practice guidance states that a public body should consult with those parties that are likely to be affected by disclosure made in response to a FOIA request, which would include a public inquiry; however, there is no duty for them to do so.[57] As a result, an inquiry may well not even be aware that a FOIA request has been received by a public body holding documents relevant to the inquiry's work and will not therefore be able to present any potential exemptions that might apply to prevent its disclosure. Disclosure of information in this way could potentially create problems for an inquiry's work.

For example, if draft witness statements are disclosed by a public body to a third party as a result of the public body receiving a FOIA request, and those draft statements are subsequently published by that third party, this could create issues relating to confidentiality for the inquiry. It could also be disruptive to the inquiry's work, if that draft evidence has yet to be finalised, heard during oral hearings and published. It may also have a detrimental impact on the inquiry's ability to fulfil its terms of reference; if confidential inquiry documents are disclosed by a third party, this may deter other witnesses from coming forward and from speaking to the inquiry as they may be concerned that their information will not be secure and controlled by the inquiry.

Once an inquiry has come to an end

In the case of statutory inquiries, after the delivery of the report of the inquiry, the inquiry comes to an end on the date on which the chair notifies the relevant minister that the inquiry has fulfilled its terms of reference, or any earlier date specified in a notice given by the minister to the chair.[58] Once the inquiry has ended, the exemption under s 32(2) of the FOIA 2000 (see above) no longer applies and the inquiry's documents are likely to be placed into the hands of public bodies, for example the sponsoring government department or the National Archives, who are susceptible to FOIA requests. At that stage, information may therefore be subject to disclosure under the FOIA (subject to any exemptions that might apply).

[57] https://ico.org.uk/media/for-organisations/documents/1624144/section-45-code-of-practice-request-handling-foia.pdf (accessed 13 August 2020).

[58] Inquiries Act 2005, s 14.

From a practical perspective, an inquiry's records will be placed in the hands of individuals who were not members of the inquiry team, do not have intimate knowledge of the inquiry's documents and who may not appreciate the extent of any confidentiality issues or other disclosure concerns. A very rigorous process of labelling must be carried out by the inquiry team prior to archiving the information.[59] There is no prescribed process that sets out how this should be managed. In the absence of a rigorous labelling process, there is a real risk that material that ought to remain confidential may be disclosed due to a lack of familiarity with, and knowledge about, the nature and sensitivities of the information in the documents and therefore the potential exemptions that may apply. (For archiving of an inquiry's materials, see chapter fifteen.)

In addition to s 32(2) of the FOIA 2000, there are a number of other exemptions that may apply in order to restrict the disclosure of information.[60] However, many of these are qualified exemptions[61] and, as time moves on following the conclusion of the inquiry, the balance between the public interest in maintaining an exemption and the public interest in disclosure is likely to shift, with a requirement for disclosure becoming more likely. An inquiry must always bear this in mind and recognise that its records may well become public in the future.

Issue – Freedom of information: why prevent the disclosure of information?

A public inquiry is just that, public; a mechanism whereby a matter of public concern is examined in order to find out happened, learn lessons and prevent recurrence. The majority of the inquiry's work is open for the public to see. So why would a public inquiry resist the disclosure of information requested under FOIA 2000 requests?

[59] Practice varies between inquiries. For some inquiries, the solicitor to the inquiry undertakes this task, and for other inquiries it is undertaken by the secretary to the inquiry; in both cases with their respective teams. The advantage of the former is that the solicitor to the inquiry tends to be more familiar with the evidence and more aware of the potential FOIA and DPA issues that could arise in the future.

[60] For example, FOIA 2000, s 23 contains an absolute exemption from the disclosure of information supplied by bodies dealing with security matters.

[61] For example, exemptions relating to information concerning commercial interests, defence, international relations, law enforcement, the economy, and the effective conduct of public affairs.

Although an inquiry is public in nature, it commonly deals with very sensitive, personal and confidential information. An inquiry needs to handle this information carefully and sensitively, not only because it is under a legal duty to do so, but also in order to foster a relationship of trust with the public and with those providing information to the inquiry. There must be safeguards in place to:

- protect witnesses and their personal information, which will often be sensitive in nature;
- protect matters that could affect national security or personal safety;
- protect the rights of whistle-blowers;
- prevent resources and costs being diverted to managing numerous information requests;
- prevent the inquiry's work from being diverted;
- allow those carrying out the inquiry to conduct a free and frank exchange of views with participants, and seek advice during the conduct of the inquiry, without fear of disclosure;
- encourage witnesses to be open and frank in their evidence.

With each of these factors in mind, a balance has to be struck, in terms of adopting an open approach and proportionality.

An inquiry should be as open and transparent in its dealings with the public as possible. Therefore, if disclosing information would not hinder the inquiry's work, consideration should be given to acceding to a request for information, even though the inquiry is not susceptible to such requests under the FOIA 2000.

In recent years, many inquiries have chosen to adopt an FOIA policy along the following lines:

'The Inquiry is not covered by the Freedom of Information Act 2000, but will endeavour to conduct proceedings in an open and transparent manner. As part of this, as much information as possible will be provided on this website. If you would like to submit a request for information, please contact the Inquiry.'

10

Evidence Taking

Introduction

The taking of witness evidence is one of the core roles of an inquiry. While documents provide a good foundation for the inquiry's investigative work, witness evidence normally provides the crucial means for obtaining a full understanding of the facts and issues by filling in any gaps and building on the documentary evidence. Depending on the nature of the inquiry, witnesses may be able to provide evidence that would be impossible for documents to reveal.

An inquiry is not required to obtain witness evidence; it can gather any form of evidence it thinks will be relevant to, and will assist it in, fulfilling its terms of reference. Nevertheless, it is very unlikely that an inquiry would not wish to obtain and analyse witness evidence. Almost every inquiry in the UK to date has obtained and relied upon witness evidence. Once an inquiry has identified the relevant documents and issues, the next stage is the taking of, or requiring witnesses to produce, written witness statements, which is the subject of this chapter.

An inquiry is not bound by the rules of evidence in the same way as adversarial civil and criminal proceedings. It is not restricted by the limitations of hearsay evidence, nor required to satisfy a particular burden of proof. The chair has a very broad discretion on how to approach the procedure and conduct of an inquiry.[1] An inquiry is an inquisitorial process and it is for the chair to determine how to approach the taking and scrutinising of evidence.

Issue – When to start gathering evidence?

Ideally, an inquiry will start to gather evidence, both witness evidence and documents, some months prior to any hearings starting. This allows a solid base of evidence to build up before any hearings start. It also reduces the need to recall witnesses to deal with issues that were not known to be relevant during their first round of oral evidence, or to respond to some later evidence, thereby reducing time and cost.

[1] Inquiries Act 2005, s 17(1).

However, in the majority of cases, time is of the essence. Inquiries are run on very tight timescales. There is often intense pressure for the inquiry to get started and then publish its findings quickly, coupled with the fact that the longer an inquiry takes the more expensive it will be. Therefore, whilst a significant lead-in time would be preferable, in some cases it is not possible, or acceptable, and a balance has to be found.

So how does the inquiry collect evidence in such circumstances?

By way of a typical example, in the case of the Mid Staffordshire NHS Foundation Trust Inquiry (being one of the swiftest inquiries undertaken to date), categories of witnesses were identified, including: victims' families, patient support organisations, those working in the hospital, the various separate health bodies and regulators with relevant responsibilities involved with the hospital, civil servants and politicians. A plan was then implemented that structured the taking of evidence by category, starting with the victims' families and patient organisations and then working through the different levels of accountability in the health service.

The inquiry team had a lead-in time of three to four weeks to prioritise gathering and analysing evidence most relevant to the first category of witnesses – the victims' families – so that that evidence was ready to be heard once the hearings opened. This model was then replicated for each subsequent category of witnesses. This rolling programme of taking evidence, and the witnesses then giving oral evidence just a matter of weeks later, continued throughout the course of that inquiry. The rolling programme was designed to commence with witnesses who were 'document light', allowing a concurrent team to analyse documents relevant to later categories of witnesses who were 'document heavy'. A similar approach was taken on the Bloody Sunday Inquiry, commencing with eye witnesses, and progressing to those with documents to consider. With the right resources in place, other inquiries could, and do, adopt a similar rolling programme.

The Power to Require the Production of Evidence

One of the main distinguishing features of a statutory inquiry, as opposed to a non-statutory inquiry, is the former's statutory power to compel witnesses to give evidence under s 21 of the Inquiries Act 2005. That power includes the power to require a witness to attend to give oral evidence to an inquiry (which is dealt with in chapter eleven) and the power to require a witness to provide a written statement of evidence. A witness may be required to attend an interview to allow the inquiry to take a written statement, or to provide written evidence directly in the form of a witness statement (see below).[2]

Even where the powers granted by the 2005 Act are not in fact exercised, their existence can provide a powerful incentive for ensuring co-operation with the inquiry.

Quote

'I found having the power to subpoena, which was probably the most critical thing if I wanted to hear from someone, simply concentrated the minds of those who might otherwise not wish to come. I never had to resort to it, but there were two occasions on which we reminded someone who was dragging his or her heels that we did have that power and ... it was enough to persuade them to appear.'

Professor Sir Ian Kennedy QC, in evidence to the House of Lords Select Committee on the Inquiries Act 2005

'We have found the Inquiries Act was very beneficial in the Azelle Rodney inquiry in that we had the powers of compulsion. We did not use them very often and we did not have to enforce them, but having that little bit of stick does help.'

Judith Kemish, in evidence to the House of Lords Select Committee on the Inquiries Act 2005

The Inquiries Act 2005 provides that the chair may give notice requiring a person to:

- provide evidence to the inquiry panel in the form of a written statement;
- provide any documents in their custody or under their control that relate to a matter in question;
- produce any other thing in their custody or under their control for inspection, examination or testing.[3]

This is often described as a 'Section 21 Notice'. The request for evidence must be made in writing. Any request for a written statement must include a description of matters or issues to be covered in a witness statement.[4]

[2] Inquiries Act 2005, s 21(1) and s 21(2) respectively.

[3] Inquiries Act 2005, s 21(2).

[4] Inquiry Rules 2006, r 9. The service requirements for written requests are dealt with in the Inquiry Rules 2006, rr 3 and 4.

The written notice must:

- explain the possible consequences of not complying;
- indicate what the recipient of the notice should do if they wish to claim that –
  - they are unable to comply with a notice under this section, or
  - it is not reasonable in all the circumstances to require them to comply.[5]

Any claim made by the recipient that they are unable to comply, or that it is not reasonable to comply, will be determined by the chair, having regard to the public interest in the information in question being obtained by the inquiry and the likely importance of the information. The chair may decide to revoke or vary the Section 21 Notice.[6] Many inquiries, however, choose to make voluntary requests for evidence and documents in the first instance, and only resort to issuing a formal Section 21 Notice if an organisation or person is refusing, or delaying, the production of evidence. Such an approach is compatible with the intended non-adversarial nature of inquiries.

Enforcement of a Section 21 Notice

If a witness is served with a Section 21 Notice and, without reasonable excuse, refuses to attend the inquiry's hearings or provide documents or other evidence as requested, including evidence in the form of a written statement, the witness will be guilty of a criminal offence[7] and the inquiry may issue enforcement proceedings to enforce the Section 21 Notice by referring the matter to the relevant court.[8]

In practice, enforcement action is rarely necessary, as receipt of a Section 21 Notice is usually sufficient to secure the attendance or cooperation of a witness. The Robert Hamill Inquiry did, however, conduct successful enforcement proceedings in the High Court in Belfast in March 2009 to compel a reluctant key witness, who had been served with a Section 21 Notice, to attend the inquiry to give evidence.

[5] Inquiries Act 2005, s 21(3).

[6] Inquiries Act 2005, s 21(4) and (5).

[7] Inquiries Act 2005, s 35.

[8] By referring the matter to the High Court, or Court of Sessions for Scottish inquiries: Inquiries Act 2005, s 36. A person who is guilty of an offence under the 2005 Act is 'liable on summary conviction to a fine not exceeding level three on the standard scale or to imprisonment for a term not exceeding the relevant maximum, or to both'.

Enforcement of a 'Section 21 Notice'

Failure to comply with a notice requiring the production of evidence under s 21 of the Inquiries Act 2005 renders the individual who is refusing to give evidence guilty of an offence.

A person who is guilty of such an offence is liable on summary conviction to a fine or imprisonment.

(Sections 35 and 36 of the Inquiries Act 2005)

When to Serve a Section 21 Notice?

In addition to having the power under s 21 of the Inquiries Act 2005 to compel a person to provide witness statements, documents and any other thing in their custody or control for inspection, examination or testing,[9] the chair of a statutory inquiry may also compel a person to attend in person at a given time or place to give evidence or produce documents or other evidence at the inquiry.[10] For example, such a notice might require an individual to attend a hearing to give evidence to the inquiry. An inquiry may also be able to use a Section 21 Notice to require an individual to attend a meeting with representatives from the inquiry to provide evidence, which could then be put into witness statement form, although as the wording of s 21 is not clear on this point, this could potentially be challenged.

There are generally two instances during a statutory inquiry when the inquiry may decide that it is necessary to exercise this power and will serve a Section 21 Notice on an individual:

- where a witness is refusing to, or is delaying in, providing evidence; or
- where a witness is willing to provide evidence, but has requested that they be served with a Section 21 Notice. This may be for a number of reasons: to give an element of protection from criticism for speaking out; to establish legal grounds to legitimise the processing and disclosure to the inquiry, of personal data (see chapter nine); or something as simple as requiring leave from work to give evidence and needing to be compelled to attend in order to obtain the necessary time off.

A witness to an inquiry should give careful consideration before refusing to provide evidence to an inquiry, and risking being served with a Section 21 Notice, because of the potential damage to reputation that may result.

[9] Inquiries Act 2005, s 21(2).
[10] Inquiries Act 2005, s 21(1).

Issue – Compelling witnesses in practice

Experience shows that most witnesses are willing to cooperate and give evidence to an inquiry. This also applies to those who may be, or have been, criticised, who will invariably wish to respond to any criticisms and add to, or comment on, the evidence as it emerges. Compelling a witness who is reluctant to give evidence, and whose evidence is not particularly relevant to the inquiry's terms of reference, can be counterproductive. It is a time consuming and costly process. The evidence obtained is likely to have reduced value as the witness may well be uncooperative. Compelling a reluctant witness to give evidence where their evidence is likely to be of limited value to the inquiry's work can also undermine the public's and participants' trust in a public inquiry; it may be viewed as an aggressive move, particularly if the witness in question is vulnerable.

Equally, an inquiry must be mindful of which evidence is key to its terms of reference and where there will be a public expectation that certain witnesses will be called. For example, if there is a public inquiry into a death at a hospital, there will be a public expectation that the chief executive of that hospital will be called to give evidence. An inquiry must bear this in mind, as well as the relative importance of the witness's evidence, when considering whether or not the witness should be compelled to give evidence.

During the Leveson Inquiry, witnesses were compelled to provide evidence by Section 21 Notice as a matter of course, whether they were willing to give evidence voluntarily or not. Many argue that this created an adversarial environment (coupled with hearings taking place in the Royal Courts of Justice). Witnesses might have felt less comfortable being open and frank when giving evidence in these circumstances, as receiving a Section 21 Notice without first being asked if they would provide evidence voluntarily might have been perceived to suggest that there was something about which they should be concerned. There is a strong argument that an inquiry should not exercise these powers routinely, but only when necessary.

Powers of Non-Statutory Inquiries

In contrast to inquiries convened under the Inquiries Act 2005, non-statutory inquiries do not have any power to compel witnesses to give evidence. In some cases this will not be significant, for example in circumstances where reliance on the cooperation of witnesses or organisations may not be key, where the information needed to investigate is already to hand, or where in-depth investigation is not necessary.

Witnesses may already feel under pressure to cooperate with an inquiry as a result of public pressure, for example from figures of public prominence. Others may be required to cooperate by virtue of their employment, for example civil servants and members of the police forces and armed services. Witnesses employed outside the public sector may also feel obliged to provide evidence to an inquiry if they have been asked to do so by their employer; the very existence of an employment relationship can be a persuasive factor. An employer may well make such a request of its employees so that, as an organisation, it is seen to be co-operating with an inquiry's work.

In other cases, however, the inability to compel witnesses to provide evidence could hinder an inquiry's progress and prevent it from obtaining evidence that could be key to its terms of reference.

The Taking of Witness Statements

Section 17 of the Inquiries Act 2005 (which provides that the procedure and conduct of the inquiry will be as the chair directs) means the chair is at liberty to determine how such written evidence should be taken.

An inquiry will determine which witnesses it wishes to receive evidence from, both by proactively identifying witnesses and requesting evidence from them and by selecting from the list of potential witnesses who have contacted the inquiry to offer evidence voluntarily.

Witnesses may be asked to produce their written statement themselves and submit the statement to the inquiry directly. If a witness or core participant is legally represented, their witness statement will usually be produced with the assistance of their legal representative. Alternatively, the chair may require statements to be prepared by the inquiry team. If so, members of the inquiry team will arrange to meet, interview the witnesses, and prepare written statements. If legally represented, the legal representative for the witness or core participant will often be present at the interview.

Issue – Who should prepare the witness statements?

Inquiries have adopted different approaches to gathering evidence. Some inquiry legal teams meet with the witnesses and prepare the witness statements, while other inquiries, often if the legal team is relatively small, will allow or encourage witnesses to provide their own statements.

There are practical difficulties that arise when witnesses prepare their own statements and, in practice, there are many instances where the only way to obtain a meaningful statement is for an inquiry to arrange to interview a witness and take the statement itself (see below).

The legislative provisions do not preclude such an approach. Under r 9 of the Inquiry Rules 2006, the 'inquiry panel must send a written request for a written statement to any person from whom the inquiry panel proposes to take evidence'. The Rules and Act are silent on who is responsible for preparing the statement. Whilst one could argue that the current wording of the Rules suggests that it should be the witnesses themselves (or their legal representatives) who prepare the statements, in 2014 the Government accepted the House of Lords Select Committee's[11] recommendation that r 9 of the Inquiry Rules 2006 should be amended to explicitly allow the inquiry's own legal team to take written statements from witnesses.[12]

Difficulties which may arise when witnesses prepare the statements

Encouraging witnesses to provide their own evidence is often done in an attempt to save costs for the inquiry. This is, however, frequently not the outcome in practice because of additional work it may create.

- It may encourage witnesses and core participants to obtain costly legal advice they do not need because, in fact, there is no realistic prospect that they will face criticism.
- Evidence provided on this basis invariably reflects what the witness wants to say, which may well be very different to the evidence the inquiry is seeking in order to further its terms of reference. The inquiry team may need to go back to the witness a number of times with additional questions and for clarification.
- Lawyers representing those who are, or are likely to be, subject to criticism will naturally adopt a cautionary and adversarial approach. They are likely to advise their client to provide the information asked of them and nothing further. Statements will be prepared based on inquiry-issued rule 9 letters; these letters may be based on the erroneous assumption that a witness is relevant only to issues 'X, Y and Z', when in truth the witness can assist with much more. However, the inquiry team cannot know in advance the full breadth of areas on which a witness may be able to assist and key evidence may be missed as a consequence. When the inquiry team takes the evidence itself, it can respond to the evidence as it is being given by the witness and adjust and broaden areas

[11] HL Select Committee, *The Inquiries Act 2005: Post-legislative Scrutiny* (HL 2013–2014 143).

[12] Ministry of Justice, *Government Response to the Report of the House of Lords Select Committee on the Inquiries Act 2005* (Cm 8093 2014).

of questioning accordingly. The inquiry legal team can thus respond to the witness in what is a truly inquisitorial approach.

- If a statement prepared by the witness is inadequate, the inquiry still has the opportunity to question the witness at an oral hearing. However, this can create its own problems. Where new evidence comes to light during oral evidence, counsel to the inquiry will not have had a chance to fully prepare. As a result, relevant documents and other evidence may not be to hand. Adjournments may be necessary. Investigating and exploring the new of line evidence may not be possible without also recalling the witness, adding to the costs of the inquiry.

Allowing witnesses to produce their own witness statements also presents practical difficulties, including:

- Issues of consistency, including the format, style and level of detail in the witness statement. Using inconsistent statements will make counsel to the inquiry's job more difficult when it comes to taking each witness through their statement during the oral hearings and for the chair when referring to them during the report-writing phase.
- A witness or core participant may not interpret the terms of reference in the same way as the inquiry and consequently may not provide the full breadth of evidence the inquiry is seeking.
- Witnesses will not be as aware as the inquiry legal team of emerging issues and documents still being provided.
- Often a memory will not be in the forefront of the mind of the witness. Memory storage and retrieval is a complex process. Specialist interviewing techniques can be used by the inquiry to assist witnesses with memory recall in order to produce fuller, and more accurate and uncontaminated statements than those produced using traditional interviewing techniques.
- Members of the inquiry team conducting witness interviews will, over time, gain a comprehensive overview of the areas of evidence given by witnesses. Areas of questioning can be broadened accordingly, to reduce missing key evidence.
- It is almost impossible, in practical terms, for an inquiry team to put all relevant documents to a witness, enquire into the possible interpretations and ask the witness to comment on them in any meaningful way, simply by correspondence. Attempting to set out all the relevant information and questions in advance, in writing, rather than during a meeting, is extremely time consuming and simply adds to the cost.
- Because of the issues of inconsistency, potential lack of detail, differing interpretations of the terms of reference, and difficulty in commenting

on documents, inevitably when a witness statement that has been prepared by the witness or their legal team is received, a process of discussion and negotiation to get the evidence improved and finalised will begin. This may result in meetings between the inquiry team and the witness, lengthy phone calls and further, often numerous, iterations of the statement. All of this substantially increases cost.

In most cases, experience suggests it is better that the inquiry legal team interviews the witnesses and prepares the witness statements if it is to be truly inquisitorial, cost-effective and serve the public interest.

Quote

'The other big change I would want to make – … is to allow the inquiry itself to take statements from witnesses if it wants to. This certainly has been a problem where you ask for a statement and it comes through, having been taken by the solicitor for the witness, and it is not adequate. We ask the witness to come in so that the inquiry can take a statement and the solicitors refuse, saying, "No, we will do it", and you have to go through iteration after iteration until you get anything useful. I know there is the fall-back position. You call them for oral evidence and you take the evidence orally, but it just takes a lot of time.'

Lee Hughes, in evidence to the House of Lords Select Committee on the Inquiries Act 2005

'An effective inquiry is proactively inquisitorial. If statements are produced by lawyers for the witnesses, they can be anodyne and self-serving. The quality of the evidence will be markedly different if it has been taken by the inquiry team. So who proofs the witnesses is critical.'

Peter Skelton QC, One Crown Office Row

Preparing for a Witness Interview

What the inquiry team will do in preparation for a witness interview

Preparatory materials

The inquiry legal team will prepare materials for the interview member or members of the legal team to review in advance of meeting the witness. This could include the following steps:

- Searching the inquiry's document management system for relevant documents to provide background information and for documents to put to the witness for comment.
- Collating evidence from oral hearings to identify any reference to the witness in the oral evidence. Is there anything the witness might want to comment on in response?
- Locating a copy of all correspondence with the witness to date, to provide background information; identify likely areas on which the witness can provide evidence; provide insight into the approach the witness is likely to take to giving evidence (eg are they likely to be hostile, or nervous about providing evidence); and to identify any additional support the witness may require (eg support for vulnerable witnesses).
- In arranging witness interviews, an inquiry might want to consider appointing particular interviewing teams to certain topics. This helps avoid duplication of reading in and research time, and allows areas of internal expertise to develop, to ensure that the witness interviews cover all necessary issues and themes.
- As witness interviews progress, in preparation for future interviews, knowledge is commonly shared both within and across the legal team about what evidence has been gathered from other witnesses and the themes and issues that are emerging from the evidence.

Logistics and support

- The inquiry team should take steps to make witnesses feel as comfortable as possible when providing their evidence. This might include providing formal, specialist witness support (see below). Other steps might include allowing a trade union representative, their recognised legal representative or lawyer, or other support figure to be present. There may also be other arrangements that might make the process easier, such as the provision of an interpreter.
- A time, date and location will be agreed for the interview. The location should be a neutral venue for the witness.
- The inquiry team will provide details in advance of who will be attending the interview and an outline of what will be discussed.
- On occasions, witnesses may make specific requests regarding additional arrangements for the interview, for example requesting a female or male-only interviewing team. The inquiry team will review such requests and put arrangements in place as appropriate.

- The inquiry team will explain what will happen after the interview (ie a statement will be prepared for the witness to review, agree and sign). If hearings are being conducted, the inquiry team will explain that the witness may subsequently be asked to give oral evidence to the inquiry.

The Witness Interview and Statement Preparation

Inquiries approach witness interviews and preparing witness statements in different ways, according to the needs of the specific inquiry. Set out below are illustrations of two approaches to the interviewing process:

Approaches to the witness interview and statement preparation

Interviewing with written notetaking
A best practice interview with written notetaking involves an interviewing team of two: one person to interview the witness and the second to take full, contemporaneous notes.

- Before the interview commences, the interviewing team should give careful consideration to the interviewing environment, to help the interviewee feel as relaxed as possible and to minimise distractions. This will include avoiding locations with negative associations for the witness, busy or noisy areas, and distractions from phones and electronic equipment. The room and seating should be comfortable, as witness interviews can be lengthy.
- The use of a two-person team enables the interviewer to focus on building rapport and trust with the witness, and to listen to the evidence whilst maintaining eye contact and full engagement with the witness, rather than having simultaneously to take detailed notes of the evidence. This should make the witness feel more relaxed and listened to, creating an atmosphere of trust and encouraging the witness to feel more able to give honest and detailed evidence.
- The role of the note-taker is to take a detailed, verbatim note of the witness's evidence, and thereafter to produce a written statement, encapsulating that evidence, as set out below.
- The use of specialist interviewing techniques, designed to enhance a witness's in-depth retrieval of memory, should be used to avoid

some of the traps normally associated with standard interviewing techniques, such as rushing the recall of witnesses and interrupting their narratives. Witnesses must feel confident that they have time to think, speak, reflect, and speak again as often as they need. Rushing witnesses sends a message to them that their information is trivial or they are not being listened to; this results in witness memory retrieval shutdown. Interviewers must give witnesses the time to concentrate and remember. It is invariably the case that witnesses who are properly interviewed provide relevant evidence that an overly proactive interviewer would not have known to seek out.

- Lines of questioning must be inquisitorial, using non-leading open questions to avoid any form of suggestion or inadvertent contamination of the evidence, whilst letting the witness feel in control of the statement taking process.
- Following the interview, the note-taker will prepare a statement, with input from the interviewer, for review by the witness. When preparing the statement, it is likely that the notes taken during the interview will have to be reordered, chronologically and logically, to make the evidence easier to follow. The statement should, however, be drafted using the witness's own words. This is not only so that the witness will be happy with, and sign, the statement but also because it provides the inquiry with the most accurate representation of the witness's evidence. Irrelevant information that does not further the terms of reference of the inquiry may be removed, to ensure the statement is focused and to save the inquiry time. The witness will have the opportunity to see and approve the witness statement in a draft form before signature. Any omissions on the grounds of irrelevance can be explained.
- A draft statement will be sent to the witness for review, any editing and for signature. Any minor amendments will generally be marked up and initialled by the witness. If there are any substantial changes, it may be necessary to prepare a further draft, or drafts.

Interviewing using a recording device

Another approach to the witness interview and statement preparation involves a single interviewer using a dictation machine, or other recording device, to record the interview. This approach has advantages and disadvantages:

- Using a single interviewer reduces initial cost.
- The interview will be captured on an audio recording, which can be referred back to in the future should there be any dispute about what was said.

- However, many witnesses dislike their evidence being recorded. It may give the impression of a police interview. It tends to make them more nervous and guarded and can prevent them being open and frank in their evidence. Being distracted by, and being overly conscious of, the presence of a recording device can also interrupt the flow of a witness's evidence, impacting negatively on their memory recall and on the quality of the evidence given.
- Once the interview is complete, the recording has to be transcribed. (Voice recognition software is not currently able to transcribe such recordings; the recordings are not always clear, do not follow grammatically correct sentence structures, and contain interruptions from both the interviewer and interviewee.) A transcription of an interview is rarely capable of standing as prime evidence; it will not be chronological, will almost certainly jump between topics, and will be very lengthy.
- Once a transcript is produced it can be converted into a witness statement. This involves a member of the inquiry team editing the transcript so that the evidence is ordered chronologically and logically, with evidence topics grouped together, and any duplicated or irrelevant material removed. In practice, the time and cost associated with producing a full transcript of a recorded interview and then converting it to a witness statement, is similar to, or may exceed, the cost of the two-person interviewing team described above.

Issue – What if a witness refuses to sign their statement?

During some inquiries, issues have arisen where a witness has provided evidence during an interview for the purpose of submitting a written witness statement to the inquiry, but has subsequently refused to sign their statement or has failed to return it to the inquiry within a reasonable period of time. Seeing their evidence written down in black and white can occasionally cause a witness to reconsider the giving of evidence, or prompt a re-think of the detail of the evidence given.

Similarly, there have been rare instances where a witness has denied giving a particular piece of evidence during an interview with members of the inquiry team once they have seen it included in their written statement. This might be because of potential repercussions if that piece of evidence becomes public, where it is particularly damaging to them, their employer, or someone else; it may be that the witness may regret having been so frank, or so strident in the criticism of others.

In many instances, any changes that a witness wants to make to a draft statement can be agreed by an inquiry; after all the witness statement is the witness's own evidence and they should be happy with how it is expressed. However, there may be rare instances where a witness has provided evidence in an interview that is crucial to the inquiry's terms of reference, which the witness later wants removed from the written statement before it is signed. In such an instance, an inquiry cannot ignore what it has heard. An inquiry legal team should not operate 'off the record'; this extends to the process of interviewing.

Most inquiries will have procedures already in place to deal with such an eventuality. These include:

- the inquiry's protocols on evidence gathering, which should specify that a witness may not materially change fundamental elements of the account of evidence given at interview;
- interviewing teams should explain, at the outset of each interview, that a record of the witness's evidence will be taken; and
- interviewing teams should avoid providing any assurance that information provided by a witness will remain confidential unless or until they consent to it being published, unless the inquiry has specifically determined in advance that it is prepared to abide by such an assurance.

In the event that a witness disagrees with the record of their evidence once they have seen it presented in a witness statement format, the inquiry has a number of options:

- Review the information that the witness is trying to alter or take out and decide how crucial it is. Is it key to the inquiry's terms of reference, issues and themes? Is it relevant to the credibility of the witness or other witnesses?
- If it is not crucial information, the inquiry may allow the witness to amend the statement as they wish; it is their statement and evidence.
- If the inquiry considers that it is crucial information, it may request that the information be put back in. This might involve showing the witness a copy of notes or audio recording of the interview, if requested, to be reminded of what was said.
- The inquiry may also explore with the witness why they do not want the information included. If it concerns personal information, the information might attract public interest immunity or be privileged. If so, the inquiry may decide to make a restriction order, specifying

that the information be redacted, thus preventing disclosure to other participants and the public without restricting access to the inquiry team. This may allay any fears the witness has, while ensuring the evidence is available to the inquiry.

If, however, the witness continues to object to the material being included in the final form of statement, or fails or refuses to return an approved and signed copy of their statement, provided the inquiry legal team is satisfied that it is an accurate reflection of the evidence provided to it in interview, a copy of the unsigned and unapproved statement can be used as evidence to the inquiry and be released in that form:

- The inquiry must make it clear where a statement is unsigned and unapproved.
- The fact that unsigned and unapproved statements may be used should be explained in the inquiry's protocols at the outset of the inquiry, so that all witnesses are aware of what action can be taken in the event they refuse to sign their witness statement.
- The inquiry's protocols should also make it clear that witnesses and their legal representatives will be given a reasonable length of time to make any representations regarding the draft being submitted as formal evidence and disclosed to other participants and the public.

Clearly, a decision as to whether or not this is the appropriate route to take will depend on the specific circumstances. For example, if a vulnerable witness is refusing to sign their statement, the inquiry may not deem it appropriate to publish a draft statement without the witness's consent.

Witness Support

It is now common for inquiries to put a witness support service in place for the duration of its work. This is particularly the case where the subject matter of an inquiry relates to loss of life or other traumatic events. When individuals in these circumstances are asked to give evidence to an inquiry, and re-live their experiences, it can result in re-traumatisation. This, therefore, is something that an inquiry should consider at the outset, and core participants and interested parties should request a support service if such a service is not already in place.

Recent examples of inquiries where support services have been established and made available to participants in the inquiry include the Grenfell Tower Inquiry, Infected Blood Inquiry and the Scottish Child Abuse Inquiry.

The type and level of the support on offer depends on the nature of the inquiry and the nature of the witnesses who may be affected.

When an inquiry is establishing a witness support service, there are a number of factors that should be considered:

- What service will be available? For example, will it be face-to-face counselling sessions, support provided over the telephone, or a combination of the two?
- Who will the support be provided to? Will it be limited to those who are core participants or interested parties to the inquiry and witnesses asked to provide evidence, or will it be available to anyone affected by the inquiry's work?
- When will support be provided? For example:
  - face-to-face support sessions may be available throughout the duration of the inquiry without limitation;
  - support may be provided to witnesses before, during and immediately after providing evidence to the inquiry (either during a meeting to provide a witness statement or by giving oral evidence during a hearing) when they may be most likely to suffer trauma, as well as during key phases of the inquiry which may be difficult for those most affected, for example when the report is published;
  - support workers may be available in person at every hearing and on the telephone at other times.
- There are number of ways in which the support may be designed and delivered. Is an individual, tailored approach needed for each witness or individual who needs support?
- What experience and qualifications are required from those delivering the service? Do they need to be qualified therapists or have a particular area of expertise?
- When will the service be available? Will the service be accessible during office hours or 24 hours a day? There are clearly cost implications for such options. If there are to be restricted hours when the service is available, an inquiry needs to bear in mind that those affected may be in crisis at any hour of the day and must therefore consider providing signposting to other services outside the restricted hours.
- Is it important that the support service provider is independent from the locality of the subject matter of the inquiry? Are there are organisations that should be avoided due to their potential involvement in the inquiry itself or any conflict of interests that could arise?
- Should there be a number of service providers to choose from if independence or other issues are likely to arise?

- How will the support service and the inquiry communicate and put in place processes for sharing information, while ensuring that confidentiality is protected?
- How will the service be funded and what are the resource implications?

Immunities

Unlike courts, neither statutory nor non-statutory inquiries have the power to rule on or determine any person's civil or criminal liability; their findings and recommendations do not have legal effect. For statutory inquiries, this is specifically set out in s 2(1) of the Inquiries Act 2005.

This does not, however, prevent an inquiry chair, or panel, from finding facts or making recommendations which are detrimental to someone or may damage their reputation. Section 2(2) of the 2005 Act states that 'an inquiry panel is not to be inhibited in the discharge of its functions by any likelihood of liability being inferred from facts that it determines or recommendations that it makes'. An inquiry's aim is to find out the truth and make recommendations for the future: 'it is not intended that the inquiry should be hampered in its investigations by a fear that responsibility may be inferred from a determination of a fact.'[13]

If an inquiry was able to rule on a person's civil or criminal liability, it might inhibit a witness's openness and willingness to give evidence. It would also increase the desire of witnesses and core participants to have legal representation, given the potential personal repercussions. In such circumstances, there would be strong arguments for witnesses to assert that they should be afforded the opportunity to put forward their own case, cross-examine witnesses and defend any criticisms directed at themselves. This would, however, lead to a more adversarial model and increase the duration and cost of an inquiry.

Quote

'It is inevitable that most, if not all, inquiries will make findings of fact that are unfavourable to certain parties. However, the inquiry is less likely to establish the truth if the witnesses are aware that what they say may be admissible in a criminal court. In our experience, finding out what really happened to those who died or were involved in a disaster is of paramount importance.'[14]

[13] Explanatory notes to the Inquiries Act 2005.

[14] Disaster Action written evidence, para 15.1. Select Committee on the Inquiries Act 2005, 'Written and corrected oral evidence', http://www.parliament.uk/documents/lords-committees/Inquiries-Act-2005/IA_Written_Oral_evidencevol.pdf (accessed 13 August 2020).

> Disaster Action, in written evidence to the House of Lords Select Committee on the Inquiries Act 2005
>
> *'An inquiry cannot determine criminal or civil liability. If it did, all the adversarial problems would just bounce back because everybody would have to have a chance to put their case because nobody should be condemned without that opportunity or certainly not be subject to a penalty in crime or potential award of damages in civil law.'*[15]
>
> Sir Brian Leveson, Chair of the Leveson Inquiry, in oral evidence to the House of Lords Select Committee on the Inquiries Act 2005

Despite the fact that an inquiry does not have the power to determine civil or criminal liability, witnesses may be reluctant to provide evidence to an inquiry for fear of potential consequences. Under s 14 of the Criminal Evidence Act 1968 and s 22 of the Inquiries Act 2005, a witness called to give evidence to an inquiry is entitled to refuse to answer questions if that evidence might be used against them in future criminal proceedings (ie a privilege against self-incrimination). In order to address this problem, and in an attempt to encourage witnesses to come forward and be open and frank in their evidence (and to prevent reliance on privilege against self-incrimination, which may prevent an inquiry receiving all relevant evidence) it is very common for inquiries to obtain various forms of undertakings to protect witnesses from self-incrimination.

Undertakings can be sought from the Attorney General, in consultation with the Director of Public Prosecutions, to the effect that evidence given by a person to an inquiry will not be used against that person in criminal proceedings (however, this would not extend to civil proceedings). Those who meet the terms of the undertaking will not face prosecution as a result of the evidence that they give. However, undertakings given by the Attorney General do not give a person immunity from prosecution, only against self-incrimination. A person may still face prosecution based on evidence produced or given to the inquiry by another person. Similarly, it does not prevent, for example, a police investigation. Any police investigation would have to gather independent evidence, rather than using the evidence provided by the witness to the inquiry, but that evidence could help direct the focus of such an investigation and help inform the areas where further investigation is necessary.

More commonly, similar undertakings to those sought from the Attorney General may be sought from relevant employers in connection with other types of proceedings, such as employer disciplinary action. For example, on the Rosemary Nelson Inquiry:

[15] Select Committee on the Inquiries Act 2005, 'Written and corrected oral evidence' (n 14) Q100.

- the Ministry of Defence provided immunity from self-incrimination for military personnel 'before a Court Martial or summary hearing before a commanding officer or appropriate superior authority';
- the Cabinet Secretary and Head of the Northern Ireland Civil Service provided a similar undertaking for civil servants in respect of disciplinary proceedings, save where an allegation of misconduct was so serious it would justify summary dismissal for gross misconduct; and
- the Chief Constable of the Police Service for Northern Ireland and Police Ombudsman for Northern Ireland gave a waiver that 'Nothing which any serving police officer provides to the Inquiry by way of evidence, whether orally or in writing, will be used in subsequent disciplinary proceedings against that officer or any other serving police officer, except where the allegations are so serious as to merit consideration by a disciplinary board of the punishments "required to resign" or "dismissed".

For most inquiries where undertakings have been given by the Attorney General, or others, the undertakings have been sought by the inquiry itself, at the outset of its work. During the Grenfell Tower Inquiry, however, a number of witnesses made an application at the commencement of the inquiry's phase 2 hearings (some two and a half years after the inquiry had been established and after phase 1 of its work had been completed) asking the chair to seek an undertaking from the Attorney General for immunity against self-incrimination in criminal proceedings. Having considered the application, the chair sought the undertaking, which was subsequently granted by the Attorney General, but the undertaking was limited in scope to cover only part of the inquiry's work (modules 1 to 3 of phase 2)[16] and did not protect corporate entities, as the Attorney General was not convinced that it was in the public interest.[17]

Issue – Nature of undertakings granting immunity

The nature of any undertaking offered will depend on the nature of the inquiry itself. In some cases, the inquiry may not consider it appropriate for undertakings to be provided, for reasons of public interest. A balance must be struck between measures taken to encourage openness and to establish the facts in accordance with the inquiry's terms of reference with the need to hold people to account.

[16] This is the position at the time of writing; an application could be made to extend the undertaking during the course of the inquiry's work.

[17] Attorney General's letter to the Chairman, available at https://assets.grenfelltowerinquiry.org.uk/inline-files/Attorney%20General%E2%80%99s%20letter%20to%20the%20Chairman%20with%20her%20decision%20on%20the%20undertaking%20February%202020.pdf.

Each request for an undertaking will be considered on a case-by-case basis and the inquiry and the Attorney General, or relevant employer or other body, will discuss whether such an undertaking should be offered and on what terms. For example, it could be limited in some way, as was the case with the Attorney General's undertaking on the Grenfell Tower Inquiry, which was limited to certain stages of the inquiry's work, and only covered natural persons, not corporate entities.

An undertaking granted to protect against self-incrimination when giving evidence will not protect against offences committed in the course of giving evidence. Such offences include giving false evidence in the course of the inquiry, or conspiring with or procuring others to do so; or one of the offences set out in s 35 of the Inquiries Act 2005, such as failing to comply with a notice to give or produce evidence, or intentionally altering, suppressing or concealing documents.

Privilege

Privileged Information

As explained earlier in the chapter, statutory inquiries have the power to compel witnesses to provide evidence to the inquiry.[18] Witnesses are, however, able to refuse to provide information if that information is privileged, in the same way as in civil proceedings.[19]

As a result, a witness may refuse to provide evidence because:

- it is covered by legal professional privilege;[20]
- it might incriminate the witness or the witness's spouse or civil partner (by virtue of s 84 of the Civil Partnerships Act 2004); or
- it relates to things said or done in Parliament and is covered by parliamentary privilege.

Public Interest Immunity

Witnesses and core participants may withhold evidence or documents from the inquiry, or from public disclosure, on the grounds of public interest immunity

[18] Inquiries Act 2005, s 21.

[19] Inquiries Act 2005, s 21.

[20] The House of Lords' decision in *Three Rivers v Bank of England* [2004] UKHL 48 made it clear that advice given to a witness in the context of an inquiry, including advice about the presentation of evidence, attracts legal advice privilege.

or 'PII', ie they are immune from disclosure in the public interest. The Inquiries Act 2005 expressly provides that public interest immunity applies in relation to statutory inquiries as in relation to civil proceedings.[21]

Applications for public interest immunity have been made in a number of inquiries by those whose duty it is to protect the information in question. The applicant is required to demonstrate that disclosure of the information requested by the inquiry would cause real risk of serious prejudice to an important public interest (such as risk to national security) and that this outweighs the public interest in open justice.[22] It is then for the chair, and panel if appointed, to carry out that balancing exercise and determine whether or not the information should be disclosed to the inquiry and disclosed publicly and, if so, on what terms (eg in a redacted form).

The Use of Classified Material

Witnesses or core participants may seek to withhold information from an inquiry on the basis that it is classified material, categorised as 'official', 'secret' and 'top secret'. Procedures and protocols managing the approach to such material are discussed in chapter eight.

Medical Evidence and Capacity

An inquiry may also face difficulties in obtaining evidence from those who refuse to cooperate on grounds of medical condition or capacity.

As explained above, the inquiry has the power to order a person to provide evidence in the form of documents and a witness statement by virtue of s 21 of the Inquiries Act 2005. If a witness fails to comply without reasonable excuse, the witness will be guilty of a criminal offence, punishable by fine or imprisonment, and the inquiry can issue enforcement proceedings to enforce the Section 21 Notices, by referring the matter to the relevant court.[23]

However, in circumstances where attendance at a hearing or the provision of evidence is refused on medical grounds, or due to issues of capacity, consideration will need to be given by the inquiry as to what further steps can be taken. The inquiry may ask to see medical evidence in order to determine whether the Section 21 Notice should be varied or revoked. If the situation cannot be resolved in this way, as an alternative to enforcing the Section 21 Notice, the inquiry may seek to agree with the witness (and, where represented, their legal representative) that

[21] Inquiries Act 2005, s 22(2).
[22] *R v H* [2004] UKHL 3.
[23] Inquiries Act 2005, ss 35 and 26.

independent medical evidence should be sought to confirm whether or not they are fit to give evidence, or to determine a method for the giving of such evidence, such as via video link from a neutral venue. Below is a list of issues the inquiry may consider when instructing an independent medical expert.

Checklist – Instructing experts to determine fitness to give evidence

- The appointed expert should be independent of the witness (ie not their current GP or consultant); the expert should be chosen by the inquiry and agreed with the witness.
- The inquiry must obtain consent from the witness for release of their medical records to the expert.
- Instructions to the expert should include seeking their opinion on whether the witness is fit to give evidence and whether particular protections should be put in place when providing such evidence (eg providing evidence from home, using a video-link, or providing only written rather than oral evidence).

11

Oral Evidence and Hearings

Introduction

Oral hearings are a key stage of the inquiry process, with witnesses presenting evidence and being questioned by counsel (or, less commonly, where counsel is not appointed, by the chair, panel members or solicitor to the inquiry). Questioning usually takes place in a public setting. It is an opportunity for the inquiry to explore and further examine witness and documentary evidence. For the witnesses, victims and survivors, families, and other participants, it can also be part of a cathartic process and is often seen as providing witnesses with a long sought-after opportunity to be heard. For members of the public, it provides the opportunity to see and hear the same evidence as the inquiry, to scrutinise the process and to draw their own conclusions.

Procedure

The chair of a statutory inquiry is generally at liberty to decide how oral hearings are managed. To that extent, statutory and non-statutory inquiry hearings often operate in a similar way.

For inquiries convened under the Inquiries Act 2005, there are few statutory provisions relating to the conduct of oral hearings.

- The chair has a broad discretion over procedure and conduct, which may be 'such as the chairman of the inquiry may direct'[1] (s 17(1)).
- The chair may take evidence on oath[2] (s 17(2)).
- The chair must act with fairness and with regard to the need to avoid any unnecessary cost (whether to public funds, witnesses or others) when making any decision regarding the procedure or conduct of an inquiry (s 17(3)).

[1] Subject to any provision of the Inquiries Act 2005 or the Inquiry Rules 2006: Inquiries Act 2005, s 17(1).

[2] One of the main distinguishing features between a statutory inquiry and non-statutory inquiry (see chapter one).

- There is a presumption that the inquiry will be held in public[3] (s 18(1)).
- The chair may compel witnesses to give oral evidence[4] (s 21).
- There is a presumption that only counsel to the inquiry, the chair and panel members may ask questions of witnesses in hearings (see the exceptions below) (r 10 of the Inquiry Rules 2006).
- A core participant, or their legal representative, may make an opening statement to the inquiry at the first oral hearing and a closing statement at the end of the Inquiry (r 11 of the Inquiry Rules 2006).

Preliminary Hearings

There are no specific provisions in the 2005 Act about conducting a preliminary hearing. In practice, most inquiries will hold at least one preliminary hearing before they begin calling witnesses to give oral evidence at the substantive hearings, under the chair's broad discretion over procedure and conduct under s 17(1).

Holding a preliminary hearing is a useful step in establishing the tone of the inquiry and setting down the ground rules, so that all those concerned with the inquiry are aware of their roles and know what to expect from the inquiry. They can help to build public confidence in the inquiry's work and ensure that there is clarity around the role, function and parameters of the inquiry.

Generally, preliminary hearings are open to the public. The date, time and location of the preliminary hearing will usually be advertised on an inquiry's website so that anyone who is interested can attend. An inquiry will often, as a matter of courtesy, contact those parties and witnesses who are, or may become formal participants to the inquiry in the future, to let them know the details of the preliminary hearing, as they may be particularly interested in attending. Preliminary hearings are usually fairly short hearings, which may take place at the same venue as the inquiry's substantive oral hearings (if the venue has been located and set up by that stage), or at another, temporary, venue.[5]

The inquiry's first preliminary hearing is its introduction to the public and it is an important opportunity to engage with the public, including the media, in a user-friendly way, setting the scene, and avoiding alienation.

[3] There is no such presumption for non-statutory inquiries.

[4] These powers to compel witnesses to give evidence do not apply to non-statutory inquiries.

[5] For example, the preliminary hearings for both the Grenfell Inquiry and the Independent Jersey Care Inquiry took place at temporary locations as the main inquiry venues had not yet been set up (see chapter three on location).

Checklist – Preliminary hearings

A preliminary hearing will usually involve the following:

- A personal statement from the chair, usually describing why the inquiry has been set up and the inquiry's purpose, as well as introducing key personnel (counsel to the inquiry, solicitors to the inquiry, secretary to the inquiry).
- Reference to the scope of the inquiry's terms of reference and how these have been, or will be, interpreted by the inquiry, so that there is no misunderstanding about what the inquiry does and does not have the power to investigate.
- Any information about how the inquiry intends to go about its work: identifying key stages and including approximate timescales.
- Reference to the inquiry's procedures and protocols, including information on where further details can be found.
- Inviting witnesses to come forward and provide evidence and communicating details for making contact with the inquiry team.
- Explaining the practical arrangements in place, such as for attending the venue in the future and specific working arrangements.
- There is usually no opportunity for other parties to speak or make any representations.

Support for attendees

Often supplemental support is provided such as the following:

- Hand-outs of material to attendees, summarising some of the key information provided during the preliminary hearing.
- Meetings at which inquiry personnel introduce themselves to participants.
- Ensuring that inquiry personnel are available after the hearing to answer any immediate questions from participants and the public.

Additional Procedural Hearings

Prior to commencing its substantive evidential hearings, an inquiry might also want to consider applications for core participant status, legal representation and public funding, anonymity, or indeed any other issues that have been raised, and give rulings on such applications.

Whilst these sorts of issues could be dealt with at the first preliminary hearing, the chair may decide to hold an opening preliminary hearing, dealing with the issues described above, in order to set the tone for the inquiry. A subsequent, procedural hearing may then be held to deal with procedural applications or other legal issues before the evidential hearings begin.

Commencing the Inquiry's Substantive Hearings

An inquiry's public hearings provide the primary opportunity for the public to see and hear the evidence laid before it. It is important that they are well organised and accessible to all.

Checklist – Practical steps that may be taken before substantive hearings commence

- Venue inspected to ensure all facilities, particularly IT facilities and microphones, are in place and working, and that there is provision for attendance for anyone with disabilities.
- Venue inspected to ensure that it is properly lit, and heated and ventilated as required.
- Desks and chairs laid out according to the chair's requirements and the number of core participants who will be attending (ensuring the stenographer's requirements are also catered for).
- Public notices placed in local papers and published on the inquiry's website to publicise the time and dates of hearings.
- All parties and witnesses informed they are required to attend, and given practical details for attendance, such as instructions to find the venue and the set up to expect when they arrive. Often an advanced detailed hearing timetable will not, however, be available and instead parties and witnesses will be given windows of time when certain evidence or phases of evidence are likely to be heard, with confirmed dates being provided at quite short notice.
- Staff briefed on their roles in the hearing process.
- The reception desk attended and, if appropriate, security put in place.
- IT technical support arranged in case of any problems arising during the hearings.

- Any catering arranged (eg water cooler and tea and coffee facilities).
- Special needs of witnesses or parties identified and provided for.
- Cultural and religious considerations appropriate to the situation taken into account (eg ensuring that the appropriate religious books are available when the oath is given).

General Structure of the Substantive Hearings

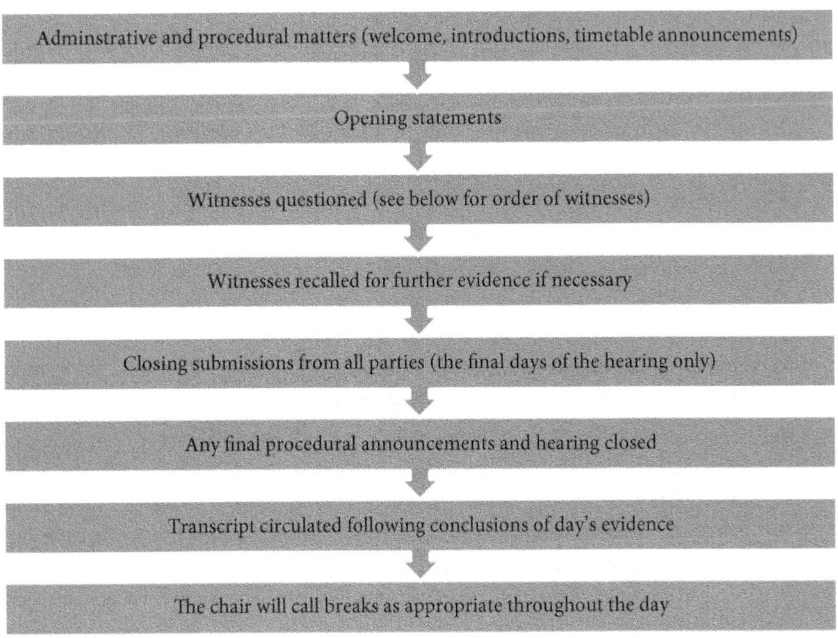

Giving Evidence to the Inquiry

The manner in which hearings are conducted during an inquiry varies from inquiry to inquiry, depending on its size, nature, subject matter and the approach the chair wishes to take. The chair may produce and publish a protocol containing guidance on how the hearings will be conducted (see chapter five) but that will not always be the case.

The following section sets out general guidance on the likely process of giving evidence at a hearing.

- During statutory inquiries, the chair may require evidence to be given on oath (or affirmation).[6]
- The length of time an individual witness takes to give oral evidence varies hugely. In some cases it might take only an hour, but in others their evidence might take several days or a week. It is usual for several witnesses of fact to give evidence in one day. If a witness has provided a detailed statement of evidence to the inquiry legal team this will substantially reduce the time needed for giving oral evidence.
- The layout of the hearing room, and where the witness will sit to give evidence, varies from inquiry to inquiry. Often witnesses will be given the opportunity to visit the hearing room in advance of giving evidence, to familiarise themselves with its layout.
- A witness is normally permitted to take short notes to the hearing and to refer to them while giving evidence.
- An inquiry will often provide a bundle of papers containing the documents to which counsel to the inquiry may wish to refer the witness. As a minimum, such bundles usually include a copy of the witness's written statement and exhibits, where one has been prepared by the inquiry.
- A witness will usually give oral evidence on their own. If a witness is particularly nervous or anxious about giving evidence, the inquiry might allow the witness to have a supporter in the hearing room. However, the supporter will not, without the permission of the chair, be allowed to sit with the witness while they are giving evidence, nor speak on their behalf.
- One exception to witnesses giving evidence on their own is 'hot-tubbing' (or the giving of 'concurrent evidence' as it is known more formally).[7] The term 'hot-tubbing' is used where more than one witness gives evidence at the same time, while physically sitting together in the witness box. This technique has been used by inquiries during the giving of expert witness evidence, for example, the Iraq Inquiry and the Leveson Inquiry, in an attempt to resolve any outstanding issues of fact or opinion.
- Consideration should always be given to the vulnerability of the witness giving evidence, including whether the witness is well enough to give oral evidence and whether further support should be put in place to assist them.[8]
- An inquiry may permit some witnesses, core participants or interested parties appearing before it to have legal representation (see chapters five and six). The role of the legal representative is to represent their interests, for example to intervene if questioning is inappropriate or if the witness is becoming particularly distressed and needs a break.

[6] Inquiries Act 2005, s 17(2).
[7] See chapter twelve.
[8] See chapter five on applications for anonymity and restrictions, and chapter ten on witness support.

- Witnesses are generally questioned by counsel to the inquiry, inquiry chair or panel (see below).
- If a witness has not been granted anonymity, and there are no restrictions on how they will give evidence, the following may be in the hearing room: the chair, panel members, assessors, counsel to the inquiry and members of counsel to the inquiry's team, the solicitor to the inquiry and members of the solicitor to the inquiry's team, core participants, legal representatives, a stenographer, IT technicians, the public and the media.
- If restrictions are imposed on how a witness will give evidence, or a witness has been granted anonymity, the inquiry may make a ruling restricting attendance in the hearing room, for example excluding the public and media, or all or certain categories of core participants and their legal representatives.
- If granted anonymity, a witness may be screened off from the rest of the hearing room so that only their voice is heard during the giving of evidence. Often, the screen operates so that the witness can still be seen by the chair,[9] as body language during oral evidence can be very helpful in allowing the chair to get a real sense of the evidence.
- Where a witness is unable to travel,[10] an inquiry may consider allowing their oral evidence to be given by video link. A screen is set up in the hearing room, so that those present in the hearing room can still see the witness giving evidence, but the witness is not physically present.
- The media will be permitted to attend the hearings as part of the public, or in a dedicated media room (see below and chapter five).
- Public recording or the taking of photographs will usually not be permitted within the hearing room.

Meeting with Witnesses in Advance of Giving Evidence?

During some inquiries, counsel to the inquiry[11] will meet with witnesses informally, shortly before they give evidence. Such an approach is intended to help put witnesses at ease. It enables counsel to explain in general terms what will happen during the hearing (such as where the witness will be asked to sit and the procedure for giving evidence), to introduce key inquiry personnel, to answer any questions. This often allows a rapport to be built between counsel to the inquiry and the witnesses.

[9] And, where there is a panel, the panel members.

[10] In other inquiries this has been used for health reasons or if a witness is located in another country and the cost of travel is considered prohibitive or disproportionate.

[11] Or the solicitor to the inquiry, chair or panel members where they are carrying out the questioning.

This approach, however, might not always be appropriate, depending on the subject matter of the inquiry. An inquiry will have to consider carefully whether meeting with a witness beforehand could undermine confidence in the independence of the process and lead to potentially damaging misunderstandings. Given that an inquiry is a non-adversarial process and counsel to the inquiry is independent of any party, as long as all witnesses are treated the same, for most inquiries, meeting witnesses shortly before they are due to give evidence will not be considered controversial. Where this approach is deemed appropriate and is adopted, for reasons of transparency it is important that, in addition to counsel to the inquiry, a member of the inquiry team is present at all times to take a full note of the discussions.

Quote

'If the subject matter of the inquiry is extremely serious … I would say that it is an extremely bad idea for counsel to meet the witnesses beforehand, since that can give rise to misunderstandings or all sorts of uncovenanted difficulties. The Leveson inquiry was unusual inasmuch as the material was softer. We were painting a picture of the culture, practices and ethics of the press, rarely deciding hard evidential dispute between witness A and witness B.

I would say that the advantage of doing it is that if you have a high-profile televised inquiry, often with very nervous witnesses, it is just common courtesy to put them at their ease, to explain in general terms the way it is going to go. The exact questions are not prefigured but the general lines of questioning are and it avoids the witness saying, "You have not warned me about that. I need time to consider".

So there are all sorts of advantages in the right sort of inquiry, but even in the Leveson inquiry I would never meet a witness without the Treasury Solicitor being there taking a careful note of the conversation. There was one occasion where at best a misunderstanding arose as to what was said.'

Mr Justice Jay, in evidence to the House of Lords Select Committee

The Order in Which Witnesses will be Called

In terms of the order in which witnesses are called, again, there is a wide variation between inquiries depending on their size and subject matter. However, the following provides a general guide:

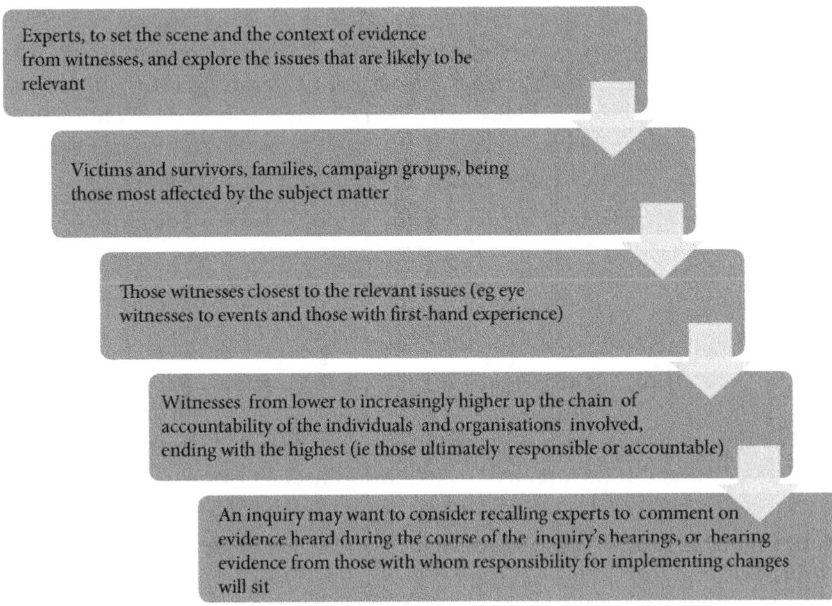

Putting Written Statements into the Inquiry Record

Not all witnesses will be called to give oral evidence. Instead, their written statements will be put into the inquiry record.

> **Quote**
>
> *'I could not possibly have conducted the inquiry without putting hundreds of statements into the inquiry record. I paid just as much attention to them as the live witnesses'*
>
> Lord Justice Leveson, in Oral Evidence to the HL Select Committee

Generally counsel to the inquiry will draw up a list of those witnesses who are to be called to give oral evidence and those whose witness statements are to be put into the record. If core participants or interested parties do not agree with the decision, they can make representations to that effect. In the event of dispute, the chair will rule on who is to be called to give oral evidence and who is not.

Inquiries have adopted different approaches to reading evidence into the inquiry record. During some inquiries, counsel read out the statements in full or key sections of the statements were read out; during some inquiries, counsel summarised the content of the witness statements; and during others, there was simply reference to a list of evidence to be 'read in', with the list read out by counsel and the evidence published on the inquiry's website. Where witness statements are to be read into the record, a suitable time slot will be found in the timetable during the hearings, perhaps when other similar evidence is being adduced, at the end of a particular topic or phase of the inquiry's work, at the conclusion of the oral hearings, or indeed to fill a gap if a slot becomes free unexpectedly.

The Role of Counsel to the Inquiry

Most inquiries appoint counsel to the inquiry to carry out the questioning of witnesses on behalf of the inquiry.[12] This leaves the chair or panel members free to concentrate and reflect on the evidence they are hearing. For some large inquiries, counsel to the inquiry may consist of a team of a QC and one or more junior barristers.

Counsel to the inquiry's role in questioning witnesses is quite different to the role of counsel in court proceedings. Inquiries are inquisitorial rather than adversarial. There are no 'sides' or 'parties' to an inquiry. Witnesses are called to give evidence to assist the inquiry, not to support a particular position or viewpoint; the inquiry responds to the evidence as it is heard, and its lines of inquiry are evidence-led. Counsel to the inquiry's role is to assist the inquiry in any line of questioning the chair or panel wishes to pursue and to ensure that the inquiry hears the witnesses' evidence, any challenges to that evidence, and the witnesses' responses to such challenges.[13]

Reviewing Evidence on a Rolling Basis

It is rare, in practice, for time constraints to permit an inquiry to wait for the completion of an evidence-gathering stage before the substantive hearings

[12] Or, if counsel has not been appointed, the solicitor to the inquiry.

[13] See chapter two for details of the other roles that counsel to the inquiry play.

commence. Evidence is often gathered, reviewed and then heard in public on a rolling basis, under very tight timescales.

During the hearing, questions may be asked of a witness without the inquiry knowing what another witness might say on that same subject, as the other witness's evidence might not be known, or may not be available at the material time. It may be necessary to revisit the evidence of that witness at a later stage to address matters that have come to light since they gave their evidence.

Questioning Witnesses

For statutory inquiries, r 10 of the Inquiry Rules 2006 places limitations on who may question witnesses during the hearings. Generally only counsel to the inquiry[14] and the inquiry chair or panel may ask a witness questions during the hearing (r 10(1)).

The three exceptions to this are:

- The chair may direct that the recognised legal representative of the witness giving evidence may ask that witness questions (r 10(2)).
- Where a witness other than a core participant is being questioned, and where their evidence directly relates to the evidence of another witness, the recognised legal representative of that other witness may ask for permission to question the witness (r 10(3)).
- A core participant's recognised legal representative may also apply for permission to question a witness who has given oral evidence (r 10(4)).

In each case, the chair has to grant the permission; there is no automatic right to question witnesses.

A practice along these lines is also followed in many non-statutory inquiries. It has the advantage that less time is taken in what could be a very burdensome and time-consuming cross-examination of witnesses by multiple interested parties, with each participant's legal representative seeking to pursue their own client's agenda, rather than helping to serve the terms of reference. However, some argue that with this approach there is a danger that not all the relevant issues are taken into account (see the section on expertise of core participants and interested parties below).

[14] Or the solicitor to the inquiry if counsel has not been appointed.

Quote

'Questioning is more coherent and proceeds at greater pace if it is left to Counsel to the Inquiry. It emphasises the inquisitorial nature of the inquiry, and de-emphasises the adversarial. It is not practical for Core Participants to ask their own questions.'

Sir Robert Francis QC, Chair of the Mid Staffordshire NHS Foundation Trust Public Inquiry

Suggesting Questions to Counsel to the Inquiry

In practice, rather than multiple, individual applications being made for permission to question witnesses during the hearing itself, many inquiries have adopted procedures whereby core participants, interested parties and recognised legal representative can suggest questions to be asked, or issues to be pursued, by counsel to the inquiry. An example of such a procedure is as follows:

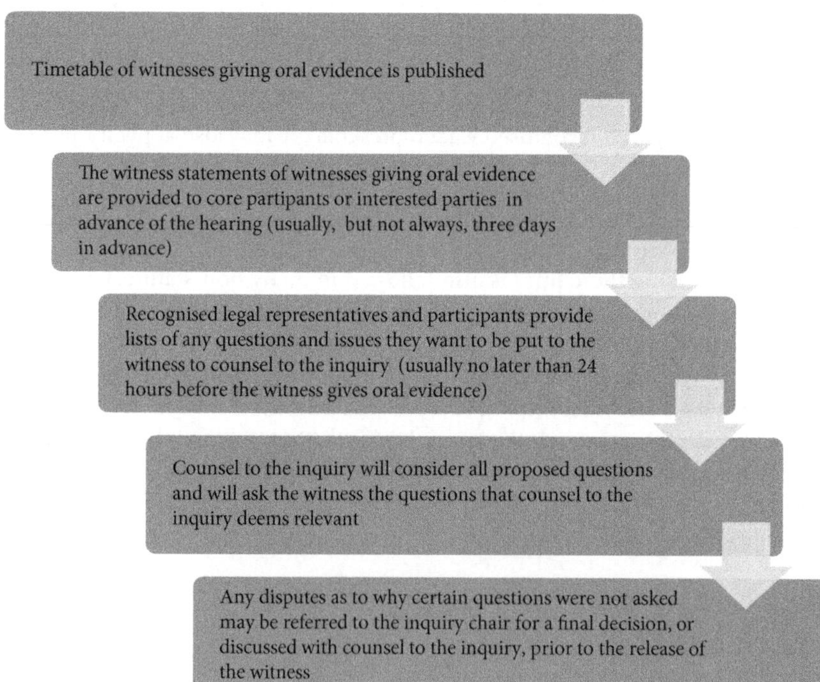

This process helps alleviate the participants' and recognised legal representatives' desire during a hearing to request that they be permitted to directly question a

witness, which in turn helps to keep the hearings running smoothly by reducing interruptions. It can also provide a level of satisfaction to core participants who have had their proposed questions at least considered. The practices that individual inquiries have put in place to adopt such a process have varied, but in general, for the procedure to work, cooperation is key.

Quote

'We had an email system in operation in the hearing room, via which Counsel for Core Participants could suggest further questions to the Counsel to the Inquiry team, as the questioning proceeded. This required very close working between the questioner and a junior member of the Counsel to the Inquiry team and proved to be a huge challenge (and distraction) if mis-used.'

Rory Phillips QC, 3 Verulam Buildings, reflecting on the practice adopted during the Rosemary Nelson Inquiry

'Inquiry hearings work best where there is faith in the judgement of Counsel to the Inquiry, and trust that they will ask the right questions.'

Peter Skelton QC, One Crown Office Row

In general, this procedure tends to work well for all concerned, provided that a dialogue between counsel and the core participants is established and maintained throughout. This process can however be undermined if counsel to the inquiry asks questions from core participants in such a way as to make the origin of the question obvious, for example by prefacing each question by identifying which core participant wanted it to be asked. Such an approach would undoubtedly have the potential to influence the response a witness might give, thereby removing any neutrality from the process.

Quote

'I do not under-estimate the difficulty of the task of Counsel to the Inquiry. However, it is possible, though demanding, to maintain a neutral stance when questioning, even when putting Core Participant points or lines of questioning. The practice which I have come across whereby Counsel to the Inquiry flags up the origin of Core Participant questions is however to be deplored: it undermines the neutrality of the questioning at precisely the moment when Counsel to the Inquiry ought to be working hardest to maintain it.'

Rory Phillips QC, 3 Verulam Buildings

Arguments for and against Limiting Questioning to Counsel to the Inquiry

Practice differs between inquiries. During the Rosemary Nelson inquiry, a strict inquisitorial model was adopted whereby questioning was entirely restricted to counsel to the inquiry. Other inquiries, such as the Al-Sweady Inquiry, have allowed all participants to ask questions as a matter of course so that, while still adopting an inquisitorial approach, allowance is also made to promote a greater feeling of participation and the responsibility of questioning is shared. In practice, however, it is customary for counsel to the inquiry to ask both their own questions and the core participants' and interested parties' questions, which are sent to counsel to the inquiry in advance. Following counsel to the inquiry's questioning of a witness, if a core participant or interested party feels that counsel to the inquiry has not asked their questions adequately, or at all, they can then seek leave of the chair to ask further questions of the witness.

The approach taken by the Rosemary Nelson Inquiry, where all questioning was restricted to counsel to the inquiry, was judicially reviewed by the Chief Constable of the Police Service of Northern Ireland (PSNI).[15] The PSNI sought to challenge the inquiry's decision to refuse permission for counsel for the PSNI to question directly certain witnesses that had made critical remarks of officers. In dismissing the application, Lord Justice Girvan commented as follows:

> Convention case law does not support the view that there is a right to cross-examine in the case of investigative procedures in the nature of an inquiry which is not dispositive of rights and in which there is no legal determination of civil or criminal liability and no determination of any right to reputation … I conclude, not without hesitation, that this court should not interfere with the Inquiry's decision on this aspect of its ruling. The Inquiry has to make a balanced judgment on the question whether opening up these lines of Inquiry would be more prejudicial to the Inquiry than probative of relevant issues. The question of the impact on the overall effectiveness of the Inquiry and the co-operativeness of other witnesses does enter into the equation.

Checklist – Limiting questioning to counsel for the inquiry

Arguments for limiting questioning to counsel for the inquiry

- Counsel to the inquiry is familiar with the facts and the wider picture and can ask questions from all sides.

[15] *Chief Constable's Application [Stephen Walker]* [2008] NIQB 145.

- Counsel's priority is to fulfil the inquiry's terms of reference and questions are asked with that aim in mind, in constrast to core participants or interested parties where their motives will inevitably be to protect and represent their client(s).
- It emphasises the inquisitorial nature of the inquiry.
- Where core participants or interested parties ask questions, it can give rise to an adversarial feel, antagonism, aggressive styles, 'grandstanding' and irrelevant questions.
- Witnesses may be more willing to provide evidence to the inquiry if they know they will only be asked questions by the inquiry itself, and not disaffected parties.
- Questioning can be dealt with fairly, courteously, comprehensively, robustly and with fewer interruptions.
- Questioning is more coherent and can proceed at greater pace, focusing questions on those issues on which the chair or panel is most concerned.
- It reduces costs, both for the inquiry (as questioning proceeds at a quicker and more efficient pace) and for the core participants or interested parties.
- It can avoid questioning becoming repetitive.

Arguments against limiting questioning to counsel for the inquiry

- An increased likelihood of judicial review and potential consequent delays to the inquiry process.
- A huge responsibility is placed on counsel to ask all the questions and elicit all the facts that are useful to the inquiry.
- A huge pressure and burden is placed on counsel due to the sheer volume of evidence to be assimilated.
- A feeling of exclusion for those closely effected by the events that form the basis of the inquiry and a missed opportunity to encourage catharsis.
- Concern from participants that counsel to the inquiry may simply pay 'lip service' to this approach and frustration arising from their proposed questions not being asked with perhaps, due to time constraints, no explanation being given as to why.
- Lawyers retained by witnesses or core participants may have specialist knowledge that would have enabled them to elicit more useful information than counsel to the inquiry.

Issue – Article 2 investigations – no right to cross-examine

Where an inquiry involves a death or series of deaths in state custody, in addition to counsel for the inquiry, in order to be compliant with Art 2 of the European Convention on Human Rights (ECHR),[16] it is vital that the victim's next of kin or their legal representative be entitled to make submissions about the questioning of witnesses. However, there is no automatic entitlement for them to cross-examine witnesses and adopting the suggested procedure above may still fulfil this obligation.

The case of *R (D) v Secretary of State for the Home Department*[17] concerned an investigation carried out by the Prison Service following a suicide attempt by a prisoner. The court was asked to consider what the procedural obligations were for an Art 2 ECHR investigation and whether this should include the right to cross-examine witnesses. On appeal, the Court of Appeal summarised the procedural obligations that apply to an Art 2 ECHR investigation, which included (i) it is for the state to decide the most effective and appropriate method of investigation, and (ii) the next of kin must be involved in such a way so as to 'safeguard his or her legitimate interests'.

The court accepted that participants or their representatives 'must in general be entitled to see the written evidence, to be present during oral evidence and to make appropriate submissions, including submissions as to what lines of enquiry should be adopted, what questions asked and, indeed, who should be permitted to ask witnesses questions about what.'[18] However, it rejected the proposition that they must be entitled to cross-examine witnesses, stating that it is for the chair of the particular inquiry to decide whether and to what extent to permit participants or their representatives to ask questions of witnesses.[19]

Expertise of Core Participants and Interested Parties

There are circumstances in which it may be particularly beneficial to involve core participants and interested parties when identifying lines of inquiry and drawing up the list of questions. The subject matter of some inquiries is highly specialised, for example inquiries into the provision of medical care at the Mid Staffordshire NHS Foundation Trust or into RUC police procedures during the

[16] 'Right to life'.
[17] *R (D) v Secretary of State for the Home Department* [2006] EWCA Civ 143.
[18] *R (D) v Secretary of State for the Home Department* [2006] EWCA Civ 143, at [42].
[19] *R (D) v Secretary of State for the Home Department* [2006] EWCA Civ 143, at [40].

Rosemary Nelson Inquiry. Core participants may have particular knowledge and expertise that would enable them to raise particular areas of concern and possible lines of questioning, thus allowing the inquiry to probe in a way that might not otherwise have been possible.

It would be for the inquiry to determine if, and in what way, core participants can contribute in this manner, but in the right circumstances, utilising the experience and expertise of core participants can add real value to an inquiry's work.

Quote

'The rule 10 procedure tends to be translated by inquiries these days to mean that the default will be that all questions for a witness will come from Counsel to the Inquiry or the panel and that the role played by other lawyers is to submit questions for the consideration of Counsel to the Inquiry to put to the witness. It can be rare to hear the legal representative of a core participant asking a witness questions themselves. The rule 10 procedure works best where Counsel to the Inquiry is an experienced advocate, used to handling witnesses and questioning them robustly if need be, with a good team behind them and whose questions are rightly and helpfully informed by the questions submitted by the Core Participants' lawyers. This leads to proceedings which are handled efficiently and fairly from the point of view of all concerned and, also importantly, which save time and money.

However, this system breaks down where one of those elements is missing. And there may be circumstances where it is arguably less appropriate in any event. For example, this might be where experts or witnesses who will give detailed or otherwise difficult evidence, possibly of particular relevance to a specific Core Participant, are to be called. Questioning of such witnesses by a Core Participant's lawyer may assist in the crystallisation of the issues and positively assist the inquiry to reach the truth.'

Nicholas Griffin QC, QEB Hollis Whiteman

Checklist – Ways in which participants or their legal representatives may provide input during oral evidence

- Where consulted by counsel to the inquiry, contributing to identifying lines of inquiry and the list of questions.
- Channelling questions through counsel to the inquiry.

- Addressing the inquiry at the close of a witness's evidence to clarify any uncertainties in the evidence.
- Written submissions to the inquiry on matters arising from the previous day's evidence which, in their view, requires further elaboration or comment.
- Before the day's hearing begins, addressing the inquiry on matters from the previous day's evidence, where counsel to the inquiry accedes to a request on the basis that written submissions to the inquiry would not suffice.
- With permission of the chair, asking sweep-up questions.
- With permission of the chair, cross examination.

Managing and Fielding Questions from Core Participants or Interested Parties

Counsel to the inquiry[20] will need to be persuaded that the particular line of inquiry proposed by a core participant or interested party is one that the inquiry wishes to pursue and is within the terms of reference. Participants must provide supporting material to justify a line of inquiry.

It can be a source of great frustration for participants who have asked for a series of questions be put to a witness when only some, or even none, are asked. A common reason why questions are not asked is that they are considered to be relevant to protect any future claims, but not the terms of reference, or are calculated to draw attention to the position or agenda of a particular party rather than to pursue the issues and line of questioning identified by the inquiry.

Participants generally do not know in advance whether their suggested questions will be asked. If their questions are not asked, they can raise objections at the conclusion of the witness's evidence. If counsel to the inquiry declines to ask the questions following discussions with the participant or their legal adviser, the core participant or interested party may seek leave of the chair to ask the questions themselves. Time pressures generally do not allow for a detailed debate at the time of questioning.

The best approach for participants is to construct their questions in such a way that they are relevant and focused on the terms of reference or raise a new issue.

[20] Or, in the absence of counsel to the inquiry, the solicitor to the inquiry, chair or panel.

Inevitably, they will want to advance their own position, or that of their client, but this must be done with the inquiry's agenda in the forefront of their mind.

Time Pressure

New evidence will come to light on a rolling basis, as the inquiry progresses. An inquiry's evidence unfolds as it proceeds. Issues and questions are often received from core participants or interested parties at the very last minute, which can make processing and assessing those requests particularly challenging. Core participants should provide as much notice as possible to enable counsel to properly consider any questions they want to suggest. Equally, core participants and interested parties should also be aware that they themselves are likely to find themselves working under very tight timescales.

It is not unusual for the core participants to receive very long statements, often many tens of pages, the night before a witness is to be heard. The evidence needs to be assimilated, and key issues and questions prepared, which will then be sent to counsel to the inquiry that night or the following morning. The pressure on counsel to the inquiry can be particularly acute when there are a large number of core participants, who are all dealing with matters the night before a hearing. On occasions, counsel to the inquiry may even receive information and requests for questions during hearings while they are actually in the process of questioning a witness. It is common for junior counsel to the inquiry to vet such email traffic while the more senior counsel is still questioning the witness.

A balance needs to be found between the need for the swift, efficient and cost effective conduct of an inquiry and allowing all concerned to have sufficient time to consider the evidence sufficiently thoroughly, and respond to new issues that arise. Establishing a good relationship between core participants and their legal representatives and counsel to the inquiry is key to the smooth running of this process.

Public Access and Restriction Notices and Orders

Where a public inquiry is convened under the Inquiries Act 2005, under s 18 of the Act there is a presumption that its hearings will be held in public. Subject to restrictions, discussed below, the chair is required to take such steps as the chair considers reasonable to secure that members of the public and media are able to attend the inquiry, or to see and hear a simultaneous transmission of proceedings of the inquiry, and to obtain or to view a record of evidence and documents provided to the inquiry.

Checklist – Steps taken by an inquiry to provide public access

Steps to provide public access may include:

- Seating within the hearing chambers for members of the public and the media.
- Dedicated facilities for the press and broadcast media (including wifi, desks, and power sockets).
- Screens in nearby rooms for simultaneous transmission of proceedings.
- Simultaneous transmission to screens at remote locations.
- Documents that are viewed by the inquiry during the hearings being displayed on screens during the hearings.
- Transcripts of hearings transmitted instantly to screens.
- Transcript of hearings published on the inquiry website at the end of the hearing.
- Broadcasting and live streaming of the hearings, but ensuring there is a short delay with the live stream and the ability to end the live stream, to ensure any sensitive information can be checked before publication, as necessary (eg if a witness refers to information that is the subject of a restriction notice).

However, s 19 recognises that openness is not always possible. It provides that restrictions may be imposed by the minister by restriction notice, or the chair by restriction order,[21] where restrictions are required by law, or considered conducive to the inquiry fulfilling its terms of reference, or necessary in the public interest. Restrictions may be imposed on attendance at the hearings themselves and on the disclosure or publication of evidence or documents provided to the inquiry.

A decision to restrict public access must be taken cautiously. For statutory inquiries, regard must be had to matters such as such as the allaying of public concern, the risk of death or injury, damage to national security, international relations or economic interests of the UK that could be avoided or reduced, issues of confidentiality, and cost and delay to or impairment of the inquiry.[22] Each of those criteria must be carefully balanced. It may be necessary to adopt laborious and time-consuming procedures to ensure that appropriate redactions are made before documents are disclosed to the public, in order to comply with any restriction

[21] In practice, once an inquiry is up and running, it is rare for a minister to become involved in issuing restriction; this usually falls to the chair. See chapter six for restriction notices and orders generally.

[22] Inquiries Act 2005, s 19(4) and (5).

notices or restrictions orders.[23] This, in turn, may have an impact on the duration and cost of the inquiry.

As a core participant of a statutory inquiry, thought should be given at all stages to whether a restriction notice should be sought to protect evidence, or to protect a particular individual or organisation. Any application to a chair to impose such a restriction should take into account the criteria, explain why the restriction is being sought and what type of restriction is being sought. Any applicant should bear in mind that the inquiry's default position is that evidence will be heard in public unless there is a good reason to do otherwise.

Where an inquiry is non-statutory, the inquiry is able to deal with such matters more simply. There are no specific requirements for chairs of non-statutory inquiries to take steps to ensure the public and media are able to attend hearings, access simultaneous transmissions or access evidence and documents provided to the inquiry. They have a wide discretion to restrict, or permit, attendance at an inquiry and the disclosure or publication of evidence or documents.

Checklist – Steps taken by an inquiry to restrict public access

Steps taken to restrict public access may include:

- Parts of the inquiry being heard in closed or 'secret' hearings.
- Permitting witnesses to give evidence anonymously from behind a screen, or from another location.
- Documents not disclosed to the public.
- Documents redacted.
- Access to hearings, or disclosure of some documents, restricted to certain groups, for example, to a witness or class of witnesses, or to core participants or interested parties and their legal advisers, with further restrictions on wider publication.

Whilst restricting public access does not restrict the evidence heard by the inquiry itself, it does have a huge impact on the transparency of the proceedings and may significantly affect the public's trust and confidence in the process. As seen during the Iraq Inquiry,[24] during which the evidence of 35 witnesses was heard in private, a perception of unnecessary secrecy may lead to claims that the decision to restrict access is motivated by an attempt to withhold evidence or to avoid accountability and political embarrassment.

[23] Redactions are dealt with in greater detail in chapter six.
[24] Also known as the Chilcot Inquiry.

Examples of Restriction Orders and Notices Made

Inquiry	Type of Restriction
Mid Staffordshire NHS Foundation Trust Public Inquiry	Restriction order for witnesses to give evidence behind a screen or in private
Litvinenko Inquiry	Restriction orders around specific evidence being heard during a closed session
Leveson Inquiry	Restriction order to prevent any statement or document provided to the inquiry being published or leaked by any party outside of the inquiry team and core participants (following the leak of a witness statement)
Billy Wright Inquiry	Restriction order prohibiting the publication or disclosure by any person of the evidence given by a specific witness who was part of RUC Special Branch
Baha Mousa Inquiry	Restriction notice issued by the Secretary of State for Defence varying the restriction orders which were imposed during the Inquiry, which enabled the Ministry of Defence to pass to the Iraq Historic Allegations Team and Service Prosecution Authority materials required in order to advance their investigation and any further prosecutions
Independent Inquiry into Child Sexual Abuse	Restriction order to render the inquiry's Truth Project (when victims and survivors of child sexual abuse will share their experiences) private and confidential, including any hearings
Renewable Heat Incentive Inquiry	Restriction order explaining that all personal information and irrelevant material in documents will be redacted prior to being published by the inquiry (save where the inquiry considers there is evidential value to publication) and prohibiting communication, reporting or disclosure, which may result in such information being revealed
Infected Blood Inquiry	General restriction order explaining four general categories of redaction that will be applied by the inquiry which briefly includes: (i) medical records, where information identifies the individual; (ii) protecting the identity of anonymous witnesses; (iii) personal information (eg date of birth, signatures); and (iv) redactions to ensure the efficiency and effectiveness of the inquiry (eg unrelated criticism of a person or organisation where a response is not required)

Issue – Criticism of the minister's power to restrict access

One of the purposes of public inquiries is to hold the government to account. Consequently, a minister's power to restrict attendance at the hearings and over the disclosure or publication of evidence or documents provided to the inquiry, gives rise to a clear conflict of interest. Many have argued that such powers should only be exercisable by the chair.

When the Inquiries Bill was introduced in November 2004, the chief criticism was of the powers granted to ministers, including the power to impose a restriction notices at any time. The House of Lord Select Committee 2013–2014 Post-legislative Scrutiny of the Inquiries Act 2005[25] recommended that the power of the minister to issue a restriction notice under s 19, restricting public access to an inquiry, should be abrogated, concluding that the chair's power to issue a restriction order was sufficient. However, the government rejected that recommendation.

The chair and the relevant minister also have the power to vary and revoke their own restriction orders and notices at any time before the end of the inquiry (they cannot vary or revoke each other's).[26] This allows for the scope of restrictions to be amended if circumstances change: more information can be made public than was originally envisaged, or made available to more people, or indeed further restrictions may be considered necessary.[27]

The Media and Hearings[28]

The chair of a statutory inquiry must take such steps as the chair considers reasonable to secure that members of the public are able to attend the inquiry, or to see and hear a simultaneous transmission of proceedings at the inquiry.[29] This requirement is expressly stated as 'including reporters'. While there is no such presumption for non-statutory inquiries, when hearings are open to the public, the chair must also consider the approach that the inquiry will take to media access to hearings.

[25] HL Select Committee, *The Inquiries Act 2005: Post-legislative Scrutiny* (HL 2013–2014, 143).
[26] Inquiries Act 2005, s 20.
[27] See chapter fifteen in relation to restrictions at the conclusion of an inquiry.
[28] See also chapter three for media facilities and chapter five for media protocols.
[29] Inquiries Act 2005, s 18.

Approaches vary between inquiries and may include some or all of the following:

- A media liaison officer is often appointed to brief and assist the media and answer any questions.
- The inquiry's approach to media access may be set out within one or more protocols issued by the inquiry,[30] and published on the inquiry's website (see chapter five).
- Some inquiries set up a media accreditation scheme, whereby members of the local and national media have to formally apply for accreditation. Consideration should also be given to who else would be considered 'the media'; for example would this include 'bloggers' or other social media outlets? Those who are granted accreditation will usually be permitted access to media facilities provided by the inquiry.[31] Those who are not eligible retain the same right of access as members of the public.
- Where an inquiry adopts an accreditation scheme, details will be published on the inquiry website.
- Facilities made available to members of the media may include allocated seats within the public seating area in the hearing room and a dedicated media room, with electronic screens displaying the live transmission of proceedings, together with working space, power sockets and wifi (see chapter five).
- Seating in the hearing room may be very limited. An inquiry will usually restrict the amount of seating available to members of the media so that they do not dominate the public seating space to the exclusion of others such as victims and survivors, family members, members of support groups, and the general public.
- Restrictions and prohibitions within the hearing room will depend on the nature of the subject matter of the inquiry. There will usually be restrictions on recording, broadcasting, photography, and the use of social media and electronic devices, such as laptops and mobile phones in the hearing rooms, for all or part of a hearing.
- Other restrictions associated with hearings may provide for:
  - temporary pausing, or the delay of live streaming of the hearing;
  - redaction of transcripts and documents;
  - prohibition on approaching members of the inquiry team during the hearings
  - prohibition on approaching members of the public and witnesses, while attending the hearings on the inquiry premises;

[30] See chapter five.
[31] With photo identification required for entry.

  - prohibition on approaching witnesses for quotes or interviews once they have been sworn in, until they have finished giving their evidence;
  - a requirement that any media interviews take place off inquiry premises.

- During an inquiry, rulings may be made that grant anonymity to certain witnesses and place a strict restriction on the publication of certain documents.

Managing Private and Closed Hearings

Since the introduction of the 2005 Act, over a third of the notable inquiries held have had some sort of restrictions on public access. This includes wholly private inquiries, such as the Penrose Inquiry, and mainly public inquiries such as the Mid Staffordshire NHS Foundation Trust Inquiry, in which a very small amount of highly sensitive material was withheld from the public domain.

Where restrictions are imposed on the hearing of evidence, this may result in the exclusion of some, or indeed all, members of the public, core participants or interested parties, or legal representatives from the oral hearings. Private hearings may be conducted where access is restricted to the inquiry team and those giving the sensitive evidence. In some cases, depending on the sensitivity or the evidence, core participants, interested parties and the public may not even be aware the private hearings are taking place. Closed hearings may be conducted where the chair will decide who may be privy to the information and which might, for example, include witnesses, core participants or interested parties with a common interest.

Where such restrictions are in place, the inquiry has to manage the hearings in such a way that the evidence in question, the individual's identity, or both, are protected.

Checklist – Steps that may be taken to manage private hearings

Steps taken to manage private hearings may include:

- Putting arrangements in place so that, where necessary, witnesses may enter and leave the inquiry premises, and the hearing room itself, without being seen.
- Requiring all 'live' electronic equipment (for displaying documents and transcripts) to be switched off.
- Requiring all screens located outside the hearing room (eg in any dedicated media room or core participants room) to be switched off.
- Ensuring that no names or details of the evidence to be given are contained in hearing timetables or on the inquiry's website.

- Ensuring that no transcripts from the hearing are uploaded to the inquiry's website.
- Taking the evidence at a location away from the inquiry hearing room.

If an inquiry does take evidence in private, the chair must proceed with care when it comes to how they can, and should, use that evidence when making findings and preparing the report. For example, if the evidence is to be relied upon to make criticisms of others, the chair will be duty bound to explain the nature of the evidence to the subject of the criticism, in accordance with the Maxwellisation process[32] and with suitable confidentiality arrangements in place.[33] Care must also need to be taken when including reference to private evidence in the final inquiry report, and ensuring that such references are suitably redacted. The inquiry will also need to make sure that assurances around the protection of information and personal data provided to those giving evidence in private are adhered to.

[32] The process of sending of letters warning of criticism arising from the inquiry, sent before the production of the inquiry report. See chapter thirteen.

[33] See chapter thirteen.

12

Assessors, Seminars and Experts

Introduction

Holding seminars and appointing assessors and expert witnesses to assist the inquiry's work are all useful ways in which an inquiry may obtain specialist assistance.

Past inquiries have adopted various approaches. Some have used seminars at the outset of the inquiry; others have concluded the inquiry's work with a series of seminars. Some inquiries have appointed assessors or expert witnesses, or both, whilst others have chosen to engage neither. An inquiry's approach will depend largely on its scale and subject matter, as well as its specific terms of reference. This chapter examines how each form of assistance works and explores the advantages and disadvantages of each.

Where provisions and guidance exist in this area, they relate to statutory inquiries. This chapter therefore focuses on statutory inquiries, but the same principles apply where a chair of a non-statutory inquiry elects to use seminars, assessors (generally referred to as 'advisers' in the case of non-statutory inquiries) and expert witnesses.

Issue – Panel members versus assessors and experts

An inquiry may be set up with an inquiry panel made up of experts in specific fields sitting alongside the chair. This provides a wider range of expertise throughout the inquiry's proceedings, its deliberations and the production of its report, than when a chair is sitting alone. Having experts on the panel may also promote participants' confidence in the inquiry and make the final recommendations more acceptable to those participants.

Inquiries, however, may last a number of years. It can be difficult to find people of distinction, with the required levels of specialist expertise, who are able to commit such a significant amount of time to an inquiry panel and away from their specialist work.[1] There are also often strong arguments in favour of a chair sitting alone. Having an inquiry panel can prolong the process. Experts who are full panel members will be involved throughout, including listening to and evaluating evidence beyond the scope of their particular expertise. Having a single chair, assisted by assessors and expert witnesses, can be much more efficient. Assessors and experts can be deployed by the chair whenever required.

Some chairs, such as judges, are chosen for their stature and reputation, together with their skills in analysing large quantities of evidence, assessing witness credibility, and resolving complex questions of fact. In most cases, however, they are not themselves experts in the subject matter of the inquiry and they may particularly benefit from advice and assistance from panel members, assessors and expert witnesses. However, other chairs are specifically appointed for their own expertise in the subject matter of the inquiry and will have less need for additional expert assistance. The key questions to be determined are the extent to which an inquiry chair or panel requires additional assistance and expertise from expert witnesses, assessors or from the holding of seminars, and whether such assistance is for a specific purpose or issue or needs to be ongoing.

The Role of Assessors

Assessors (or 'advisers' in the case of non-statutory inquiries) provide expert advice and assistance to inquiry chairs and panels. For a statutory inquiry, under s 11 of the Inquiries Act 2005, both the convening minister and the chair of the inquiry have the discretionary power to appoint one or more assessors to assist and advise the inquiry. The minister may exercise this power before the setting-up date, first consulting with the chair. The chair may exercise this power during the course of the inquiry (irrespective of whether or not the minister has already appointed assessors).

Other than being appointed to 'assist' the inquiry, there are no provisions in either the Inquiries Act 2005 Act or the Inquiry Rules 2006 regarding the role of

[1] See Dr Judith Smith's oral evidence taken before the HL Select Committee (4 December 2013) Q295 'Select Committee on the Inquiries Act 2002: Written and Corrected Oral Evidence' www.parliament.uk/documents/lords-committees/Inquiries-Act-2005/IA_Written_Oral_evidencevol.pdf (accessed 12 August 2020).

an assessor and the term is not defined. The explanatory notes to the 2005 Act state simply

> The role of assessors will vary from inquiry to inquiry, but in essence they are experts in their own particular field whose knowledge, where necessary, can provide the panel with the expertise it needs in order to fulfil an inquiry's terms of reference.

It is therefore a matter for the chair to determine their role and extent of their assistance.[2] What is clear, however, is that, while the chair or panel may ask for the advice and assistance of assessors, the chair or panel alone will have the final word on what goes into the report.[3]

An assessor of a statutory inquiry has immunity from suit for any action or omission in the execution of their duty as an assessor to the inquiry, under s 37 of the Inquiries Act 2005, in the same way as the chair, panel members, counsel and the solicitors to the inquiry and other persons engaged to provide assistance to the inquiry. An assessor or adviser in a non-statutory inquiry does not have immunity from suit.

Issue – Transparency and assessors

Unlike expert witnesses, assessors do not give written or oral evidence to the inquiry and are not, therefore, subject to public examination by the inquiry or, if permitted, the core participants. The substance of the advice they give may be disclosed to the core participants and public, but this is not usually the case. This can give rise to concerns from participants about transparency, which need to be addressed by the inquiry (see below).

Quotes: Differing views on panels, assessors and experts

Opinions differ on the use of panels, assessors and experts and much will depend on the nature of the inquiries concerned.

'I would prefer in all cases that the chairman should act alone. If you have access to expert advice, that advice should not come through the medium of an assessor or a member of the panel. It should come through the use of an expert as a witness to the inquiry. There are two reasons for that. The first is that if you have an expert witness to the inquiry, he is seen to be detached from the decision-maker and that instils confidence in the core participants.

[2] The chair, under the chair's general power to determine the procedure and conduct of an inquiry: Inquiries Act 2005, s 17(1).

[3] Explanatory notes to the 2005 Act, para 18.

> *The second reason is that if an expert is seen to be an assessor at an inquiry, the parties always wonder what evidence he is giving to the chairman when they retire into closed session to discuss things, whereas if he is a witness everyone knows exactly where they stand.'*
>
> Lord Gill, Chair of the inquiry into the ICL disaster in Glasgow in oral evidence to the House of Lords Select Committee on the Inquiries Act 2005 (30 October 2003)
>
> *'My view is a bit different [to Lord Gills']. For a start, I would not be in favour of any rule for there being a panel of a number of chairmen acting together. I see no need for that and I see it causing complications. As regards assessors, I do not share the misgiving that Lord Gill has had about assessors, since it is made perfectly clear that they are not a source of evidence but a form of assistance to the chairman in going about his work.'*
>
> Lord Cullen of Whitekirk, Chair of inquiries into the Piper Alpha Disaster, the Dunblane Primary School Massacre, and the Labroke Grove Rail Crash in oral evidence to the House of Lords Select Committee on the Inquiries Act 2005 (30 October 2003)

In order to determine what the role of an assessor may entail, one can look at past inquiries:

Victoria Climbié Inquiry

- During the inquiry into the circumstances surrounding the tragic death of Victoria Climbié, Lord Laming appointed four assessors to assist him during the inquiry. As noted in Lord Laming's report, in this instance the assessors assisted the chairman in analysing the evidence and giving advice on areas within their expertise.[4]

The Mid Staffordshire NHS Foundation Trust Public Inquiry

- At the commencement of its proceedings, the Mid Staffordshire NHS Foundation Trust Public Inquiry published a protocol setting out the role of its assessors.

[4] Secretary of State for Health and the Secretary of State for the Home Department, *The Victoria Climbié Inquiry* (Cm 5730, 2003).

- Four assessors were appointed by the chair at the outset, having been chosen for their experience and knowledge, both within the NHS and other fields, in key areas of interest for the inquiry. They were asked to provide advice to the chair.
- A further four assessors were then appointed to join the existing panel of assessors, at the conclusion of the oral evidence, prior to the chairman finalising his report. The assessors' role at this stage was to provide advice on the practical implications of implementing draft recommendations proposed by the chair and whether they would achieve what was intended.

Mid Staffordshire Protocol on Assessors

'4. An Assessor will assist the Chairman in dealing with a matter in which the assessor has expertise.

5. An assessor will take such part in the proceedings of the Inquiry as the Chairman may request, and in particular the Chairman may at any time request an assessor to –

(a) prepare a report for the Chairman on any matter relevant to the Inquiry within the expertise of the assessor; and/or

(b) attend the whole or any part of the public hearings to advise the Chairman on any such matter; and/or

(c) provide the Chairman with advice on any matter relevant to the Inquiry within the expertise of the assessor.

6. If an assessor prepares a report for the Chairman which the Chairman intends to take into account, in whole or in part, in reaching his conclusions –

(a) the Chairman will send a copy of the report, or such part(s) of it which he intends to take into account, to each of the Core Participants; …'

The Leveson Inquiry

- During the Leveson Inquiry, a panel of six assessors was appointed to assist the inquiry with its work. The assessors were appointed by the prime minister, and were chosen for their expertise in the range of issues being considered by the inquiry.
- The inquiry adopted a similar protocol to that of the Mid Staffordshire NHS Foundation Trust Public Inquiry in respect of its assessors, but the protocol envisaged the assessors playing a much more central and full-time role.

The Leveson Inquiry Protocol on Assessors

'3. An assessor will take such part in the proceedings of the Inquiry as the Chairman may request, and in particular the Chairman may at any time request an assessor to –

(a) Attend the whole or part of any hearing, seminar or briefing; and/or
(b) Chair the whole or part of any seminar in an area of his or her expertise; and/or
(c) Prepare a report for the Chairman on any matter relevant to the Inquiry within the area of expertise of the assessor; and/or
(d) Provide to Counsel to the Inquiry suggested lines of questioning for witnesses, in respect of any matters within his or her expertise; and
(e) Provide the Chairman with any other assistance, or advice, on any matter relevant to the Inquiry within the expertise of the assessor.'

- In practice, the assessors on the Leveson Inquiry were given a more active role in the hearings than during the Mid Staffordshire NHS Foundation Trust Public Inquiry. At any one time, at least one assessor was asked to attend the daily hearings. The assessors were also asked to read all witness statements and evidence submitted to the inquiry, and to provide suggested lines of questioning to counsel.
- On 28 July 20111, during opening remarks at the commencement of the inquiry, Lord Leveson made a statement about the role of the assessors: 'I intend that each should have a central role in the work and that the final report will be a collaborative effort. I will strive for unanimity; if any particular recommendation is not unanimous, I shall make the contrary view clear.'[5]

Issue – Leveson Inquiry: retaining a distinction between assessors and panel members

- Concerns were raised by a core participant during the Leveson Inquiry about the role of the assessors, expressing the view that their

[5] On 28 July 2011, https://webarchive.nationalarchives.gov.uk/20140122144927/http://www.levesoninquiry.org.uk/about/opening-remarks/ (accessed 12 August 2020).

role appeared to be more akin to a hybrid between a panel member and assessor. Lord Leveson addressed these concerns during a hearing on 17 October 2011:

'I must make it clear that I do not accept that the assessors are in some way a hybrid between assessors (within the meaning of s. 11 of the 2005 Act) and members of the determining panel (as set out in s. 4) …

What then is the role of the assessors? By reason of s. 11(4) of the 2005 Act, it is clear that the Ministers considered that each had expertise that made him or her a suitable person to provide assistance to the Inquiry panel …

As I said at the hearing, I am very conscious that in chairing this Inquiry, I am stepping into a profession that is not the one in which I have spent 40 years of life. It is obviously desirable (as the Prime Minister and others have identified) that I obtain advice and assistance from those who have made their lives and careers in the various areas covered by the Inquiry … Not least, this is because I would be keen to understand any flaws or unintended consequences that might flow from suggestions that are advanced that my lack of experience would not otherwise identify …

The assessors bring their expertise to bear in a number of ways. First and foremost, on pre-reading evidence which has been submitted to the Inquiry, they may suggest additional lines of investigation or potential lines for questioning; essentially, these would not be for me to receive or to act upon but, rather, will be considered by Counsel to the Inquiry who may take them up or not as they consider appropriate …

It is also clear from the Protocol that if an assessor prepares a report for me which I intend to take into account, it shall be disclosed to the core participants and will form part of the Inquiry record: there will then be an opportunity for representations to be made upon it (see para 4 of the Protocol). Further, if I receive any advice not contained within a report but which I intend to take into account, to such extent as it is necessary for the fair and proportionate conduct of the Inquiry, I will similarly disclose it and allow observations to be made upon it (see para. 5).

The assessors also bring an understanding of the practical implications of potential ways forward – what may, or may not, work in the fields of their respective expertise. It is that to which I refer when I speak of being collaborative and "striving for unanimity". There is absolutely no point in my suggesting a way forward (if different from the present system) that everyone decries as unworkable; if that were my provisional view, I would want to be told …

Ultimately, however, as I have made very clear, my conclusions shall be solely my conclusions.'

The Independent Inquiry into Child Sexual Abuse (IICSA)

- At the outset, the inquiry appointed two separate panels of advisers:
  - The Victims and Survivors' Consultative Panel: an eight-member panel set up to provide advice and guidance to the chair and panel, with each member bringing experience of providing support and advocacy for victims and survivors of child sexual abuse.
  - The Academic Advisory Board (AAB): a board of five individuals, all experts in the field of child protection, to oversee and guide the inquiry's research project and advise the chair and panel members on a range of matters. (The inquiry subsequently revised its governance structure and, as a result, the AAB was dissolved,[6] but former members continue to give expert academic and ethical advice to the Panel regarding the Inquiry's research, as requested.[7])

Issue – The IICSA and a combined role as expert and assessor

The advisers to the IICSA, however, were not formally appointed as assessors under s 11 of the Inquiries Act 2005. Instead they seem to have been appointed as 'expert advisers', for which there are no specific legislative provisions.

In this sense their appointment is quite different to the traditional role of an expert witness in a public inquiry, who is a witness of fact and opinion and generally detached and independent from the internal workings of the inquiry. Instead, the IICSA appears to have adopted an unusual approach, whereby its advisers are termed 'experts', when truly their role is that of an assessor.

The Grenfell Tower Inquiry

- Shortly after the inquiry was established, three assessors, with specific experience and expertise that was felt to be of value to the inquiry,[8] were appointed to

[6] With its work being taken forward by a research steering group.

[7] https://www.iicsa.org.uk/news/inquiry-updates-research-governance-structure (accessed 12 August 2020).

[8] The three assessors appointed by the Grenfell Tower Inquiry in November 2017 had expertise in civil engineering, social housing and local government.

assist the chair. The inquiry's website explained the expectations of the assessors' role and how any advice they gave would be treated:

> *'An assessor's function is to provide advice to the Inquiry Chairman. This is likely to involve reading relevant documents, witness statements and any experts' reports. Assessors will normally be expected to attend hearings when evidence is being taken in relation to matters within the scope of their expertise. Assessors are not expected to ask questions of witnesses, but before a witness is called they may suggest lines of questioning to Counsel to the Inquiry.'*
>
> *'The Chairman expects that most advice and assistance will be given informally, but if he obtains formal advice in writing from an assessor, which he intends to take into account in reaching his decision, he will provide a copy to Core Participants and publish on the Inquiry's website.'*

As can be seen, there is no particular precedent for an inquiry to follow when defining the role of an assessor to an inquiry (or an 'adviser' in the case of non-statutory inquiries); the Inquiries Act 2005 is silent on their role and obligations in statutory inquiries. Common themes can, however, be drawn from past inquiries. The circumstances in which advice will be given, whether that advice will be made public and the form that the advice should take, is entirely at the discretion of the individual chair, to best support the particular inquiry in question.

Advantages and Disadvantages of Appointing Assessors or Advisers

Advantages

- Their appointment can give the inquiry credibility
- Their expert knowledge fills gaps in chair or panel's knowledge or experience
- Their advice on the potential recommendations provides gravitas for the inquiry report
- They give informed advice as to lines of questioning to use when questioning witnesses
- Their appointment can ensure 'buy-in' from sceptical stakeholders because of their expertise and the element of independence from the inquiry
- They can input ideas and act as a sounding board to the chair and provide a different perspective
- They can 'dip in and out' depending on need and therefore are not a constant drain on the inquiry's budget

Disadvantages

Assessors' and advisors' advice is not subject to external scrutiny and so can be perceived to lack reliability or provide an untested and 'one-sided' view. Core participants and members of the public are often not privy to their advice

They can be perceived as lacking independence from the inquiry as their advice is usually given to the chair in private

There can be cost implications, although assessors or advisers can be a more cost effective solution than permanent panel members

Quote

'Many inquiries find engaging assessors very useful:

For example, they will help [the chair] to put a setting for the evidence, give [the chair] a sense of what may or may not be significant. They may help [the chair] to some extent in putting questions and they may also help [the chair] in putting together parts of the report where they are peculiarly qualified to help. That is not to say that it is easy to find assessors. Sometimes it is extremely difficult, but if you can get good assessors they are invaluable, as far as I am concerned.'

Lord Cullen of Whitekirk, in evidence to the House of Lords Select Committee on the Inquiries Act 2005

Checklist – Practicalities the minister or chair will consider when appointing assessors

- Whether the assessor holds the necessary credentials and expertise to assist with the inquiry's terms of reference.
- Whether the individual(s) are free from any potential conflicts, including perceived conflicts, to the extent that the chair is comfortable with their appointment (there may be others who raise conflict issues in

any event). The inquiry may decide to publish a declaration of interests for each of the assessors for transparency purposes.

- Will the appointee be objective? The assessor's role is to be a sounding board, and an adviser to the chair. It is important that the assessor can do this impartially.
- What will be the extent of the assessor's intended role? The assessor's role should be defined at the outset, so that both the chair and any assessors are aware of their duties and obligations from the outset:
  - Will the chair seek advice on specific issues as and when required?
  - Will the assessor provide advice at certain defined stages?
  - Will the assessor be required to attend the daily hearings and review all evidence?
  - Will the assessor be asked to devise lines of questioning?
  - Will the assessor be asked to input into the report or comment on the proposed recommendations only?
- What time commitment will be required from the assessor? Is the time commitment a daily one, or does it fall at certain intervals during the inquiry? Will individuals with the necessary expertise (ie leading experts in the field) be able to commit the amount of time needed? Will only retired experts be able to commit the required time and, if so, will the fact that they are no longer practising raise issues?
- Many inquiries will prepare a protocol or written procedure to set out the role of an assessor. The protocol or procedure should explain the role of an assessor and the appointment process; it is likely to allow some flexibility since the role can develop and evolve as the inquiry's work progresses.
- Care needs to be taken to ensure assessors do not effectively become quasi panel members or expert witnesses to the inquiry. The assessor's role is to advise and assist with the inquiry's internal workings, not to give evidence as part of the inquiry.
- Consideration will also need to be given to the remuneration of any assessors.

Issue – Should advice given by assessors be published?

An issue that often arises is the extent to which any advice offered by an assessor should be made public. In the past, most inquiries have chosen not to report the detail of discussions between the chair and the assessors. There have been exceptions. For example, in the Grenfell Tower Inquiry's Protocol on the Role of the Assessors, it provides:

'The Chairman expects that most advice and assistance will be given informally, but if he obtains formal advice in writing from an assessor which he intends to take into account in reaching his decision, he will provide a copy to the Core Participants and publish it on the Inquiry's website, unless he considers that it would be inappropriate to do so.'[9]

But does this go against the very tenor of a public inquiry? Section 18 of the Inquiries Act 2005 creates a presumption that information relied upon by the inquiry should be made public. Assessors have influence and one could argue that their advice should be published, as it could be regarded as being, in part, evidence relied on by the chair.

A counter argument would be that the 2005 Act does not provide that 'advice' must be made public. Section 18(1)(b) provides that evidence and documents will be made public, stating: '*The chairman must take such steps as he considers reasonable to secure that members of the public (including reporters) are able – … (b) to obtain or to view a record of evidence and documents given, produced or provided to the inquiry or inquiry panel.*' However, there is no equivalent provision for advice provided by assessors.

The danger of publishing all advice received is, of course, that assessors may not feel comfortable giving honest and frank advice in such circumstances. Instead, qualified and guarded advice may be given which is of little use to a chair who requires clear, expert guidance. The deliberative process that occurs between the chair and the assessors should be open and challenging; there is a real danger that this would be lost if all advice were to be published.

If advice were to be published, it is difficult to determine where the line should be drawn. If there is a panel assisting the chair, should all discussions between panel members and the chair be published? Should all communications between the chair and the inquiry team be published? This would not only be impractical but could completely de-rail an inquiry's work as a result of time being spent publishing internal inquiry correspondence

[9] https://www.grenfelltowerinquiry.org.uk/sites/default/files/inline-files/Protocol-on-the-Role-of-Assessors.pdf (accessed 12 August 2020).

rather than focusing on gathering evidence in order to fulfil the inquiry's terms of reference.

Whilst the issue of transparency is important, great care (and restraint) is needed before publishing advice of this nature as it could open the flood-gates of requests for all advice to be published. Where advice crosses the line into an expert opinion, then consideration should be given to documenting the opinion formally and submitting it as evidence to the inquiry, which would then lead to publication. This may in turn call into question an assessor's role, and result in that person becoming an expert witness to the inquiry, having to forfeit their role as an assessor for reasons of independence and impartiality.

Expert Witnesses

The use of expert witnesses during an inquiry is common. Past inquiries have utilised the expertise of all manner of experts: from ballistics experts to medical experts, to experts on policy and management procedures, to statisticians and handwriting experts.

In some ways experts are similar to assessors, in that they are there to provide professional assistance to an inquiry and are selected because of their area of expertise. The capacity in which an expert witness assists the inquiry is, however, very different to that of an assessor.

Expert witnesses are witnesses of opinion. They are independent from the chair and the chair's team. As with other witnesses, they are asked to prepare written evidence (usually an expert's report rather than a witness statement); they provide oral evidence to the inquiry based on that evidence, and are questioned further by counsel to the inquiry during that oral evidence.

Expert witnesses to an inquiry are, however, different to expert witnesses in civil or criminal proceedings, where it is not uncommon for the court to grant the parties permission to obtain their own expert witness to support their case. During an inquiry, expert witnesses are usually chosen by the inquiry alone; core participants or other participants are rarely permitted to instruct their own expert witness to give evidence, although they may be afforded the opportunity to comment on the intended expert appointment by the inquiry.

In respect of statutory inquiries, there are no express statutory provisions that provide for the instruction of expert witnesses; expert witnesses are not referred to either in the Inquiries Act 2005 or the Inquiry Rules 2006. Where an inquiry instructs an expert witness, it does so using the chair's power under s 17 of the Inquiries Act 2005, which allows the chair to determine the inquiry's procedures and conduct proceedings as the chair sees fit.

Advantages and Disadvantages of using Expert Witnesses

Advantages

Expert witnesses are independent of the decision-making of the inquiry in a way that assessors are not. This can instil more public confidence in the inquiry's work. In some senses experts are the only really independent witness to give evidence during an inquiry

Expert evidence is often used at the outset of an inquiry's hearings to help provide background information and set the scene and tone of the evidence

An inquiry may find it useful for expert witnesses to be called back at the end of an inquiry's oral evidence, to comment on the evidence heard and provide their independent expert view

Evidence given by expert witnesses is made public. An expert's report is published and the experts' evidence is given in public and is subject to public scrutiny. This is in contrast to the position for assessors, who usually provide the chair with advice and assistance privately

Expert witnesses enable an inquiry to address and examine any specialist aspects of the terms of reference

Disadvantages

From the perspective of core participants to an inquiry, they have no control over the choice of an expert nor the scope of their instructions (but may have an opportunity to comment), but expert evidence can often carry great weight in an inquiry

For specialist inquiries, the potential pool of skilled experts can be very small, which can make it challenging to identify experts who are entirely independent from all parties involved with the inquiry

There is the potential for an expert to have an interest in certain outcomes from an inquiry's conclusions, for example if it furthers their academic research or business interests, which could damage the credibility of the evidence given. Careful checks of any potential conflicts are required. This is also one reason why core participants may be invited to comment on any proposed appointment

A Dual Role

There have been examples of individuals taking a dual role, first as an expert witness and later as an assessor to an inquiry. For example, Dr Judith Smith was initially appointed as an expert witness to the Mid Staffordshire NHS Foundation Trust Inquiry, where she gave evidence at the outset of the oral hearings as an expert on the structure and organisation of the NHS. Later, at the point when the chair was considering his recommendations, Dr Smith was appointed as an assessor.

Whilst there are circumstances where an individual can fulfil both roles, it would be difficult for someone to conduct these roles simultaneously. It would raise questions about the individual's independence from the inquiry and whether all evidence was fully on the record. A chair and an assessor have a different relationship to that of a chair and expert witness; in the former case, issues can be discussed and debated. If a dual role of expert witness and assessor exists, discussions that have taken place between the chair and the assessor could influence the evidence given by the assessor in their role as an expert witness.

Hot-tubbing

One method used by some inquiries to receive expert evidence during hearings is a technique referred to as 'hot-tubbing'. The term 'hot-tubbing' describes the process of witnesses giving evidence concurrently, in this case expert witnesses, and is known formally as 'concurrent evidence'. The experts are asked to collaborate and give evidence to the inquiry collectively, in an attempt to resolve any outstanding issues of fact or opinion. The phrase 'hot-tubbing' is used because the expert witnesses physically sit together in the witness box at all times.

The experts remain together during the entirety of their evidence, as opposed to the traditional approach where each expert presents their evidence separately. This approach facilitates a discussion between the experts, counsel to the inquiry and the chair or panel, and helps to narrow the issues in dispute during the hearing itself.

The process usually involves the following steps:

- Identification of the issues upon which expert evidence is required.
- Preparation of individual expert reports.
- A conference between the experts to discuss the matters upon which there is agreement and the matters that remain in issue and, if required, the preparation of a joint report to setting out the details.
- The experts are called to give evidence together and question each other on issues raised during the evidence.

Hot-tubbing was used during the Leveson Inquiry to question expert witnesses (eg academics providing evidence together on 'public interest') and other witnesses (eg the evidence of regional news editors was heard in a 'hot tub' format).

There is no reason why other non-expert witnesses could not provide evidence using a 'hot-tubbing' approach, provided the circumstances were appropriate. Set out below are a few of the advantages and disadvantages of 'hot-tubbing' expert witnesses:

Advantages	Disadvantages
Enables expert evidence to be subject to expert criticism or questioning	Can increase the adversarial nature of the hearing if two experts have opposing views
Increases the quality of discussion and therefore the quality of evidence	Can also lead to experts simply agreeing with one another on the stand, due to professional politeness, and therefore not adding much to their written evidence
Reduces delays and cost by questioning witnesses together, potentially avoiding having to recall witnesses to deal with other issues raised	A confident expert, or someone who sees him or herself as a budding advocate, could dominate the evidence

Seminars

Purpose of Seminars

Using seminars as a means of assisting an inquiry is a concept that has been used more and more frequently by inquiries. Formal seminars have been used successfully on the Leveson Inquiry, the Mid Staffordshire NHS Foundation Trust Inquiry, the Victoria Climbié Inquiry and the IICSA. Seminars are usually used to bring together a group of key stakeholders and experts to examine, at a high level (ie without reference to detailed evidence), the key issues and themes that the inquiry needs to explore and the experiences and views of those key stakeholders. They may well focus on ideas and suggestion for the future to, assist the inquiry in developing recommendations.

Mid Staffordshire NHS Foundation Trust Public Inquiry

By way of an example of this, during the Mid Staffordshire NHS Foundation Trust Public Inquiry, seven seminars were held after the conclusion of the oral evidence to 'explore the "forward-looking" part of the inquiry's terms of reference', ie focusing on recommendations for change. The seminars enabled a broader discussion to take place on some of the key themes raised by the evidence and to provide an opportunity for key stakeholders and experts to provide ideas and information to the inquiry to help inform the chair when it came to making recommendations for the future.

Quote

Dr Judith Smith, expert witness and assessor to the Mid Staffordshire NHS Foundation Trust Public Inquiry, discussed the positive aspects of the seminars held during the Inquiry:

'I want to return to the point about the inquiry seminars that we held during the Francis inquiry. These took place just after the conclusion of taking oral evidence, and there were seven of them, which were held in different places around the country. They involved some of us who had been formally appointed as experts, as well as many other people who could be considered to be experts. The people attending included the core participants – for example, the families of the people at Stafford – and the seminars were on a range of topics such as healthcare regulation, the role of NHS boards and nursing. They were filmed, were very public and were independently facilitated. People wrote papers in advance for them, and they were all on the website. There was significant debate and discussion at the seminars. The reason I mention them is that they were very deliberative, interactive and engaging. They just had a different feel to them. They were more like a seminar or workshop but they brought out some different perspectives and there was a lot of challenge.

They were very helpful to the Chairman and the Inquiry team. It just leaves me to wonder: clearly, they were fed into the Francis inquiry and that is a different way of using experts and potentially assessors, to have some of that challenge and debate in a public setting. It is partly about it being on the public record, and there is a slightly different, less formal feel … It was a very rich part of the inquiry process.'

Dr Judith Smith, in evidence to the House of Lords Select Committee on the Inquiries Act 2005 (4 December 2013)

Leveson Inquiry

The seminars held during the Leveson Inquiry adopted a slightly different approach, particularly as they were held at the beginning of the inquiry's proceedings. Three seminars were held at the outset of the inquiry, and before any oral evidence had been heard. The Leveson Inquiry's website explained the purpose behind holding the seminars:

> Lord Justice Leveson announced that he would hold a number of seminars to enable consideration of the central public policy issues in the Inquiry's terms of reference to be enriched by and examined from across a range of informed perspectives.
>
> Each of the seminars will be chaired by one or more of the Inquiry's assessors, and to ensure that the seminars are informed by professional opinion in the field, Lord Justice Leveson will invite a small number of influential experts and key people in the area to make a personal contribution by presenting brief papers to stimulate debate among an invited audience of opinion-formers.
>
> The seminars will be recorded and available for anyone to view on the website. The intention is that these seminars will provide the stimulus for an open invitation for both media professionals and members of the public to continue the debate online, and provide further evidence to the Inquiry which Lord Justice Leveson will take into account.
>
> These seminars will constitute a part of the Inquiry's procedures. Lord Justice Leveson will be present and listening throughout, and the papers and debates will be important parts of the Inquiry's records. But the seminars are in addition to, and quite distinct from, the forensic fact-finding exercise that is also being undertaken by way of formally seeking witness evidence as to the circumstances surrounding the phone-hacking scandal itself and the other issues that the Inquiry has been asked to consider and where Lord Justice Leveson is separately inviting or requiring first-hand accounts from a range of witnesses, to the facts and the approach. The seminars, by contrast, are an opportunity for the Inquiry to take a broad brush look at the wider picture – to hear opinions and debate.[10]

Victoria Climbié Inquiry

During the final phase of the Victoria Climbié Inquiry, five seminars were held on topics that were relevant to the elements of good childcare practice and the processes designed to secure the safety and well-being of children. Representatives of those interested in the inquiry's work were invited, who were drawn from across the country and from a wide range of professional backgrounds.

[10] http://webarchive.nationalarchives.gov.uk/20140122152757/http://www.levesoninquiry.org.uk/news-and-events/events/ (accessed 12 August 2020).

In his report, Lord Laming said: 'These seminars proved to be of great value to this Inquiry. They provided the opportunity to consider, in a wider forum, many of the issues raised in evidence … during Phase One'.[11] (Phase One was the retrospective phase of the inquiry.)

Lord Laming's report also made it clear that the seminars were to help fulfil the forward-looking element of the inquiry's terms of reference, namely, to make recommendations on how safeguards for children might be strengthened in order to prevent a tragedy of that kind happening again.

IICSA

As well as encompassing a number of different investigations, the IICSA was divided into three projects: the Truth Project, the Research Project and the Public Hearings Project. The Research Project of IICSA was a dedicated research function that had been set up to bring together in one place what was already known about child sexual abuse and find out, and fill, the knowledge gaps, and support the inquiry to ask the right questions of the institutions it was investigating. It is the Research Project which has undertaken the inquiry's seminars.

This has resulted in a number of seminars being held to date. The purpose of the seminars was described as being:

> to gather information and views about important topics, to help the Inquiry to identify areas for further investigation and scrutiny. They do this by
>
> (1) Providing information for current investigations and future hearings to consider.
> (2) Gathering the latest views on topics that may not yet be publicly available.
> (3) Consider the implications for the four themes for change set out in the Chair's December 2016 review: cultural; structural; financial; and professional & political.[12]

Relevant participants (including experts, victim and survivor groups, and key stakeholders, some of whom were core participants) were invited to attend and take part in structured discussions. Members of the public also attended the seminars and observed.

Managing Seminars

The Inquiries Act 2005 and the Inquiry Rules 2006 make no reference to holding seminars during a statutory inquiry. However, by virtue of section 17 of

[11] Looking into the circumstances leading to and surrounding the death of Victoria Secretary of State for Health and the Secretary of State for the Home Department, *The Victoria Climbié Inquiry* (Cm 5730, 2003).

[12] https://www.iicsa.org.uk/about-seminars (accessed 12 August 2020).

the 2005 Act, a chair is at liberty to use the methods they believe will best fulfil the inquiry's terms of reference in the most efficient and cost-effective way. Seminars are likely to be most appropriate for inquiries that are examining questions of policy, where recommendations for the future are a key cornerstone of the inquiry's remit, rather than for very fact-specific inquiries.

Checklist – Seminars: some important considerations

Timing

- Seminars may take place before or after any oral hearings.
- If seminars are held in advance of any oral hearings, they can help to set the scene, narrow down some of the issues, focus minds, and facilitate and 'buy-in' support and participation from those who may be sceptical of the inquiry process. However, it is more difficult at that stage for the inquiry to select the seminar topics, and indeed determine whether seminars are necessary, given that the inquiry has yet to receive oral evidence and the documentary evidence it will have received at that stage may well be limited.
- If seminars are held after the oral hearings phase, an inquiry can select the seminar topics most pertinent and relevant to the evidence already heard, as well as the issues and themes that have been identified as potential areas in which recommendations may be made. Seminars can draw on the evidence and may make considered recommendations. By adopting this approach, an inquiry may, however, miss an important opportunity to narrow the issues early on and to focus questioning more narrowly during the evidence gathering phase and oral hearings. Holding seminars at an earlier stage can help to ensure that all relevant topics are covered with witnesses during evidence gathering and oral hearings, avoiding a potential need to re-call any witnesses.

Attendees

- The inquiry should draw up a list of invitees to take part in the seminars. It will need to consider a variety of issues such as:
  - The breadth of expertise required for each topic.
  - Whether representatives from the core participants will be invited to attend and, if so, how many and whether representatives of any family, survivor or victims group will be permitted a higher number of attendees.

- Whether legal representatives will be permitted to attend. If so, will there be restrictions around formal submissions being made, to prevent it simply being another 'legal process'?
- Whether members of the public will be permitted to attend as observers. If so, what limit will be placed on numbers?

Location

- Careful consideration should be given to the location of the seminars. Depending on the remit of the inquiry, they may be held at the inquiry's premises, nationwide or internationally, to allow the fullest participation of relevant stakeholders, experts and members of the public.

Format

- The format of seminars varies between inquiries. They may involve a series of presentations, papers prepared and submitted in advance, key speakers, round-table discussions, exercises, workshops, and question-and-answer sessions.

Facilitators

- Some inquiries use an independent organisation to chair and facilitate discussions, which can provide a level of independence to the seminars and demonstrate the fact the inquiry has not pre-judged any outcomes. Other inquiries use assessors, or a member of the inquiry team, to chair and facilitate the seminars.

Outcome

- Some inquiries produce a report of the outcomes from the seminars.
- Discussions may be audio-recorded and transcripts published. Notes may be made of the discussions, which then feed into a final report or are published on the inquiry's website.
- Some inquiries will attribute comments to individuals, but others will produce a more general report of information received. An inquiry may choose to publish the papers and presentations prepared for the seminars.

13

Warning Letters and Rules 13, 14 and 15

Introduction

The sending of letters warning of criticism, which is known as 'the rule 13 process' for a statutory public inquiry, or 'Salmon letters' and 'Maxwellisation' for a non-statutory inquiry,[1] is the process by which individuals or organisations are warned that they may be criticised in the final inquiry report. This chapter focuses primarily on the rule 13 process and statutory inquiries. Most non-statutory inquiries adopt a similar form of warning letter process, but they are not bound by the prescriptive nature of these rules. The essence is one of being fair and applying natural justice. The extent to which the issues discussed below apply to a non-statutory inquiry will depend on the form of the process adopted by that particular inquiry. It is important that a non-statutory inquiry is aware of the challenges and issues presented by the rule 13 process, so that it may seek to avoid and circumvent these challenges and issues as far as possible when considering if and how to adopt its own warning letter process.

Over the years, there has been an ongoing debate about how public inquiries should approach a warning letter process, to ensure fair treatment of individuals who might be singled out for criticism, and indeed the extent to which this process is in fact necessary or appropriate at all. There is a commonly held view amongst many that the highly prescriptive rule 13 process simply does not work in practice. There is much debate about how to minimise the impact of what is an extremely onerous process, while still fulfilling the inquiry's duty of fairness to those who may face criticism by the inquiry.

[1] Salmon letters are warning letters sent prior to oral hearings and Maxwellisation is the process whereby warnings are sent after oral hearings but before production of the inquiry report.

Quote

In his oral evidence to the Select Committee on the Inquiries Act 2005, Ashley Underwood QC, Leading Counsel to the Robert Hamill Inquiry, put his views quite simply:

'I think Rodney [the Azelle Rodney Inquiry] would have been cheaper if it had been non-statutory because of the whole rule 13 nonsense. That is one where we did not need the powers, I think ... I think it is a complete waste of space. In fact, it is much more than a waste of space; it is a huge waste of money and effort.'[2]

Mr Justice Jay, leading counsel to the Leveson inquiry, supported this view in his oral evidence to the Select Committee, saying that the rule 13 process is 'extremely time consuming' and:

'Rule 15 caused us huge grief and a huge amount of work and incurring of public expense. I think literally thousands of hours of work went into the generic letter, but had we not done it more or less in full compliance with rule 15, I think the inquiry would have been derailed.'

Sir Robert Francis QC also commented that the rule 13 process took nearly as long as the report writing phase of the Mid Staffordshire NHS Foundation Trust Public Inquiry; and has stated that 'Rule 13 is profoundly unsatisfactory'.

The Salmon Principles, Maxwellisation and the Evolution of Warning Letters

The origin of rule 13 warning letters is to be found in the report of the Royal Commission on Tribunals of Inquiry,[3] also known as the Salmon Report. The 1966 Commission, chaired by Lord Justice Salmon, was convened following dissatisfaction with procedural aspects of Lord Denning's inquiry into the Profumo affair. Lord Salmon devised six cardinal principles of fair procedure for inquiries

[2] Oral evidence taken before the HL Select Committee (20 November 2013) QQ 248–271 'Select Committee on the Inquiries Act 2005: Written and Corrected Oral Evidence', available at https://www.parliament.uk/documents/lords-committees/Inquiries-Act-2005/ucINQUIRIES201113ev11.pdf (accessed 12 August 2020).

[3] Cmnd 3121, 1996.

set up under the Tribunals and Inquiries Act 1921. The second of those Salmon principles was:

> Before any person who is involved in an inquiry is called as a witness, they should be informed of any allegations made against them and the substance of the evidence in support of them.

Letters sent out before witnesses are called to give evidence, where they might face criticism, became known as Salmon letters. The procedure of sending Salmon letters was never given statutory authority, but became widely adopted by inquiries as evidencing fair procedure.

Salmon letters have been severely criticised by many, including Sir Richard Scott in the Arms to Iraq Inquiry in 1997. In his report, Sir Richard Scott said that whilst the Salmon principles may be appropriate to some inquiries, 'it really makes very little sense when applied to an inquisitorial inquiry' such as his own, where the substance of allegations and any conclusions remain unclear until the latter stages of an inquiry. He said that 'the point of inquisitorial inquiries is to investigate and, at the end of the investigation, to draw such conclusions as the evidence allows'. Sir Richard also concluded that the Salmon principles were 'too heavily based on procedural requirements of fairness in an adversarial system'.

A further practice has also evolved whereby an inquiry intending to criticise an individual in its final report will send that individual the relevant section of the final report, in advance of publication, providing an opportunity to respond to the proposed criticism. This process has become known as Maxwellisation, following a case brought by Robert Maxwell against the Department of Trade and Industry[4] during which Mr Maxwell complained that he had not seen a draft of the inspectors' report containing criticism of his business practices, which he alleged breached the rules of natural justice.

Mr Maxwell's challenge was ultimately unsuccessful and Lord Justice Lawton in the Court of Appeal made it clear that fairness did not require that those likely to be criticised in a report be given an opportunity to refute tentative conclusions:

> Those who conduct inquiries have to base their decisions, findings, conclusions or opinions (whichever is the appropriate word to describe what they have a duty to do) on the evidence. In my judgment they are no more bound to tell a witness likely to be criticised in their report what they have in mind to say about him than has a judge sitting alone who has to decide which of two conflicting witnesses is telling the truth.

Notwithstanding the court's decision, following the case, Maxwellisation began to be adopted by subsequent inquiries in an attempt to stop any factual errors or misinterpretations getting into the public domain.

An amended version of the use of Salmon letters and Maxwellisation was subsequently formally incorporated into the Inquiry Rules 2006, with the process

[4] *Maxwell v Department of Trade and Industry* [1974] QB 523.

being set out in rules 13 to 15. This was in the face of objections from practitioners who could foresee the inherent problems in the process. The details of the approach taken by inquiries differs depending on what is most appropriate in the specific circumstances.

Although non-statutory inquiries are not subject to the legislative provisions of rules 13 to 15, most continue to adopt Salmon letters and or Maxwellisation. Many of the issues relating to the operation of rules 13 to 15, including a significant increase of the time and cost of the inquiry because of the potential number of warning letters and vast quantities of evidence involved, apply equally to non-statutory inquiries.

Issue – Warning Letters: time and cost

One of the most serious criticisms of the warning letter process in recent years relates to the significant time and cost incurred by the process and resultant delays to publication of the final inquiry report. Warning letters and responses can run into hundreds of pages and result in significant amounts of additional evidence being provided to the inquiry to support those responses.

Examples that demonstrate the scale of time and work that goes into this process include:

- Thousands of hours of work went into producing the generic warning letter for the Leveson Inquiry.[5]
- The Mid Staffordshire Inquiry was extended by at least six months by having to undertake the rule 13 process, sending out the letters and processing substantive responses.[6]
- The Iraq Inquiry received a huge amount of public and media criticism because of the delay caused by the Maxwellisation process. Although the inquiry was non-statutory, and therefore there was no statutory requirement to undertake a warning letter process, the chair, Sir John Chilcot, chose to adopt a thorough Maxwellisation process, which

[5] Mr Justice Jay, oral evidence to the House of Lords Select Committee on the Inquiries Act (16 October 2013) Q125 'Select Committee on the Inquiries Act 2005: Written and Corrected Oral Evidence', available at https://www.parliament.uk/documents/lords-committees/Inquiries-Act-2005/IA_Written_Oral_evidencevol.pdf (accessed 12 August 2020).

[6] Sir Robert Francis QC, oral evidence to the House of Lords Select Committee on the Inquiries Act (n 5) (30 October 2013) Q216.

he said was 'essential not only to the fairness but the accuracy and completeness of our report'.[7]

- The HBOS Review, a non-statutory inquiry, whose report, the HBOS Report, was published by the Financial Conduct Authority and the Prudential Regulation Authority in November 2015, was also criticised for delays caused by the Maxwellisation process, which was said to have taken 14 months.[8]

Optional and Mandatory Warning Letters

Rule 13

(1) The chairman may send a warning letter to any person –
   (a) he considers may be, or who has been, subject to criticism in the inquiry proceedings; or
   (b) about whom criticism may be inferred from evidence that has been given during the inquiry proceedings; or
   (c) who may be subject to criticism in the report, or any interim report.

(2) The recipient of a warning letter may disclose it to his recognised legal representative.

(3) The inquiry panel must not include any explicit or significant criticism of a person in the report, or in any interim report, unless –
   (a) the chairman has sent that person a warning letter; and
   (b) the person has been given a reasonable opportunity to respond to the warning letter.

[7] Sir John Chilcot's statement published on the Iraq Inquiry's website on 26 August 2015, available at https://webarchive.nationalarchives.gov.uk/20171123123237/http://www.iraqinquiry.org.uk/ (accessed 12 August 2020).

[8] Parliament Publication: A Review of Maxwellisation for the Treasury Committee dated November 2016, paragraph 115 available at https://publications.parliament.uk/pa/cm201617/cmselect/cmtreasy/maxwellisation/a-review-of-maxwellisation-24-11-16.pdf (accessed 12 August 2020).

Rule 13 does not place a mandatory obligation on the inquiry to send a warning letter whenever a criticism is made of a person or organisation. Instead, it states when a warning letter *may* be sent and when a warning letter *must* be sent.

The chair '*may* send a warning letter' to a person:

During the proceedings:

- where the chair considers the person may be, or has been, subject to criticism in the inquiry proceedings;
- about whom criticism may be *inferred from evidence* given during the proceedings.

In relation to the report:

- who may be subject to criticism in the report, or any interim report.[9]

The chair *must* send a warning letter to a person:

- If the report, or any interim report, is to include any 'explicit or significant criticism' of the person (see below on the meaning of 'explicit or significant criticism').

When determining the procedure and conduct of a statutory inquiry,[10] the chair will decide whether the inquiry will send warning letters whenever a person is subject to criticism during the inquiry's proceedings, or only if the report is to include any explicit or significant criticism.

Practical Difficulties Associated with Serving Warning Letters before Evidence is Given

Quote

Sir Louis Blom-Cooper QC has suggested that sending a warning letter after oral evidence, but before the final report, presents a 'closing the door after the horse has bolted' scenario.

Sir Louis said:

'Fairness, in Lord Salmon's eyes, demanded a species of further and better particulars of an allegation, in order that the witness could know in advance of giving his or her evidence what he or she had to meet. It did not contemplate evidence being given by an alleger, untrammelled by scrupulous examination at the time of its being brought forward for consideration.'[11]

[9] Inquiry Rules 2006, r 13(1).

[10] Under the Inquiries Act 2005, s 17(1).

[11] Sir Louis Blom-Cooper QC, 'Witnesses before public inquiries: an example of unfairness' [1996] PL, Spring, 11.

The Rules do not specify the timing of rule 13 letters, save to say that the recipient should be given 'a reasonable opportunity to respond to the warning letter'.[12]

It may be, in an ideal world, as Sir Louis Blom-Cooper QC suggested, that a person will be given notice in advance of giving evidence, where a chair considers the person may be subject to criticism. However, the very nature of an inquiry, being investigative and exploratory, means that evidence emerges as the inquiry progresses. It is therefore often not possible for an inquiry to warn a witness of all potential criticisms they may face before they give evidence. In many cases, criticisms will be made after an individual has given evidence. However, when taking statements from a witness the solicitor to an inquiry will invariably put any adverse material to the witness, so that the response can be captured in the witness statement. If such statements are prepared by the witnesses themselves, the statement will invariably not comment on such adverse matters. Further, the existence of a continuing duty to indicate an inquiry's perceptions and preliminary thoughts is incompatible with an open-minded examination of the evidence and an inquisitorial approach, which follows the evidence wherever it may lead.[13]

Public inquiries have adopted different approaches when determining when warning letters should be sent. The Leveson Inquiry, Mid Staffordshire NHS Foundation Trust Inquiry, Iraq Inquiry and Historical Institutional Abuse Inquiry issued warning letters after the oral hearings had concluded and once a draft report had been prepared, and this is the approach commonly taken by inquiries. The Billy Wright Inquiry originally intended to notify participants about all criticisms arising in advance of oral hearings. But,

> this procedure proved to be harder to follow than had originally been anticipated. The outcome was that the nature of the Inquiry's investigation and the way in which evidence was provided to the Inquiry made the process of sending out detailed warning letters in advance impossible to fulfil.[14]

The Al-Sweady Inquiry took a two-stage approach. As set out in the directions hearing on 19 July 2012, Sir Thayne Forbes explained that the inquiry would send a first warning letter to a witness who may be subject to criticism not later than 14 days before the witness was scheduled to give oral evidence. However, recognising that issues of potential criticism may only arise, or become evident to the inquiry, after a witness has given oral evidence, a second warning letter would be sent before any explicit or significant criticism of that person was included in the final report, with a reasonable opportunity to respond being given.[15]

[12] Inquiry Rules 2006, r 13(3)(b).

[13] See MC Harris, 'Fairness and the adversarial paradigm: an Australian perspective' (1996) PL Aut 508.

[14] The Billy Wright Inquiry – Report HC 431 p 29 available at http://cain.ulst.ac.uk/issues/collusion/docs/wright_140910.pdf (accessed 12 August 2020).

[15] The Al-Sweady Inquiry Directions RE: Inquiry Management Following Hearing on 19th July 2012', paras 22–26, available at http://webarchive.nationalarchives.gov.uk/20150115114913/http://www.alsweadyinquiry.org/key_documents/index.htm (accessed 12 August 2020).

The Infected Blood Inquiry published a statement on 31 January 2019 setting out its intended approach to warning witnesses and individuals of criticisms that may be made of them. This essentially said that there was not a 'one size fits all approach' and that 'judgements will have to be made by the Inquiry on a case-by-case basis as to the best way of ensuring fairness while avoiding unnecessary delay'. While that inquiry intends to send confidential warning letters to those who are to be explicitly or substantially criticised in the final report, the inquiry has made it clear that the period for responding to warning letters will be short, since significant criticisms should already have been aired by that stage.[16] The inquiry also intends to explore all criticisms during the course of its public proceedings, thereby offering individuals and organisations the right of reply during the course of the inquiry.

The Infected Blood Inquiry has stated that notification of criticisms during the course of proceedings may be done in a number of ways, including:

(a) drawing criticisms to the attention of an individual or organisation and requesting (under Rule 9 of the Inquiry Rules) the provision of a written statement and/or relevant documents in response;
(b) sending warning letters under Rule 13(1) to the individual or organisation during the course of the Inquiry's investigation or prior to the conclusion of the Inquiry's hearings;
(c) ensuring that significant criticisms are explored during an individual's oral evidence;
(d) where criticisms or relevant documents come to light after a witness has given oral evidence, by recalling that witness in order that they might be asked questions about the issue.[17]

This approach is intended to reduce the time involved in sending warning letters and considering responses prior to finalising the inquiry report. The chair acknowledged:

> 'Over recent years concerns have been expressed, for example in press reports and to Parliament, that some inquiries have been too slow in producing their reports and that this delay has been caused by the warning letter procedure'.[18]

Are Warning Letters before Evidence is Given Necessary?

Section 17(3) of the Inquiries Act 2005 already requires 'the chairman [to] act with fairness and with regard also to the need to avoid any unnecessary cost'

[16] See the Infected Blood Inquiry's Statement of Approach: The Warning Letter Procedure, available at https://www.infectedbloodinquiry.org.uk/sites/default/files/Statement%20of%20approach%20-%20warning%20letter%20procedure.pdf (accessed 12 August 2020).
[17] Infected Blood Inquiry's Statement of Approach: The Warning Letter Procedure (n 16).
[18] Infected Blood Inquiry's Statement of Approach: The Warning Letter Procedure (n 16).

when making decisions as to the procedure or conduct of the inquiry. An inquiry is therefore already bound by the principles of natural justice and fairness and a well-conducted inquiry will give notice of prospective criticism at various stages in any event.

Quote

Warnings of criticisms can come after the giving of evidence without raising issues of unfairness:

'... the procedure set out in Rule 13 of the 2006 Rules is specifically designed to meet issues such as these. In particular, Rule 13(3)(b) requires me to allow a recipient of the letter a reasonable opportunity to respond. If that response requests the further opportunity to give evidence, or to allow further evidence to be called, I would, in any event, consider such an application with care: my duty of fairness both and common law and under s.17 of the 2005 Act requires no less.'

Lord Justice Leveson, Application of Rule 13 of the Inquiry Rules 2006 in Relation to the Metropolitan Police Service Ruling 4 May 2012[19]

'Even if you did not have them [the Inquiry Rules 2006], the common law would fill in the gaps in any event, in my view. The general requirement that the person who is going to be criticised knows what the basic case against him or her is ordinary common law fairness. It is nothing more, nothing less, than that. These inquiries must be fair, if they are nothing else.'

Mr Justice Jay, in oral evidence to the House of Lords Select Committee on the Inquiries Act 2005

'There is no benefit to warning everyone before the inquiry even starts ... At the beginning it would effectively be saying we will be examining your conduct on [x], without the suggestion that necessarily we are going to criticise you. That is not what is intended by the rules. I believe it would be better later, once all the evidence has been drawn in. Dealing with it piecemeal would be very difficult.'

Sir Robert Francis QC, Chair of the Mid Staffordshire NHS Foundation Trust Public Inquiry

[19] Available at http://webarchive.nationalarchives.gov.uk/20140122203432/http://www.levesoninquiry.org.uk/wp-content/uploads/2011/11/Application-of-Rule-13-of-the-Inquiry-Rules-in-relation-to-the-MPS-4-May-2012.pdf (accessed 12 August 2020).

Whatever the approach taken, if a chair considers it appropriate to send a warning letter in advance of oral evidence being given, it is highly likely that the process will have to be repeated at the conclusion of the oral evidence, for the majority of those witnesses. This is due to the ongoing inquisitorial nature of an inquiry and the fact that, in many cases, criticisms may be made after an individual has given evidence (see above).

The key issue is that a witness properly treated will know of adverse evidence and potential criticism when signing a witness statement. The witness may be questioned on it again in public hearings. What purpose does it therefore serve to repeat the criticism a third time under Rule 13, other than to waste time and money?

An alternative approach an inquiry may adopt is to use counsel to deliver the inquiry's final submissions (usually delivered in both oral and written form), drawing together all potential criticisms, effectively as the 'warning letter' and to then regard the participants' or witnesses' final submissions as the response to that 'warning letter'.

To Whom Will the Warning Letter be Sent?

Rule 13 provides that a warning letter must be sent to 'any person' who is the subject of the criticism, or about whom criticism may be inferred from evidence. This is straight forward in the case of an individual, but less so in the case of an organisation, government department or other body.

'Person' is not defined in the Inquiry Rules 2006, nor the Inquiries Act 2005. In circumstances where a word is not defined, s 5 of the Interpretation Act 1978 provides that 'In any Act, unless the contrary intention appears, words and expressions listed in Schedule 1 to this Act are to be construed according to that Schedule'. Schedule 1 to the 1978 Act provides that '"Person" includes a body of persons corporate or unincorporate'. Therefore, the provisions of r 13 apply to government departments and other bodies, both corporate or non-corporate, as well as to an individual.

Where criticisms are made about organisations, government departments or other bodies, an inquiry must determine to whom the letter should be addressed. For example, should it be to the chief executive or the chair or, in the case of the Government, the relevant minister or the Permanent Secretary, as the most senior civil servant? It may be that a particular criticism is aimed at the organisation itself, acting through its board or its executive, or an individual who was acting on behalf of the organisation, or both. Determining these issues can be a painstaking and time consuming process. It is not always as straightforward as asking for guidance from the relevant body or organisation itself since, by doing so, the inquiry might breach the confidentiality obligations under r 14 (see below).

Identifying who is being criticised sounds an easy and quick task, but rarely is in practice. Where there is some ambiguity as to whether a criticism is aimed at the actions of a particular individual or at the relevant organisation, it is likely that the inquiry will send a warning letter to both parties. The letter may, for example, explain that although the criticism is not, on the face of it, directed at the recipient, it may potentially be interpreted as criticism of the recipient and so notification is being given. Thus a criticism directed at a decision of an organisation may be sent to the executive, or the whole board, or both.

Similarly, where it is unclear who within an organisation or body should be the recipient of the letter, in the first instance the letter is likely to be sent to the most senior individual within that organisation or body. The letter should explain that, if the recipient considers that the letter would be more appropriately addressed to someone else, they should notify the inquiry, which will redirect the letter. A recipient must not redirect a warning letter, due to the obligations of confidentiality under r 14 of the Inquiry Rules 2006.

Any letter sent should remind the recipient that they are bound by an obligation of confidentiality.

What does a Warning Letter Contain?

Rule 15 of the Inquiry Rules 2006 requires an inquiry to:

- state what the criticism or proposed criticism is;
- state the facts the chair considers substantiate the criticism or proposed criticism; and
- refer to any evidence that supports those facts.

The nature and the level of detail of the information provided can vary. An inquiry may provide a summary of the criticism, facts and evidence, or may choose to provide an extract from the draft report containing the proposed criticism. Providing extracts from the draft report can, however, create contextual difficulties, which may in turn create unfairness issues and the potential for challenge by judicial review. An inquiry must therefore decide if it also needs to provide additional extracts, or detail, to give the necessary context. If so, care must be taken not to prematurely reveal criticisms of others, in breach of the confidentiality requirements under r 14.

Recipients of warning letters may well ask an inquiry to confirm whether their response to the proposed criticism has been accepted and whether the draft report will be changed as a result. This is dealt with further below but, in general terms, an inquiry must consider the fairness of its chosen approach to the warning letter process and its various stages, within the context of practical time constraints. The priority is to find a process that is fair, while being proportionate and appropriate to the inquiry's particular subject matter and circumstances.

Quote

In his evidence to the House of Lords Select Committee on the Inquiries Act, Sir Brian Leveson, chair of the Leveson Inquiry into the role of the press and police in the phone-hacking scandal, described the rule 13 warning letter process as being far too prescriptive. Instead he provided participants with generic commentary, gave them the opportunity to respond and, if they wished to say something new, they were encouraged to do so by setting the information out in a witness statement:

'if I had obeyed it to the letter, [it] would have killed any prospect of doing the report in time' ...

Rule 13 is the opportunity to give witnesses the chance to respond to possible criticisms and that is absolutely critical as a matter of pure fairness. I think it is rule 15 that required me to set out the potential criticism, the facts forming the basis of the criticism, and all the evidence. Had I done that in terms, I need never have finished because they were all very specific. I decided that I wanted to approach it in a different way [by providing generic commentary in warning letters, rather than the full criticism] and I invited submissions on that different way. I gave a ruling as to how I would proceed deliberately before I did the work so that, if anybody wanted to challenge it, they could go to the Divisional Court and challenge it. Nobody did.'[20]

'I do not believe that one should be sending letters that set out in minute detail all that you are about to write. As long as you make the person aware, in general terms, of the nature of the criticism that will be made, in my view that is sufficient.'

Lord Gill, Chair of the ICL inquiry[21]

Mandatory Warning Letters: What is an 'Explicit or Significant Criticism'?

Rule 13(3) of the Inquiry Rules 2006 is clear that any explicit or significant criticism must not be contained in the report, or any interim report, if a warning letter has not been sent. This is the point at which sending a warning letter becomes mandatory. So when is a criticism 'significant or explicit'?

[20] Oral evidence taken before the HL Select Committee (9 October 2013) Q93 'Select Committee on the Inquiries Act 2005: Written and Corrected Oral Evidence', available at https://www.parliament.uk/documents/lords-committees/Inquiries-Act-2005/IA_Written_Oral_evidencevol.pdf (accessed 12 August 2020).

[21] Oral evidence taken before the HL Select Committee (n 20) (30 October 2013) QQ190–201.

The phrase 'explicit or significant' criticism is not defined in the Rules. Jason Beer QC suggests that:

> It is to be expected, however, given the purpose of the warning letter regime, that those words will be given a broad definition and it is suggested that an inquiry should interpret the provision as requiring it to send a warning letter to anyone who might be identified as being associated, either positively or by implication, with any criticism being made by an inquiry in its report.[22]

Determining whether wording amounts to criticism and, if so, if it is 'explicit and significant', can be very subjective and difficult to assess. While an inquiry may consider the drafting of a report to be anodyne, individuals who are the subject matter of the material may feel quite differently, particularly given their reputation could be at stake.

In order to obtain a balanced view, an inquiry will often ask a number of members of the inquiry team to review the material to determine whether there is an 'explicit or significant' criticism of a person in the report, applying a low threshold to 'explicit or substantial', on the basis that a combination of views should lead to a more balanced and fair approach. This might reduce the potential for future challenges.

Alternatively, an inquiry may choose to err on the side of caution by sending a warning letter to every subject of a potential criticism in the report or interim report, regardless of whether the criticism is explicit or significant. This may prevent potential future judicial review challenges, but it can become a huge and costly undertaking for an inquiry.

What Happens after a Response is made to a Warning Letter?

Where an inquiry wishes to include any explicit or significant criticism of a person in the inquiry report, or in any interim report, in addition to requiring a warning letter to be sent, r 13(3) also states that the recipient of that letter must be given a 'reasonable opportunity to respond to the warning letter'.

That means the recipient can challenge the proposed criticisms in a response to the inquiry. Although the 2006 Rules do not expressly provide for this, statutory[23] and common law rules of fairness require an inquiry to take into account any response received and consider if the draft criticisms should be altered. The reality is that the recipient will already have responded in their written and oral evidence. There is, however, no obligation on the inquiry to reply to the responses received nor provide the recipient with a further draft of the report.

[22] Jason Beer and others, *Public Inquiries* (OUP 2011), para 9.37.
[23] Inquiries Act 2005, s 17.

Where recipients of a warning letter have sent a response, inquiries have adopted different approaches. Most inquiries have simply acknowledged receipt and have not engaged in any further correspondence or debate. This avoids an ongoing debate, usually fruitless, on the appropriateness of the criticism. Some inquiries have, however, engaged in correspondence with recipients of warning letters about whether their response or additional evidence has been accepted and if or how the criticism will be amended. This is sometimes termed the 're-Maxwellisation process'. Such a process is not required under the statutory and common law rules of fairness.

An issue does arise where information provided by the recipient significantly alters the nature of the criticism made and it results in an amendment to a draft report, giving rise to a different criticism. For reasons of fairness, the inquiry should respond to the recipient of the warning letter, notify them of the new criticism, and give them an opportunity to respond to the new criticism only.

Issue – Responding too much or too little?

An inquiry may choose to send a reply to a recipient of a warning letter, where the recipient responded to the warning letter by providing further information that altered the inquiry's view on the nature or emphasis of the criticism. An inquiry may also choose to send the recipient further iterations of relevant extracts from the draft report. However, in doing so, the inquiry could find itself drawn into a seemingly never-ending process of protracted correspondence, with the recipient repeatedly providing further information, or making submissions, in an attempt to alter the criticism made.

During some past inquiries, recipients of warning letters who provided a response, but did not receive a reply or a further iteration of the relevant extract from the draft report despite their request for one, threatened either to apply for judicial review of the inquiry's decision or to apply to injunct publication of the report.

In practice, no such application has yet been made, and the merits of such an application are doubtful; however, such threats can disrupt an inquiry's work. Inquiries will consider the potential for a challenge carefully before deciding how, or if, to respond to a response to a warning letter.

In reality, if the recipient has dealt with the criticism in written and oral evidence, further (usually repetitive) responses at the eleventh hour will be very unlikely to change the chair's, or inquiry panel's, view of the criticism.

This is hugely problematic, and impractical, and is at the heart of the frustration with the regime prescribed by the rules.

Confidentiality

There are strict confidentiality requirements associated with the warning letters process.

Rule 14 of the Inquiry Rules 2006 states that the contents of a warning letter are to be treated as subject to an obligation of confidence owed:

(a) separately by each member of the inquiry team to the recipient of the warning letter;
(b) by the recipient to the chair; and
(c) by the recipient's recognised legal representative to the chair (where the recipient has disclosed the letter to their legal representative).

Any breach of the obligation is actionable at the suit of the person to whom the obligation is owed. The 2006 Rules allow the obligation of confidence to be waived, in writing, at any time by either the chair or the recipient of the warning letter. The inquiry's obligation of confidence comes to an end when the report is finalised and signed, and the obligations of all other persons come to an end once the report is published.[24]

Confidentiality

Confidentiality and the recipient of a warning letter

The recipient may:

- Show the warning letter to their recognised legal adviser[25] and discuss its contents with them
- Seek a waiver of confidentiality from the inquiry. Any request for a waiver should be limited only to those who need to see a copy, rather than a blanket waiver, for example any other individuals within an organisation from whom assistance may be needed to respond to the warning letter.

Unless the obligation of confidence has been waived, the recipient must *not*:

- Show the letter to other witnesses, participants nor their recognised legal advisers, including those also in receipt of a warning letter or those within the same organisation. For example, if criticisms are made

[24] Inquiry Rules 2006, rr 14(2)–14(4).
[25] Recognised legal adviser as defined in the Inquiry Rules 2006, r 6.

of a corporate entity, and each board member of that entity receives their own, identical criticism letter, they are still not entitled to share the fact they have received the letter, the detail within it or discuss a proper response to it, with any other board member, unless the inquiry agrees to waive confidentiality.

- Disclose the warning letter or its content publicly.
- Disclose the content of a warning letter during submissions.
- Inadvertently refer to the fact that they have received a warning letter in other documentation or correspondence.

Confidentiality and the inquiry team

The inquiry team may:

- Discuss the warning letter, or acknowledge its existence, with the recipient only.

Unless the obligation of confidence has been waived, the inquiry team must *not*:

- Disclose a warning letter to another witness, participant or legal representative or acknowledge its existence.
- Publish a warning letter or its content on its website or elsewhere.
- Disclose the content of a warning letter when questioning witnesses or in submissions.
- Inadvertently refer to the fact that warning letters have been sent to certain individuals in other documentation or correspondence.

The Practical Steps to Preserve Confidentiality

Applying the confidentiality provisions in practice is logistically very challenging. Where a recipient of a letter wants to disclose their letter to other parties, for example to help in formulating a response, waivers of the obligation of confidence must be obtained. This requires consent from the chair of the inquiry for each individual waiver. A meticulous audit trail must be kept by the inquiry of each waiver granted and a list of all individuals who have seen a copy of the warning letter or letters and have permission to do so.

Prior to granting the waiver, an inquiry is likely to ask for a signed confidentiality undertaking from each person who will have sight of a warning letter, confirming they understand the duty of confidence that they owe to the chair. If the inquiry needs to send a large number of warning letters, this can be a huge administrative burden.

During the Magnox Inquiry, although a non-statutory inquiry, the chair, Steven Holliday, adopted similar procedures to those under r 14, concerning the confidentiality of draft extracts of the report containing proposed criticisms. Requests for waivers of confidentiality were then refused by the inquiry, leading to an application for permission to apply for judicial review.[26]

One of the grounds of challenge was based on the refusal to permit the sharing of extracts from the inquiry's draft report, to enable board members to submit representations in response, where they were the subject of the same, similar, or overlapping potential criticisms, particularly when represented by the same legal team. Another ground was that the chair had failed to disclose material that might undermine criticisms made of them or support their defence. The court refused permission to apply for judicial review on both grounds, stating:

- The requirement that each recipient maintain the confidentiality of material disclosed to them and their representatives during the warning letter process is entirely conventional and lawful and is consistent with the statutory rules for public inquiries.
- The need for confidentiality is particularly important given the sensitivity of the material, including material that is subject to legal privilege, and the need to protect against premature unauthorised disclosure of the substance of the draft report.
- The chair had indicated that he was willing to entertain reasoned requests to share any material between the claimants, on a case-by-case basis, even if that did create practical difficulties for the claimants and those representing them.

This case serves to highlight to real practical difficulties stemming from r 14, for those in receipt of warning letters, those representing them, and inquiries.

Issue – Confidentiality and responses to warning letters

The obligation of confidence applies to warning letters because the inquiry may ultimately decide not to include the criticism referred to in the warning letter in the final report.

An inquiry may, however, find itself in a position where it is considering material submitted in response to a warning letter, which is unpublished because of the obligation of confidence. As a result, no one else has had an opportunity to comment on that material, or examine or investigate it further. If the inquiry wants to rely on this material, it must first be

[26] *John Clarke and others v Chairman of the Magnox Inquiry and Secretary of State for BEIS and others* [2019] EWHC 3596 (Admin).

published. However, great care has to be taken when doing so, to ensure that this will not reveal, or suggest, who has received the warning letter, thereby breaching the obligations of confidence.

A further complication may arise where a recipient of a warning letter responds by blaming others. If, as a result, new criticism of others is added to the inquiry report, the inquiry must then send a warning letter to those who are now also criticised in the report. However, the inquiry cannot tell them how it came to learn of that information and must be very careful about how this is communicated, because of the obligations of confidence to other recipients of warning letters.

Quote

'The real problems however are the issues of confidentiality. I do not see why it all has to be done behind closed doors. It is after all a public inquiry.'

Sir Robert Francis QC, Chair of the Mid Staffordshire NHS Foundation Trust Public Inquiry

Future of Rule 13?

Given that a public inquiry's proceedings are just that, public, there is an argument that the confidentiality provisions are superfluous. Witnesses will be aware, from the evidence heard and published by the inquiry to date, and from the process of giving a statement to the inquiry legal team (if the inquiry team takes statements rather than witnesses preparing statements themselves), of the likely criticisms that they may face. In practice, responses to warning letters rarely bring anything new to bear.

The Independent Jersey Care Inquiry,[27] an inquiry not subject to the Inquiry Rules 2006, took a different approach, as set out in its protocols:

> Individuals, institutions, organisations and/or other bodies may be subject to criticism in the Inquiry's final report, or any interim reports, arising out of evidence that the Inquiry has heard. The Inquiry does not intend to give any forewarning to the subject of such criticisms prior to the publication of any report unless it would be unfair not to do so in the judgment of the Inquiry.[28]

[27] A public inquiry conducted in Jersey into historical institutional child abuse.

[28] Available at www.jerseycareinquiry.org/Key%20Documents/Final_Inquiry_Protocol_Protective_Measures.pdf (accessed 12 August 2020).

This allowed that inquiry to deal with criticisms in written and oral evidence, negating the need for a 'rule 13' style procedure thereafter, unless a new issue or piece of evidence had arisen.

The 2014 post-legislative report prepared by the House of Lords Select Committee on the Inquiries Act, recommended that rr 13 to 15 should be revoked and replaced with a more flexible arrangement.[29] The proposed amendment to the 2006 Rules envisaged the chair being given the discretion to decide whether to send a warning letter at all.

The recommended re-draft was:

> If the chair is considering including in the report significant criticism of a person, and he believes that that person should have an opportunity to make a submission or further submission, he should send that person a warning letter and give him a reasonable opportunity to respond.[30]

Despite the weight of evidence from those highly experienced in inquiry work who spoke about the practical difficulties and additional expense created by the existing rules, and the lack of any legal basis to require such rigid rules, in June 2014, the Government published a response to the post-legislative report and rejected the recommendation stating:

> The Government rejects this recommendation because rule 13 encapsulates what was the practice of most pre-2005 Act inquiries (and is still the practice of many non-statutory investigations) in (i) sending a 'Salmon letter' giving notice of potential criticism to a person before he or she is called to give evidence, and (ii) giving a participant who is to be criticised in an interim or final report the opportunity to comment on a proposed criticism before publication. The power to send a warning letter contained in rule 13(1) is discretionary, although in the Treasury Solicitor's Department's experience is almost universally adopted by inquiry chairs; only the requirement to give an opportunity to respond to criticism contained in rule 13(3) is mandatory. The Treasury Solicitor's Department has advised that the drafting of rule 13 is not defective.[31]

The government's response was badly received, as was evident from the House of Lords debate on the Select Committee Report, which took place on 19 March 2015.[32] During the debate, the Select Committee's proposed amendment was supported. It was pointed out that there is no comparable warning letter procedure in a court of law and the rules of natural justice do not require such a procedure in a public inquiry, particularly as a public inquiry does not have the power to impose any criminal or civil liability.[33]

[29] HL Select Committee, The Inquiries Act 2005: Post-legislative Scrutiny (HL 2013–2014 143) recommendation 25.

[30] HL Select Committee, The Inquiries Act 2005: Post-legislative Scrutiny (n 29) para 251.

[31] Ministry of Justice, *Government Response to the Report of the House of Lords Select Committee on the Inquiries Act 2005* (Cm 8093 2014) paras 78–80.

[32] HL Deb 19 March 2015, vol 760, cols 1134–1179.

[33] HL Deb 19 March 2015, vol 760, cols 1142 and 1153.

Quote

'... even in a court of law, once a fair hearing has been given to the witnesses, the rules of natural justice do not require the judge to present a draft judgment on which the parties are then entitled to comment before the judge hands down the final decision. If that is right in a court of law, it is all the more so when we are talking about the report of an inquiry – which, however important, imposes no criminal or civil liability on anyone.'

Lord Pannick QC, House of Lords Debate 19 March 2015[34]

'In short, the Government's bland rejection of this recommendation is surely to be regarded as deeply unsatisfactory and indeed somewhat disingenuous. Nothing could be more obviously calculated to result in future inquiries needlessly suffering the same problems of delay and expense. I say "needlessly" because the rule proposed to substitute for Rules 13 to 15 would provide the flexibility required to enable chairmen in future to ensure fairness in the particular circumstances of each case. The recommendation makes obvious good sense and should be accepted and implemented without further delay.'

Lord Brown of Eaton-under-Heywood, House of Lords Debate 19 March 2015[35]

Such was the strength of feeling during the House of Lords debate in March 2015 that subsequently, on 21 July 2015, Caroline Dineage MP,[36] the Minister responsible for the policy area, wrote to Lord Sewel to confirm:

> In light of the strength of argument in the debate on 19 March we accept that the process of Maxwellisation and the related rules should be reconsidered to see whether greater clarity can be given to both chairmen and those who may be criticised in inquiry reports. Rules 13 to 15 will therefore be reviewed as we take forward work to amend the Inquiry Rules 2006 ... The changes to the Rules are in hand and other recommendations that require primary legislation will be made when a suitable legislative vehicle becomes available.[37]

Subsequently, in 2016, the Treasury Committee commissioned a review of 'Maxwellisation'[38] which included a review of both non-statutory and statutory

[34] HL Deb 19 March 2015, vol 760, col 1153.

[35] HL Deb 19 March 2015, vol 760, cols 1158 and 1159.

[36] Then Parliamentary Under Secretary of State for Women, Equalities and Family Justice.

[37] Available at https://www.parliament.uk/documents/lords-committees/liaison/Inquiries-Act-2005-Committee-follow-up.pdf.

[38] By Andrew Green QC, Tony Peto QC, Pushpinder Saini QC, Fraser Campbell and Ajay Ratan.

inquiry warning letter processes.[39] Its principal conclusions included a call for inquiries to adopt a narrower approach, including the following:

> We endorse the recommendation of the House of Lords Select Committee on the Inquiries Act 2005 that Rules 13 to 15 should be revoked. The Government initially rejected this recommendation, but then agreed (in July 2015) to reconsider the position. It does not appear yet to have done so. It should now do so, and it should revoke Rules 13 to 15.

At the time of writing, the government has yet to confirm that it has reconsidered its position and no legislative changes are currently tabled. Therefore, for the time being, the challenges around implementing the requirements of rr 13 to 15 remain.

[39] While the review had a particular focus on public inquiries of a financial nature, it addressed public inquiries generally.

14

Preparing and Publishing the Report

Introduction

Once all of the evidence has been collated, the oral hearings concluded and any seminars conducted, the inquiry chair is then responsible for preparing and delivering the inquiry's report to the minister who convened the inquiry. Where a panel is appointed, panel members will be consulted and are likely to play a key role in assisting the chair in producing the report.

What is Included in the Report?

Requirements

For statutory inquiries, s 24 of the Inquiries Act 2005 requires the report to set out:

(a) the facts determined by the inquiry;
(b) the recommendations of the inquiry (where the terms of reference required the inquiry to make recommendations).

Section 24 states that the report may also contain anything else that the panel considers to be relevant to the terms of reference (including any recommendations the panel sees fit to make despite not being required to do so by the terms of reference).

For non-statutory inquiries, there are no specific requirements for the content of the inquiry report; this will be at the discretion of the chair and any panel members. In practice, for past non-statutory inquiries, the reports have generally been drawn up along similar lines to those set out above for statutory inquiries.

Content

- The report must address the matters set out in the terms of reference and must not go beyond the terms of reference.

- Provided the inquiry's terms of reference have been addressed, the chair may prepare the report as they see fit. The format, content and style of both non-statutory and statutory inquiry reports are completely at the discretion of the chair. Where a report is produced by a number of individuals (eg a chair and panel members), it is important that the style is consistent throughout.
- The report should use clear, simple and jargon-free language, with any technical terms used being explained. The report is a public document, and should be accessible to all.
- The inquiry may consider splitting up the report in such a way as to make it clear how the terms of reference have been addressed.
- The report must demonstrate how the conclusions reached are supported by evidence and that all the recommendations have a clear evidential basis.
- Inquiry reports are often quite lengthy, so inquiries frequently produce an executive summary, and separate the report into volumes, to make it more user-friendly. Many people reading the report will only read the executive summary and the press will generally report from the information in the executive summary. An inquiry should therefore ensure that all key information is contained in that summary and that there is nothing in the summary that does not appear in the text of the report itself.
- The report may be translated into other languages where appropriate.

Who Writes the Report?

While responsibility for drafting the report and its content ultimately rests with the chair of the inquiry, preparing an inquiry report is a huge task and inevitably chairs of inquiries need assistance from others to complete the task. This assistance may be in the form of, for example, identifying supporting evidence, reviewing draft sections of the report, testing and challenging proposed findings, editing, proof-reading or preparing draft sections of the report for the approval of the chair at the chair's discretion.

Assistance may be provided by:

- Counsel to the inquiry – an experienced drafter with detailed knowledge of the witness evidence and the chair's general approach to the inquiry, as well as having an established working relationship with the chair.
- The solicitor to the inquiry or inquiry legal team – again, experienced drafters with detailed knowledge of the evidence. They also have an additional, objective view to offer, given that they will not have been involved in the questioning of witnesses during the hearings or in preparing the closing submissions.

- The secretary to the inquiry – also with knowledge of the evidence and an additional, objective view, having not been involved in questioning witnesses. Assistance from the secretary to the inquiry in this way, however, is the exception and is not the norm as the role of the secretary to the inquiry usually involves administrative, logistical and contract-management tasks. Further, where the secretary is sourced from the sponsoring department particular care must be taken by the inquiry to avoid any suggestion of influence, or the perception of influence, from the sponsoring department over the content of the report. It is essential that the report is independent, and seen to be independent.
- The inquiry administrative team – for proofing the drafts, formatting and checking document references.
- An editor or copy-editor to ensure consistent style and accuracy of the language of the text.
- Some past inquiries have also used a professional scriptwriter, for example the Bichard Inquiry.[1] The Bloody Sunday Inquiry also enlisted the help of a professional historian.

However it is approached, an inquiry must find a way to communicate the findings of the inquiry and its recommendations clearly and effectively to the minister, Parliament, participants, the public and the media, or much of the value of the public inquiry is lost.

Reviews and Checks

- There will be a full scale and thorough review of the final draft of the report, prior to publication, to identify any personal data or protected information that must be redacted.
- An audit trail of all reviews and checks undertaken by the inquiry team will be kept. This will serve as evidence that all reasonable steps were taken to protect information and ensure accuracy, should any issues arises in the future.
- Numerous checks will also be undertaken for any typographical and grammatical errors, and to ensure that all references to evidence are accurate.
- The final report should also be checked to ensure that no criticisms are made that have escaped the Maxwellisation process (see chapter thirteen).

[1] Inquiry Into the Events Surrounding the Murders of Holly Wells and Jessica Chapman in Soham, Cambridgeshire, in 2001.

Issue – Approaches to writing

Chairs of past inquiries have tackled the task of writing the report in a variety of ways:

- Leveson Inquiry – under the chair's oversight and direction, junior barristers wrote the first drafts of specific parts of the report. Counsel to the inquiry then assisted with the drafting and the chair finalised and approved the final version. The report was 1,987 pages long, with four volumes and 92 recommendations.
- Bichard Inquiry – counsel to the inquiry wrote the first drafts of the report, which was finalised by the chair. The final draft was then refined by a scriptwriter. The report was 189 pages long, with one volume and 31 recommendations.
- Mid Staffordshire Inquiry – the chair took control of drafting the report, with editing assistance from the inquiry team. The report was 1,781 pages long, with three volumes and 290 recommendations.
- Independent Jersey Care Inquiry – the chair and panel members drafted the report, with assistance from counsel to the inquiry in fact checking and testing the findings, and proof reading from the solicitor's team. The report was 1,321 pages long, with eight recommendations.
- Some chairs of inquiries have prepared sections of the report during the course of the inquiry's work; others have prepared notes but have not started to draft the report until the conclusion of all evidence.

Quote

'I also felt, as has been said, that a report written by a committee is a rather different animal from one that an individual chairman, for better or for worse, takes responsibility for. You can disagree with the report of a chairman and you can disagree with the report of a committee, but what you know about the report of a committee is that it is more likely to be a compromise, for obvious reasons. I think there are disadvantages with that.'

Sir Robert Francis QC, Chair of the Mid Staffordshire NHS Foundation Trust Public Inquiry, in evidence to the House of Lords Select Committee on the Inquiries Act 2005[2]

[2] Oral evidence of Sir Robert Francis QC taken before the Lords Select Committee on the Inquiries Act 2005 (30 October 2013) Q210, www.parliament.uk/documents/lords-committees/Inquiries-Act-2005/IA_Written_Oral_evidencevol.pdf (accessed 12 August 2020).

> *'The second decision I took, egged on by my team, was that we had to produce this report in language that anyone could understand. It was not just for the professional stakeholders. This was an issue the country was concerned about and therefore I spent an obsessive amount of time rewriting and rewriting this report. Right at the end it was suggested to me, and I thought it was a fantastic idea, that I get a scriptwriter in to take my final draft and rewrite it yet again. So the final report was written by a professional scriptwriter and I think that had a real impact in terms of people being able to read through it.'*
>
> Lord Bichard, chair to the Soham Inquiry, in evidence to the House of Lords Select Committee on the Inquiries Act 2005[3]

Number of Recommendations and Public Understanding

An inquiry must consider carefully how many recommendations it should make; there is a balance to be found. Fewer recommendations makes implementation more achievable. However, there is a risk that restricting the number of recommendations too far may result in a failure to adequately address some of the areas of public concern the inquiry is seeking to address. The best approach will depend both on the subject matter of the inquiry and the scope of the inquiry's terms of reference.

Where recommendations are wide-ranging and extensive, to facilitate implementation an inquiry will often group the recommendations into themes, or by organisation, to ensure it is clear at whom each recommendation is targeted (see section below on implementation).

Of key importance is ensuring that the minister, Parliament, participants, the public, and those affected understand the findings and recommendations in the report when it is published. The challenge is how best to achieve that. Approaches have differed between inquiries.

Lord Bichard who chaired the non-statutory inquiry into the Soham murders decided that in order to produce a report with impact, the number of recommendations would be limited to 30, with five key recommendations. He also employed a scriptwriter to refine the final draft of the report, to maximise its readability and impact.[4]

[3] Oral evidence of Lord Bichard, taken before the Lords Select Committee on the Inquiries Act 2005 (30 October 2013) (n 2) Q222.

[4] As explained by Lord Bichard in evidence given to the House of Lords Select Committee on the Inquiries Act 2005 (30 October 2013).

The Mid Staffordshire NHS Trust Inquiry, by way of contrast, was criticised for producing a report that was 1,790 pages long and contained 290 recommendations (although it had a very wide remit). In reality, very few members of the public are likely to have read the report in full. To assist in addressing the wide remit of the inquiry, and to help embed some of the recommendations, after the conclusion of the inquiry, members of the inquiry team, including the chair, solicitor and counsel to the inquiry as well as the inquiry's assessors, were invited to speak at numerous conferences and spent significant amounts of time with the health service and stakeholders to promote understanding of the conclusions of the report and its recommendations.

The approach in recent years to recommendations has, however, continued to vary between inquiries.[5]

Inquiry	Year of publication of report	Number of recommendations
Leveson Inquiry (statutory)	2012	92
The Detainee Inquiry (non-statutory)	2013	0
Azelle Rodney Inquiry (statutory)	2013	3
Al-Sweady Inquiry (statutory)	2014	9
The Morecambe Bay Investigation (non-statutory)	2015	44
The Harris Review (non-statutory)	2015	108
Litvinenko Inquiry (statutory)	2016	1
Iraq Inquiry (non-statutory)	2016	0

The approach taken is largely influenced by the chair's own preference and the width and purpose of the inquiry's terms of reference. As shown above, some inquiries do not make any recommendations if this does not form part of their remit.

In formulating the recommendations, however, inquiry chair and panels will often seek expert assistance to ensure that the recommendations they propose are workable, realistic and practical. Inquiry chairs are often not experts in the subject matter of the inquiry (see chapter two on the appointment of the chair) and therefore this additional support can be necessary. They may do this by appointing assessors, specifically with a view to 'sense checking' the practicality of the recommendations to be made.

[5] National Audit Office, '*Investigation into government-funded inquiries*' (2018) HC 836 Session 2017–2019.

Quote

'To develop robust, implementable recommendations, expertise on the issues at hand is needed – for instance, specialist knowledge of the intricacies of child heart surgery, or of fire safety during building construction, or an understanding of the information-sharing practices of different public services. Additionally, knowledge of how to construct policy recommendations in a form that is likely to have traction in government is an aid to effectiveness. It is not realistic to expect inquiry chairs to possess all these skills or knowledge. Therefore, inquiries should adopt a seminar process to involve expert witnesses when developing recommendations, as happened, for example, during the Bristol Royal Infirmary Inquiry and the Mid Staffordshire NHS Foundation Trust Inquiry.'

Institute for Government report *'How public inquiries can lead to change'* dated December 2017

Publication, Withholding of Information and Laying before Parliament

Responsibility for Publication

Once the report has been drafted and warning letters sent to those who may be criticised,[6] the report is then finalised and the concluding stage of the inquiry's work is to publish the report.

For non-statutory inquiries, the process by which a report is published (eg who is responsible for publishing the report, and how much, if any, material might be withheld; will any parties will be given advance access to the report; how will any 'lock-in'[7] period be managed) is that which the chair sees fit, or which is agreed between the chair and the sponsoring department.[8] For statutory inquiries, s 25 of the 2005 Act sets out who is responsible for publishing the report and when material within the report may be withheld from publication. The Act provides that the minister is responsible for publishing the report; however, the minister can delegate this responsibility to the chair and this often happens in practice. In most cases, the inquiry will be informed well in advance (often at the time that the terms of reference are framed or within the terms of reference themselves) if the minister is delegating the responsibility for publishing the report to the chair.

[6] See chapter eleven.

[7] The process by which certain specific categories of persons are provided with an opportunity for pre-publication access to the report, see below.

[8] If it is a government-commissioned non-statutory inquiry.

Withholding of Information

The party responsible for arranging publication of the report is under a duty to publish the inquiry report in full. However, that duty is subject to the provisions in s 25(4), which state that the party arranging publication may withhold material in the report from publication to such extent as is required by any statutory provision or rule of law, or as they consider to be necessary in the public interest, having regard to the factors listed in s 25(5) and (6). Those factors include the allaying of public concern, any risk of harm or damage that could be avoided or reduced, and issues of confidentiality.

In practice, where information is withheld from publication in an inquiry report, it is usually as a result of data protection obligations, with such information being redacted. There are, however, some examples of information being withheld on the grounds of public interest. For example, the inquiry report of the Litvinenko Inquiry, a 2005 Act statutory inquiry, included a section on the analysis and conclusions arising from evidence heard during the inquiry's closed hearings, and contained the inquiry's single recommendation. That part of the report was not published as it concerned the closed evidence, the publication of which was prohibited by restriction notices made by the then Home Secretary, Theresa May, in relation to specific sensitive material information, on the grounds of public interest immunity.

Laying before Parliament

Whoever is responsible for publishing the report, whether this is the minister or the chair, they must also lay the report before Parliament at the time of publication or as soon afterwards as is reasonably practicable.[9]

Where the minister is responsible for publishing the report, the parliamentary clerk within the sponsoring department will be responsible for liaising with the Parliamentary authorities to arrange the laying of the report before both Houses.

As explained above, it is generally more common, however, for the chair of an inquiry to be delegated the responsibility of publishing the report and laying the report before Parliament. The inquiry secretary, or another member of the inquiry team, will often oversee the arrangements for laying the report before Parliament.

[9] Inquiries Act 2005, s 25(6).

Procedure for Publication of the Report

A suggested procedure for publication is as follows:

- Once finalised and signed off by the chair (and panel if appointed), the report is forwarded to the printers for printing and binding
- Only a relatively small print run of bound copies is made (enough to be provided to all core participants and interested parties), as most people access inquiry reports electronically on the inquiry's website
- The inquiry will make arrangements for advanced access to the report for limited categories of persons, via a lock-in procedure prior to publication (see further detail below)
- An advanced copy of the report will be provided to the minister (r 17 of the Inquiry Rules 2006)
- The lock-in procedure takes place. Advanced copies of the report are provided to certain individuals (see section below on advance access to the report), including core participants and their recognised legal representatives (r 17 of the Inquiry Rules 2006)
- The report is formally published on the inquiry's website. The chair makes a public statement, and delivers a prepared written statement, to broadcast the key findings of the report. The chair may also decide to give further press interviews
- Where the report is to be laid before Parliament, there is a long-standing precedent whereby the prime minister allows leaders of the main opposition parties access to the report prior to any statement in the House
- The sponsoring minister will make a statement to the House and will usually respond publicly to the content of the report shortly after publication

Advance Access to the Report and the Lock-in Procedure

For statutory inquiries, under r 17 of the Inquiry Rules 2006, the inquiry chair is required to provide advance copies of the report (or any interim report) to the minister, core participants and their legal advisers, subject to confidentiality obligations. The chair of statutory inquiries may also choose to grant access to a number of other specific categories of persons, for example recipients of warning letters or representatives of the media (see below). Non-statutory inquiries may decide to adopt a similar approach.

Where advance access to an inquiry report is to be provided to recipients of warning letters, care must be taken by the inquiry to ensure that these individuals are not identified during this process. Under r 14 of the Inquiry Rules 2006, each member of the inquiry team, and the chair, is under an obligation of confidence in respect of the content of a warning letter, which arguably includes the identity of the recipient of the warning letter (inquiries have adopted this interpretation in the past). This obligation of confidence continues until the report has been published or the obligation is waived by the recipient. The procedures for publishing the report should therefore take this into account.

In reality, advance access to an inquiry report, or interim report, is usually only a matter of hours. Each recipient of advance copies must treat the content of the report as confidential until the report has been published. An inquiry may choose to administer this process by requiring each recipient of an advance copy of the report to sign a separate confidentiality undertaking. A breach of this obligation may result in a claim being brought against the recipient by the chair of the inquiry for breach of confidence. No one granted advance access to the inquiry report will have any opportunity to influence or edit the content of the report prior to publication.

The Lock-in

The process by which certain specific categories of persons are provided with an opportunity for pre-publication access to the report is known as a 'lock-in'. During a 'lock-in', those persons who choose to attend are required to attend at a specified venue, shortly before publication of the report, to view the report in private. Past inquiries have managed this in a variety of ways. Set out below is a list of issues an inquiry will consider when organising the lock-in process.

Checklist – Managing the lock-in

- The venue for the lock-in might be the inquiry's premises or, alternatively, a neutral venue. Often inquiries use conference centres or other buildings with similar facilities. The venue must have sufficient space for all the parties, and sufficient security.

- Depending on the subject matter and nature of the inquiry, the inquiry will decide whether all participants should be in the same room or separate rooms. If the latter, the inquiry will decide how participants would be best grouped.
- Invitations will be sent to those who will be granted advance access, ie the core participants and their legal representative,[10] as well as any other additional specific categories of persons that may be identified by the chair (eg selected members of the media and recipients of warning letters). In the case of the latter, the chair will decide whether or not the advance access granted to those additional categories will be on the same or on different terms to that granted to the core participants and their legal advisers, for example whether some categories will be granted a longer period of pre-publication access than others.
- Where a core participant is an organisation, the inquiry may impose a limit on the number of representatives who may attend. Similarly, an inquiry may impose a limit on the number of core participants' legal representatives who may attend. On occasions, limits on numbers may be relaxed for specific categories of participants, for example victims and families.
- The invitation to attend the lock-in should include a requirement to RSVP and to provide a signed undertaking in advance which confirms that the invitee will adhere to the rules of the lock-in and undertake to keep the content of the report confidential until the time of publication (see below).
- There will be rigorous checks in place on the day of the lock-in. These may include checking individuals' names off the invite and acceptance list, asking for proof of identification and escorting people to specific rooms. On arrival, there should be someone available to explain the procedure for the lock-in.
- The venue will have security at the entrance, as well as security for the copies of the report.
- Many past inquiries have adopted a staggered approach to timings for advance access. For example, core participants may be given only three hours' advance access and warning letter recipients who are not core participants and the media may be given only two hours' advance access. The justification for the difference between the two is often that core participants and interested parties are likely to be most impacted

[10] Inquiry Rules 2006, r 17(1).

by the report, and therefore should be provided with a longer period to digest the key findings and recommendations, before they are made more widely available.

- If recipients of warning letters are to be allowed advance access to the report, the inquiry must take steps to ensure that those recipients cannot be identified as a result, because the chair's obligation of confidence[11] continues until the point the report is published. Past inquiries have achieved this, for example, by locating these individuals in a private room and giving them access to the building via a different entrance to the other attendees and by not publishing the fact that recipients of warning letters will be at the lock-in, so that they cannot be easily identified.
- Inquiries may put a variety of security precautions in place during the lock-in. Some inquiries will require participants to surrender their mobile phones and other electronic devices on arrival, but others may simply require confirmation that they have been switched off. The inquiry may make arrangements for wifi facilities at the venue to be shut down during the lock-in. Attendees may be required to be escorted during toilet breaks.
- Where advance access is given to the minister and the report is to be laid before Parliament, there is a long-standing precedent that the prime minister will allow leaders of the main opposition parties advance access to the report prior to any statement in the House. The chair of the inquiry may wish to be involved in discussions concerning how and when any advance access to the report should take place, for example requesting that access be given only once the lock-in procedure has begun, so the victim and families are given sight of the report before the politicians.

Issue – Advance copies to the sponsoring minister

In terms of timing, the sponsoring minister often seeks several days or a week's advance sight of the report, to allow time to digest the content of the report (which is likely to be lengthy) and to prepare a public response. The sponsoring minister is also likely to ask for the copy to be shared with senior personnel in the sponsoring department, or other personnel

[11] Inquiry Rules 2006, r 14.

in the department who have been involved in the team managing the department's response to the inquiry, to assist with this task.

For both statutory and non-statutory inquiries, the chair is obliged to deliver the report to the minister.[12] However, there are no prescribed timings and it is for the chair to decide how much time to allow the minister to consider the report pre-publication. Victims, and other similar groups, may take the view that ministers should not have more time than them to see the report prior to publication, to maintain a level playing field, and to dispel notions that the minister could influence the content at the eleventh hour. The chair will therefore be wary of allowing a lengthy period of time between delivery to the minister and publication, for reasons of perception of independence. It is important for the chair to avoid circumstances that may give rise to any suggestion that the minister has had the opportunity to edit or influence the content of the report.

The chair will also be wary of providing unlimited access to the minister's team, particularly where the sponsoring department is also a core participant to the inquiry and individuals within the sponsoring department have been witnesses to the inquiry, and therefore may be named in the report. Those individuals should be treated in the same way as any other witness to the inquiry.

Understandably, however, the minister may need assistance with assimilating what is likely to be a large report and with preparing a statement in response. The chair may decide that advance copies should be restricted to the relevant minister and those who are essential to helping prepare a statement in response. Again, this is largely an issue of perception, ensuring that the inquiry is seen to be maintaining its integrity and independence.

As discussed above, under s 25(4) of the Inquiries Act 2005, the party responsible for publication of the report may withhold evidence from publication where those restrictions are required by law, or are considered necessary in the public interest, having regard to matters such as the extent to which doing so might inhibit the allaying of public concern, would reduce the risk of death or injury, damage to national security, international relations, or the economic interests of the UK. Therefore, depending on the circumstances and subject matter of an inquiry, the minister and the sponsoring department may be anxious to ensure that there is no such material in the report that should be withheld for these reason. (In fact, denying the government an opportunity to do so could be fertile grounds for a judicial review challenge.) However, from the public's point of view, this can give

[12] For statutory inquiries, Inquiries Act 2005, s 24.

rise to a perception that the government is being given an advantage over others, and may lead to concerns that conclusions in the report could be altered, thereby undermining confidence in the inquiry system.

There are however potential solutions to this. For example, during the Billy Wright Inquiry, the Secretary of State for Northern Ireland announced measures to address similar concerns, which included setting up a small team of officials and legal advisers to review the report and identify information that might need to be withheld on the grounds identified in s 25(4). The inquiry retained physical custody of the report whilst the work was being carried out, with the government officials and legal advisers being under strict terms of confidentiality, and members of the inquiry team present throughout the checking process.[13] A similar procedure was adopted for the Bloody Sunday Inquiry report.

Checklist – Security measures

An inquiry will take steps to ensure the security of the advance copies of the report to help reduce the possibility of leaks:

- Possible example wording of an undertaking a recipient of an advance copy of an inquiry report will be asked to sign to maintain the confidence of the report is as follows:

'I [insert name] of [address] acknowledge the access to the [name of report] in advance of publication is confidential and I hereby undertake to [inquiry chair] that in consideration of being provided with a copy of [name of the report] and/or access to a copy of [name of the report] that I will take all necessary steps to preserve that confidentiality. I acknowledge that access is provided to me solely for the purposes of assisting me in the provision of information about the [name of report] after publication and for no other reason.

I undertake to [inquiry chair], not to disclose, publish or pass on to any third party any of the contents or information contained within the [name of report] prior to publication. I understand that the confidentiality of the [name of report] and the contents and information contained within it must be preserved until after publication.'

[13] See HC Deb vol 513, col 3WS, 6 July 2010.

- An inquiry will produce only a limited number of advance copies, and will mark each with an individual number for identification.
- Each individual copy may be marked with a watermark (across the whole page) identifying to whom the copy was disclosed; this may deter individuals from leaking the report as they could be identified as the source of the leak.
- Advance copies are often distributed by hand, with copies only being sent electronically once the report has been made publicly available.

Implementation

Once an inquiry report has been delivered to the relevant minister, and the chair has notified the minister that the inquiry has fulfilled its terms of reference, the inquiry comes to an end.[14]

Public inquiry recommendations are non-binding and unenforceable; a minister is not obliged to accept or act on all, or indeed any, of the recommendations of a public inquiry. Other than potentially facing public criticism, there is no recourse if the government fails to implement recommendations or fails to explain the reasons for non-implementation.

The implementation of an inquiry's recommendations is, however, seen as being key to the perceived effectiveness of an inquiry and to public confidence in the inquiry system. Many chairs of public inquiries have expressed their frustration at failures on the part of government to fully implement their inquiry's recommendations.

Quote

'... the main reason for most inquiries is to find out how we can avoid something like that happening again and what changes to systems, training and procedures would help to avoid that happening. Therefore, I think it is absolutely about action. Once you have made recommendations about action, personally ... I find it very difficult then to just walk away and watch nothing happening.'

Lord Bichard, chair to the Soham Inquiry, in evidence to the House of Lords Select Committee on the Inquiries Act 2005

[14] Inquiries Act 2005, s 14.

The consequences of the lack of implementation of recommendations can be seen quite starkly if one compares the recommendations made by the Bristol Royal Infirmary Inquiry to that of the Mid Staffordshire NHS Foundation Trust Public Inquiry. The Bristol Royal Infirmary Inquiry made a number of recommendations which sought to put patients' needs at the centre of healthcare delivery and make improvements to systems to ensure the safety and quality of care in the NHS. This mirrored the intention behind a large number of the recommendations made by the Mid Staffordshire NHS Foundation Trust Public Inquiry. Arguably, if the recommendations from Bristol had been fully implemented, many of the issues and failures that were identified 10 years later during the Mid Staffordshire NHS Foundation Trust Public Inquiry would not have occurred. The Leveson Inquiry was another notable example of an inquiry's recommendations appearing to fall on deaf ears, or at least with no obvious implementation.

But, beyond exerting public criticism and political pressure, there is currently no recourse for the public if the government fails to implement recommendations or fails to explain its reasons for non-implementation. There is, therefore, a risk that key recommendations will be ignored or pushed aside in the hope that, in time, they will be forgotten. In practice, policies may already have been formed by the time the inquiry has taken place and the inquiry will either endorse what was already intended or its recommendations will simply be shelved if they do not meet the existing policy objectives.[15] It is common for government departments, or other core participants to inquiries, to try and pre-empt the conclusions and recommendations that may be made at the end of an inquiry and make changes and improvements in advance, to try and dilute any criticism for lack of action. In some senses this is a good strategy. It does mean, however, that any changes or improvements made in advance of an inquiry reporting may not address the full extent of the recommendations ultimately made by the inquiry.

Some inquiry chairs feel personal responsibility to ensure that their recommendations are implemented. There have been examples of inquiry chairs who have proactively sought to impose procedures to monitor the implementation of recommendations. The chair of the Mid Staffordshire NHS Foundation Trust Public Inquiry, now Sir Robert Francis QC, made a specific recommendation that organisations should announce the extent to which they intended to implement all relevant recommendations, and should publish their progress against that planned implementation in annual reports. He also invited the House of Commons Select Committee on Health to consider incorporating into its own reviews the performance of those organisations that are accountable to Parliament, measured against those recommendations.

[15] See the oral evidence of Sir Stephen Sedley taken before the Lords Select Committee on the Inquiries Act 2005 (10 July 2013) Q23, www.parliament.uk/documents/lords-committees/Inquiries-Act-2005/IA_Written_Oral_evidencevol.pdf (accessed 12 August 2020).

Lord Bichard, seemingly of his own volition, conducted a review of the recommendations from the Soham Inquiry six months after the conclusion of the inquiry. The inquiry panel on the Independent Jersey Care Inquiry included a recommendation that the panel should return in two years to carry out an independent review and consider the extent to which the inquiry's recommendations had been implemented. The States of Jersey accepted that recommendation, and Jersey's Children's Commissioner invited the inquiry panel back to conduct this independent review. The review took place in June 2019 when a number of key parties gave evidence.

Other chairs have chosen to adjourn their inquiry, rather than formally bringing the inquiry to an end by the chair informing the minister that the inquiry's terms of reference have been fulfilled,[16] to enable them to have an ongoing, authoritative voice on the implementation of recommendations (see below).

Quote

The implementation of an inquiry's recommendations, and a potential power to oversee or monitor their implementation, was an issue explored by the 2013–2014 House of Lords Select Committee on the Inquiries Act 2005. Those giving evidence to the Committee held a variety of views:

'Implementation is, of course, everything, but sometimes it is not possible, when running an inquiry, to micro-manage, in terms of the recommendations, what should happen because there are a number of perfectly legitimate options. Therefore, there has to be executive discretion at some point. That is the sort of thing that can properly be reviewed by the Health Select Committee or whoever else it is in Parliament, and bring to account those who ought to be brought to account for implementation of the spirit of what is there.'

Sir Robert Francis QC, Chair of the Mid Staffordshire NHS Foundation Trust Public Inquiry

'... there ought to be a watching brief. We can disagree whether that should be vested in the chair or some other constitutional mechanism. I do not think it should necessarily be the chairman whose expertise is there, but things have moved on.'

Professor Sir Ian Kennedy

'... in Azelle Rodney the chairman made recommendations and he has been waiting for a report from the IPCC and the Metropolitan Police Service as to whether they have implemented them. He has had a response back but

[16] See Inquiries Act 2005, s 14.

> *I think, in his view, he felt, suddenly because his position was functus, he could not then write angry letters or say what is happening about my recommendations. So I think if there could be a period after the report has been delivered, for example, three to six months, when people report to him on the status of the implementation of the recommendations, that may help.'*
>
> Judi Kemish, Solicitor for the Mark Duggan Inquest
>
> '*... we do not think the chairman should be involved in implementing or monitoring recommendations made after the inquiry has concluded. That is really outside of the scope of the role of the chairman and raises constitutional issues about who has responsibility. A far more appropriate suggestion is along the lines of a departmental or thematic committee dealing with the issues raised. To have the function of querying whether recommendations are being implemented, of questioning relevant authorities about their approach to the recommendations on an ongoing basis, is a good way to approach implementation and oversight ...*
>
> *That [a select committee] is certainly one obvious way of doing it. For example, if it raises home affairs issues it could be the Home Affairs Select Committee, or health issues then similarly. That is one good way of ensuring that we keep the focus on the recommendations and that those with responsibility for implementing them or those who have it in their gift to implement them are effectively tested and questioned and asked to explain why they have or have not implemented certain recommendations.'*
>
> Rachel Robinson, Policy Officer, Liberty

Once an inquiry has delivered its report and recommendations to the minister, and then notifies the minister that the inquiry has fulfilled its terms of reference, the inquiry comes to an end.[17] Therefore, in order for the chair or inquiry panel to formally monitor or oversee implementation of an inquiry's recommendations, the inquiry has to reconvene, or adjourn, after delivering the report, but before notifying the minister that the terms of reference have been fulfilled, to allow for a subsequent review. Some witnesses before the House of Lords Select Committee on the Inquiries Act 2005 argued that that would be useful. However, others pointed out the limitations of that approach as it was very likely that members of the inquiry team would have moved on to other projects. Many thought it would, in any event, be inappropriate for the chair and any panel members to be involved in monitoring implementation. The Select Committee agreed with the majority of

[17] See Inquiries Act 2005, s 14.

witnesses before it; that inquiry chairs and panels should not be responsible for the implementation of their recommendations.

The 2014 report of the House of Lords Select Committee on the Inquiries Act 2005 ultimately recommended the following:

- The publication of the formal government response to an inquiry report should invariably be accompanied by statements to both Houses, stating exactly which recommendations are accepted.
- If an inquiry specifies that particular recommendations are for implementation by particular public bodies, those bodies should have a statutory duty to say within a specified time whether they accept the recommendations, and if so, what plans they have for implementation.
- In all cases, the response should be published not more than three months after receipt of an inquiry report, with reasons given for not accepting recommendations and, for those which are accepted, details of when and how they will be implemented, an implementation plan, and a commitment to issue further reports to Parliament at 12-monthly intervals.[18]

This was broadly accepted by the government in its response to the report, subject to a six-month timeframe, albeit the government did not accept this needed to be a statutory duty. This new process will provide greater transparency and should provide greater accountability. However, there was no response to the report's suggestion that the Commons Department Select Committee is best placed to monitor implementation and it is unclear who at present oversees the implementation process.

Since the government's response to the Select Committee's report in June 2014, inquiry reports have been published by the Al-Sweady Inquiry (December 2014) and the Iraq Inquiry (July 2016), although the latter did not make any recommendations. In respect of the former, three months after publication of the report a ministerial statement was made, in March 2015, updating the House on the implementation of recommendations in the report. The statement explained that a number of the recommendations had already been implemented and the remaining recommendations were partly implemented or were intending to be implemented.

The Anthony Grainger report was published and laid before Parliament on 11 July 2019. The government published its response in May 2020, noting that the organisations to whom the recommendations were addressed accepted the recommendations and that progress had been made on implementing some of the recommendations.[19] It is not clear how ongoing implementation will

[18] Select Committee on the Inquiries Act 2005, *The Inquiries Act 2005: Post-legislative Scrutiny* (HL 2013–14, 143) recommendations 30 to 32.

[19] Home Office, *Government Response to the Anthony Grainger public inquiry* (May 2020) available at https://assets.publishing.service.gov.uk/government/uploads/system/uploads/attachment_data/file/885961/AGI-Open-Report-Response_v2.pdf (accessed 19 August 2020).

be monitored. The report of the Independent Inquiry into the Issues raised by Paterson was published on 4 February 2020 and the Renewable Heat Incentive Inquiry report was published on 13 March 2020. A formal government response has yet to be published.[20]

It remains to be seen to what extent the Select Committee's recommendation regarding publishing a response to inquiry reports, and explaining how any recommendations will be implemented, will be adopted.

Challenging Decisions

Decisions made by ministers and the chair or inquiry panel during the convening, and course, of a public inquiry may be challenged by way of judicial review. Judicial review is a means of monitoring and challenging the lawfulness of the actions of the government and public bodies, or bodies exercising functions that are of a public nature. It is a form of court proceedings where an individual or an organisation ('the applicant') affected by such a decision or actions asks the court to determine whether or not the decision-making process exercised by that body was lawful, fair and complied with the rules of natural justice. The court in judicial review proceedings is not concerned with the merits of the decision reached but, rather, whether the process followed in reaching the decision was procedurally correct.

In the context of public inquiries, the most frequent judicial review challenges have related to decisions by a minister not to convene a public inquiry.[21] As this book focuses on the practice and procedure of public inquiries once convened, what is of note is those challenges that have been made once an inquiry has been established.

> **Quote**
>
> *'In general, the very limited number of reported JRs of inquiries in mid-flow in England is the clearest possible evidence that the Courts give Chairs/Panels a very wide degree of latitude in running their own procedures and in conducting their own hearings.'*
>
> Rory Phillips QC, 3 Verulam Buildings

[20] At the time of writing (in Summer 2020).

[21] For example: *R v Secretary of State for the Home Department, ex p Amin* [2003] UKHL 51 (Mubarek Inquiry); *R (on the application of Al-Skeini) v Secretary of State for Defence* [2007] UKHL 26 (Baha Mousa Inquiry); *R (Al-Sweady) v Secretary of State for Defence* [2009] EWHC 2387 (Admin) (Al-Sweady Inquiry).

The court's approach to reviewing decisions made by ministers, chairs and inquiry panels has been one of deliberate restraint and reluctance to interfere. The majority of challenges have been unsuccessful. Examples of challenges include challenges to the scope of the terms of reference;[22] to the appointment of panel members;[23] to a decision not to allow certain witnesses to give evidence from behind a screen;[24] and a challenge to the decision to restrict all questioning of certain witnesses to counsel to the inquiry.[25]

Quote

It is recognised that challenging the content of an inquiry's report is difficult. Core participants may have advance sight of the report before publication, but for such a short period that there is little opportunity, in practice, to bring a challenge. Once a report is published, any resulting damage to reputations will already have been done.

'*However it is possible to envisage circumstances in which a report contains material damaging to individuals or organisations which is either perverse, not supported by evidence or is outside the terms of reference. There appears to be no practical check on this. A statutory inquiry panel has immunity from suit in respect of anything done in the course of the inquiry in good faith and enjoys the same immunity in relation to defamation as if the inquiry were court proceedings, i.e. an absolute privilege. If this were not enough, the Minister must lay a statutory inquiry report before Parliament either at the time of publication or as soon as reasonably practicable thereafter. Usually formal publication takes place by the report being laid before Parliament at which point it attracts Parliamentary privilege. In theory it might be possible to mount urgent judicial review proceedings before publication, but the circumstances in which this would [be] practical are likely to be very limited. In any event the damage is already done. These are difficulties which are inevitable if interested parties are not given an appropriate length of time to consider the report in draft before it is published. In practice access by core participants to reports before publication is restricted to a few hours of a "lock-in" under stringent conditions of confidentiality. The difficulty with granting a longer period is that the contents of the report would be likely to*

[22] *Re an application by Steven Davis for permission to apply for judicial review* (NIQB, 6 August 2007) (Billy Wright Inquiry).

[23] *R (on the application of Da Silva) v Secretary of State for the Home Department* [2018] EWHC 3001 (Admin) 2018 WL 05822983 (Undercover Policing Inquiry).

[24] *R (on the application of E) v Chairman of the Inquiry into the Death of Azelle Rodney Inquiry* [2012] EWHC 563 para 26 (Azelle Rodney Inquiry).

[25] Chief Constable's Application [Stephen Walker] [2008] NIQB 145.

be selectively and non-attributably leaked in an attempt to gain some media related advantage. However as there is the possibility of significant injustice being caused to individuals and organisations, it may be worth considering whether some more extensive post publication remedy to require correction of the report might be beneficial, or perhaps alteration of the warning letter regime considered above.'

Sir Robert Francis QC, in written evidence to the House of Lords Select Committee on the Inquiries Act 2005[26]

When a Challenge may be Brought

The traditional test for establishing whether or not a body is exercising functions of a public nature has been to look at their 'source of power', including whether the power to make the decision in question was derived from public law, including statute. A public inquiry established under the 2005 Act would clearly fall within this category.

Following *Datafin*, a Court of Appeal decision in 1987,[27] the 'source of the power' was not, however, considered to be the determining factor of whether or not a body was carrying out a public function, as the nature of the power, and whether or not this was relevant to the public, was also considered relevant. On this basis, although their powers are not derived from statute, non-statutory inquiries may also be carrying out a public function and therefore be susceptible to judicial review.

The justiciability of non-statutory inquiries was considered in 2019 during proceedings relating to the Magnox Inquiry. The defendant maintained that the inquiry in question was not subject to judicial review as the chair was not a public body but an individual tasked by the minister to prepare a report following a non-statutory inquiry conducted privately, with no public powers and no powers of compulsion. The defendant argued that any judicial review claim should be brought against the minister to prevent publication.[28]

The claimants were challenging the procedure followed by the inquiry during the interview process and subsequent Maxwellisation process.[29] The claimants

[26] House of Lords Select Committee on the Inquiries Act 2005, 'Written and corrected oral evidence' www.parliament.uk/documents/lords-committees/Inquiries-Act-2005/IA_Written_Oral_evidencevol.pdf (accessed 12 August 2020).

[27] *R (Datafin plc) v Panel on Takeovers and Mergers* [1987] QB 815, [1987] WLR 699, [1987] 1 All ER 564.

[28] *John Clarke and others v Chairman of the Magnox Inquiry and Secretary of State for BEIS and others* [2019] EWHC 3596 (Admin). The claimants sought leave to appeal the decision, but this was refused.

[29] See chapter thirteen where Maxwellisation is discussed.

argued that, although the inquiry was non-statutory and the evidence was being heard in private, the inquiry was still carrying out a public function. The claimants submitted:

> It was set up after a public procurement process that went wrong, involving a substantial expenditure of public money. The Inquiry is being conducted for the benefit of the public to determine what happened, to establish lessons learned and to make recommendations for the future. It is not essential for the Inquiry to have been sitting in public in order for Mr Holliday [the chair] to be carrying out a public function.[30]

The judge accepted the argument in relation to the Magnox Inquiry's justiciability, but with the caveat: 'This is a fact-specific conclusion, and it is not my view that the work of a non statutory inquiry is necessarily always amenable to judicial review.'

It is therefore clear that whether or not a non-statutory inquiry can be challenged by way of judicial review must be assessed on an individual basis, depending on the facts. Non-statutory inquiries need to be aware that their decisions and procedures may be capable of legal challenge, and must act accordingly.

Key Features of a Judicial Review Challenge

This book does not contain a comprehensive guide to the process by which decisions relating to a public inquiry can be judicially reviewed, nor the potential grounds for such an application; that would be a book in and of itself. Instead, this section summarises the key features of a judicial review challenge and process, as well as the potential challenges of taking such action.

Judicial review is a two-stage process:

- First, the applicant must obtain permission to apply for judicial review from the court. Permission to bring a claim for judicial review will not normally be granted if there is an adequate alternative remedy available to the applicant. The applicant must therefore demonstrate that they have exhausted all other means of obtaining the remedy sought.
  - In order to challenge a decision, the court must also be satisfied that the claim gives rise to an arguable case with a realistic prospect of success, and that the applicant has 'standing' to bring a claim.
  - To have 'standing' the applicant must have a sufficient interest in the matter to which the application relates. What amounts to 'a sufficient interest' is a matter for each case, but the courts have interpreted this broadly, to include any person with a real and genuine interest in obtaining the relief sought.
- If permission is granted, the second stage is the substantive challenge or claim.

[30] See chapter thirteen.

Any challenge to review a decision made by the relevant minister in relation to an inquiry, or by a member of an inquiry panel (including the chair) must be brought within 14 days after the day on which the applicant became aware of the decision, unless that time limit is extended by the court.[31] This time limit, however, does not apply if the decision being challenged relates to the content of the report, or an interim report, of the inquiry or a decision of which the applicant could not have become aware until the publication of the report, or an interim report.[32] In these circumstances, applications should be made promptly, and no later than three months from the date on which the grounds for the application arose, as the courts can refuse permission or relief if there is a delay with the application.

In addition to claimants and defendants, or applicants and respondents,[33] 'interested parties' may also be a party to judicial review proceedings. An 'interested party' is classified as any person or organisation, other than the claimant or defendant, who is directly affected by the claim; they can participate in the proceedings, rather than having to bring separate judicial review proceedings themselves. In addition, an 'intervener' is any other person or organisation who wishes to apply to file evidence or make representations in the proceedings.[34] Interveners are not parties to the proceedings and, typically, are not directly affected by the claim.

Grounds for Challenge

The potential grounds of challenge fall into three broad categories:

- Illegality – this includes errors of law, improper delegation, abuse or fettering of discretion, taking into account irrelevant considerations, or acting without or in excess of authority.
- Irrationality – this is where the decision is so unreasonable that no other reasonable authority could ever have come to the same decision.[35] (The approach of the courts has resulted, over time, in this threshold becoming increasingly more difficult to meet and it is usually argued alongside other grounds.)
- Procedural impropriety or unfairness – this includes a failure to comply with the relevant procedure, or the principles of natural justice have not been observed in the decision-making process, such as a failure to have a fair hearing or actual or apparent bias.

[31] Inquiries Act 2005, s 38(1).
[32] Inquiries Act 2005, s 38(3).
[33] Claimants and defendants in the Administrative Court and the applicants and respondents in the Upper Tribunal.
[34] Civil Procedure Rules (CPR), r 54.17.
[35] *Associated Provincial Picture Houses Ltd v Wednesbury Corporation* (1948) 1 KB 223.

- Breach of legitimate expectation – often associated with procedural impropriety and sometimes considered to be a discrete ground in itself, this is where steps are taken in breach of a legitimate expectation (ie that the minister or inquiry will act in a certain way); this could be a procedural expectation that a certain procedure would be followed, or a substantive expectation that a person or organisation will receive some sort of assistance or benefit.

Remedies

There are six remedies available to a successful applicant in judicial review proceedings:

- Mandatory order – to compel the inquiry to act in a particular way.
- Quashing order – which quashes or sets aside the decision, thereby confirming that the challenged decision has no lawful force and no legal effect.
- Prohibiting order – which prohibits the inquiry from taking an action that the inquiry has indicated an intention to take, but has not yet taken.
- Ordinary declaration – a statement by the court as to what the law is on a particular point.
- Declaration of incompatibility – this is made when an Act of Parliament is incompatible with a right derived from the European Convention on Human Rights.
- Injunctions – an order to act in a particular way or to refrain from acting in a particular way.

Damages can also be awarded alongside one of the above remedies.

Considerations before Bringing a Judicial Review Challenge

Historically, successfully challenging an inquiry has been difficult, because of the need to overcome the hurdles required to be granted permission to apply and the fact that the court's approach to reviewing decisions made by ministers, and chairs and inquiry panels, has been one of deliberate restraint and reluctance to interfere. As a result, careful thought must be given before making such a challenge.

Applicants must also be wary of pyrrhic victories. A successful judicial review challenge may result in an inquiry's decision on a procedural matter being quashed, for example for failure to take relevant criteria into account. However, when reconsidering the decision while taking that criteria into account, the inquiry may ultimately reach the same conclusions. Making such an application may also bring an increased focus on the applicant as a participant in an inquiry's work, and expose them to greater criticism than would otherwise have been the case.

Inquiries must be aware of other wider consequences of judicial review challenges. They can cause significant delay to the inquiry's work (on occasion, this can be a major motivating factor for an applicant, who may wish to delay any anticipated reputational damage, for example to reduce impact on upcoming crucial commercial activities). Judicial review challenges of an inquiry's decisions can also be hugely disruptive to an inquiry's work and can cause reputational damage to the inquiry itself and undermine public support for its work.

Quote

'The effect of judicial review can be similar to an appeal, in particular where the error is a straightforward error of law or misconstruction of a statute. But the classic grounds of judicial review include breach of the rules of natural justice or procedural fairness, and the portfolio ground of Wednesbury unreasonableness or irrationality. A challenge based on bias, procedural unfairness or irrationality may be seen as damaging the perception that the judge conducting an inquiry so challenged is impartial or that the process is fair, whether or not it succeeds. It must be recognised that this will also be the case for inquiries which are not chaired by judges.'

Lord Justice Beatson, in written evidence to the House of Lords Select Committee on the Inquiries Act 2005

Cost of a Judicial Review Challenge for an Inquiry

From an inquiry's perspective, avoiding judicial review challenges, where possible, is of course important given the delay and likely disruption that they cause, and the potential negative impact on the inquiry's reputation. Cost must also be considered.

As explored in chapter two, for statutory inquiries, during the operation of the inquiry, the chair, panel, and members of the inquiry team will receive immunity from civil proceedings in respect of any act or omission relating to the inquiry's work. That immunity extends to judicial review proceedings and that immunity relates to acts or omissions made in the execution of that person's duty, or in good faith in the purported execution of that duty, during the course of the inquiry.

Given that immunity, in practice it will be the inquiry that bears the cost of defending any judicial review challenges, and meeting any costs award, if an applicant is successful in challenging the decision of an inquiry chair or panel. Thought should be given to that fact by the inquiry at the budgeting stage. This can, however, be difficult to estimate. Some inquiries do not face any judicial review challenges;

others may face a number. Those setting an inquiry's budget at the outset may need to be persuaded that provision should be made for such costs. An inquiry must also bear in mind the fact that if repeated, successful challenges are made, the cost of defending such satellite proceedings may be difficult to justify.

Whether for a participant, or an inquiry, it is clear that judicial review should be seen as a remedy of last resort.

15

Closing Down the Inquiry

Introduction

The work of an inquiry does not end when the final report is published. It is essential that inquiry documents are saved, correctly archived and preserved for the future. An inquiry team also has to consider other practical logistics of closing down the inquiry. As explained below, much of the planning for closing down the inquiry, and putting effective procedures into place, in fact should commence during the early stages of an inquiry and continue as the inquiry progresses.

In the case of statutory inquiries, an inquiry comes to an end on the date, after the delivery of the report of the inquiry, on which the chair notifies the relevant minister that the inquiry has fulfilled its terms of reference, or any earlier date specified in a notice given by the minister to the chair.[1] In practice, the point at which this happens has varied between inquiries; some inquiry chairs have delayed notifying the minister that the inquiry is at an end in order to monitor the implementation of recommendations.[2]

An inquiry may set an absolute cut-off date on which it will cease to operate. Alternatively, there may be a phased closing down, which will allow witnesses and members of the public a longer period during which to remain in contact with the inquiry and to raise queries. This decision is one for the inquiry team to make. Organisations and individuals who are involved in, and have an interest in an inquiry's work will need to ensure they know how, and until what date, the inquiry will be operational.

Below is a checklist illustrating the types of issues that should be considered when planning for the closing down of the inquiry.

[1] Inquiries Act 2005, s 14.

[2] See chapter fourteen.

Checklist – Closing down an inquiry: issues to consider

Termination of contracts

- All inquiries have contracts that need to be terminated at the end of the inquiry. These contracts range from building leases, to contracts for telephone landlines, mobile phones, e-mail accounts, leases for equipment (eg printers, computers, drinks machines), utilities and internet service providers, as well as fixed-term contracts for inquiry staff. It is advisable for an inquiry to maintain such contracts for a short period after any public hearings come to an end, in case any last minute applications are made or any unexpected events occur following the hearings. This reduces the possibility of serving notice but then needing to revisit and extend a contract. This will need to be planned in advance, taking into account the timescales involved, by examining the terms of the contracts, particularly the relevant notice periods, to ensure the termination of contracts is well coordinated and cost effective.

When contact with the inquiry will cease

- An inquiry should communicate clearly with core participants or interested parties, and the public generally, about when the inquiry will no longer be contactable (ie when phone lines and e-mail addresses will no longer be in use). The communication should take place well in advance, in order to provide plenty of notice. Those involved with an inquiry should be mindful of this date when considering whether there is any further information they need from the inquiry or that they wish to send to the inquiry. Once the inquiry has closed down, it will be difficult for any queries to be dealt with.

Support for witnesses

- Where the nature and subject matter of an inquiry has necessitated support being put in place for witnesses and those involved with the inquiry, the inquiry will need to consider whether, and in what form, this support should continue and who will fund it. This should be discussed and agreed with the relevant sponsoring department well in advance of the closing down of the inquiry.

The inquiry's website

- The website for an inquiry often remains live for some years after the inquiry's work has concluded so that the public can access evidence and details of the inquiry's work. Arrangements should be made for maintaining the website during this period, as the inquiry team will no longer be in place. The associated cost will have to be discussed with the relevant sponsoring department, although the cost of ongoing maintenance of the inquiry website is likely to be low given that the inquiry has concluded and the website is unlikely to require updating.

- Ultimately, most inquiry websites are moved, in their entirety, to the National Archives as part of the archiving process (see below). This process may be managed by the inquiry team if the transfer takes place immediately after the conclusion of the inquiry or by the relevant sponsoring department if the website remains live for a period of time following the transfer.

Indexing and destruction of non-archived documents

- At the conclusion of the inquiry, all inquiry documents (including electronic documents) have to be fully indexed, to assist with any document requests and searches at a later stage. Document management systems, referred to in chapter four, assist with this process.
- The section below describes how inquiry documents are archived. The destruction of documents is, however, also a key element of the archiving process. Inevitably, the inquiry will hold documents that do not need to be archived and therefore have to be destroyed. Most commonly this occurs where the inquiry holds hard copies of documents that are also held electronically and the hard copy duplicates do not need to be retained. All documents that are destroyed must be recorded and indexed to ensure the destruction is carried out in a methodical and organised manner. The record of destruction itself will be an important document, in the event that any questions are raised in the future about the archiving and destruction of material. An appropriate shredding method must also be used (ie documents shredded to a certain security grade, by shred size or particle size) particularly if any of the documents contain particularly sensitive or secret material.[3]

[3] There may be specific shredding requirements for protectively marked information. See in particular the 'Cabinet Office's Government Security Classifications May 2018', which refers to the guidance provided by the Centre for the Protection of National Infrastructure and the specifications of HMG Information Assurance Standard No 5 – Secure Sanitisation of Protectively Marked or Sensitive Information.

Document Retention and Archiving: Planning and Implementation

The key task when archiving an inquiry's records is the processing, transfer and archiving of documents. Retaining and preserving the material that was used or created during the course of an inquiry's work, and formed the basis of the inquiry's report and recommendations, is very important.

For statutory public inquiries, the chair is under a duty to ensure that the record of the inquiry is comprehensive and well-ordered. At the end of the inquiry, the chair is required to transfer the inquiry record to a government department, or an appropriate public record office, as the sponsoring minister directs (for England and Wales this is the National Archives).[4]

Planning for retaining and archiving the inquiry's records is something that needs to be considered right at the outset of the inquiry and revisited throughout its duration. Decisions made in respect of document management and storage during the life of an inquiry will have an impact on archiving the documents at the end. Witnesses may be less willing to give evidence if they are concerned that anonymity will not be preserved during archiving. Inquiries usually receive, create and store a huge volume of documents (both electronic and hard copy). The potential time and cost that can be incurred in archiving should not be underestimated and, as such, should be addressed at an early stage to reduce the potential cost.

The National Archives has published guidance on archiving an inquiry record, which includes general guidance on what material should be archived, how the material should be transferred for archive and additional technical considerations.[5] Set out below is a further checklist of some of the key points to will bear in mind:

Checklist – Archiving inquiry documents: key points to bear in mind both during and at the end of an inquiry

- There is no obligation to archive all material, only that which the chair considers ought to be preserved.
- There is a limit to the quantity of hard copy documents that can be archived. Unless there is good reason to the contrary, there is likely to be an expectation that documents should be stored electronically and hard copies should be destroyed.

[4] Inquiry Rules 2006, r 18(1).

[5] The National Archive, 'Public Inquiry Guidance' http://www.nationalarchives.gov.uk/information-management/manage-information/public-inquiry-guidance/ (accessed 12 August 2020).

- Where transcripts, witness statements and other evidence relied on by the inquiry have been published on a website, it may be sufficient for the website to be archived in its final form, as the principal point of reference.
- Having regard to an inquiry's obligation under s 18 of the Inquiries Act 2005, it is important that an inquiry draws up a records management policy in the initial stages of its work. This policy document should outline the way in which the inquiry intends to treat documents during the inquiry, which will help with organising and archiving documents at later stages in the inquiry.[6]
- A records management policy should also ensure that a full audit history of all decisions taken by the inquiry is retained, should any queries arise at a later date. This includes minutes from all meetings, copies of all incoming and outgoing correspondence, voicemail recordings and handwritten notes from interviews.
- Details of all documents received by the inquiry (such as disclosure from a core participant or from a witness) should also be recorded and catalogued to ensure that there is a full record of all incoming documents and their source.
- Documents must be categorised as they are received, so that each category of documents can be processed and stored appropriately. For example:
  - 'Public Documents' – documents that have been used in public hearings and referred to in evidence (these documents are likely to have been made publicly available, with redactions if necessary);
  - 'Restricted Documents' – documents that are subject to a restriction notice or restriction order, or are privileged, secret or are otherwise highly sensitive documents and should not be published or made public;[7]
  - 'Non-public Documents' – documents provided to the inquiry as relevant to the terms of reference, which have not been used in public hearings or relied on when preparing the report. These documents will be available to the inquiry chair, any panel members and assessors, and the inquiry legal team. They will not necessarily have been redacted if they have not been used in public hearings or otherwise published on the inquiry's website.

[6] See chapter five and the references to a protocol on the treatment of evidence.
[7] See below for discussion on duration of restriction notices and restriction orders.

- Destruction of documents is also a key part of the archiving and records management process. This process:
  - avoids unnecessary storage costs and reduces the time spent on archiving material unnecessarily;
  - supports compliance with data protection legislation and the obligation to retain personal information for only as long as is necessary; and
  - makes finding and retrieving information quicker and easier because there is less material to search.

Restricted documents and archiving

All documents must be handled carefully when it comes to archiving. In the future, they may become susceptible to disclosure, for example via a Freedom of Information Act request, but they will not have been prepared for publication (ie reviewed by the inquiry team to consider whether any information requires redaction in advance of onward disclosure or publication). Therefore care must be taken by the inquiry when archiving this material, to ensure that clear instructions about the status of the documents, and how they should be handled, are provided to those who are responsible for them once archived.

Of particular concern will be information and documents covered by restriction orders and restriction notices. Section 19 of the Inquiries Act 2005 provides that restrictions may be imposed by the minister by restriction notice, or the chair by restriction order,[8] to prevent the disclosure or publication of evidence or documents provided to the inquiry.[9] Restrictions imposed under s 19 continue indefinitely if not varied or revoked, unless the terms of the restriction notice or order specify that the restrictions will cease at the end of the inquiry, or some other date.[10] For example, if a restriction order provided for the identity of a particular 'at risk' witness to be kept confidential, that order would continue in order to protect that individual even once the inquiry ceases to exist.

Those restrictions do not, however, apply to information in the possession of a public authority after the end of an inquiry, unless it is held as a result of a breach of any such restriction.[11] This means that a public authority that holds an inquiry's

[8] In practice, once an inquiry is up and running, it is rare for a minister to become involved in issuing restrictions; this usually falls to the chair. See chapter six for restriction notices and orders generally.

[9] See further at chapter eleven.

[10] Inquiries Act 2005, s 20(5) and (7).

[11] Inquiries Act 2005, s 20(6).

records after an inquiry has come to an end[12] will not be able to rely on the existence of a restriction order or notice to prevent disclosure of inquiry records if requested via the Freedom of Information Act 2000.[13]

This creates real practical difficulties when it comes to archiving material, and distinguishing what information will, or will not, be protected by ongoing restrictions, particularly if those responsible for holding the material at the end of the inquiry are not familiar with the documents and their different sensitivities.

Issue – Challenges arising regarding access to archived documents and freedom of information requests

Following completion of an inquiry's work, there may well be subsequent requests for information: either information that was made available to the inquiry during its work (such as documents disclosed to the inquiry by others) or documents created by the inquiry itself (such as correspondence with witnesses or witness statements).

A public inquiry, whether statutory or non-statutory, is not susceptible to Freedom of Information Act (FOIA) requests during its lifetime.[14] This position, however, changes once the inquiry ends and its records are transferred to the sponsoring department or national archiving body, which are susceptible to FOIA requests (subject to any exemptions which may apply). From a practical perspective, the issue that then arises is that the inquiry's records have been placed with individuals who were not members of the inquiry team and therefore do not have the same in-depth knowledge of the nature of the material, nor whether there are any particular sensitivities or other disclosure concerns relating to particular documents. It is therefore essential that when the documents are archived there is a very rigorous labelling process in place. The archiving process must be organised in such a way as to ensure that no inadvertent disclosure is made and that the status of material is clear.

Given the subject matter of public inquiries, some of the documents are likely to be privileged; other documents are likely to be confidential or extremely sensitive. Some documents may be protectively marked 'official',

[12] Inquiry Rules 2006, r 2 defines 'inquiry record' as 'all documents given to or created by the inquiry' – a very wide definition.

[13] See chapter nine in relation to Freedom of Information (FOIA) requests made to an inquiry and after an inquiry has ended.

[14] See chapter five.

'secret' or 'top secret'.[15] There may be documents that compromise national security, breach confidentiality undertakings or restriction orders or restriction notices (where these orders or notices continue indefinitely under s 20(5) of the Inquiries Act 2005), or contain personal material of a distressing and personal nature (eg medical records or details of abuse suffered). Particular care must be taken with these documents, both when recording and retaining the material as well as when archiving it, to prevent any future breaches of confidentiality, data protection obligations or waiver of privilege, even if inadvertent. A party or witness to an inquiry, who may have provided privileged or confidential material, will also want to be reassured that the information they have provided will be archived and stored appropriately, to preserve the protected nature of that material once the inquiry has concluded.

At the archiving stage, the inquiry team therefore need to identify any information that may need to be withheld, and to which exemptions may potentially apply, in order to assist those dealing with any FOIA requests in the future. These documents should be clearly marked and organised in such a way so that those dealing with FOIA requests can clearly see where potential issues with disclosure may arise.

Treatment of confidential and sensitive material

As stated above, public inquiries often deal with information of a very sensitive nature. There may also be information that is subject to restriction orders or restriction notices, where their terms mean that they continue indefinitely (see above). When archiving such material, particular care will need to be taken.

Core participants and interested parties who provide sensitive documents to an inquiry will want to be assured that the information will be treated with the utmost care. For example, an individual may provide very personal and sensitive information, such as details of abuse suffered, on the basis of assurances from the inquiry that this will remain confidential. That individual will expect that information to remain protected even once the inquiry's work has come to an end.

Appropriate handling of this information is essential. The majority of documents that are archived are likely to be in an electronic form, which may make

[15] See the 'Cabinet Office's Government Security Classifications May 2018' for further details on the protection of documents belonging to Her Majesty's Government. See also chapter eight on the use of classified material. It should be noted that the former classification of public sector documents, for example 'Restricted', 'Unclassified' or 'Confidential' may also be encountered if historical documents are of relevance to the particular inquiry's subject matter.

reviewing the nature of the documents more difficult. There is a risk that a storage system may not make it sufficiently clear which documents are particularly sensitive, especially where they are stored alongside other documents that are not similarly sensitive. Electronic documents are quicker and easier to search than hard copies, and large volumes are easier to process, but this can mean that warnings about onward disclosure and publication of certain documents are missed or lost. It is important that there is a clear process in place to ensure that the relevant sensitivities of individual documents are made clear on any electronic archiving system.

An inquiry should ensure that its records management policy includes a process by which sensitive material is marked and identified, and that the nature of any restriction to be applied should be made explicit at the time of transfer for archiving. This might include, for example, individual headers or watermarks on every page of a document or separate bundles for separate categories of confidential or sensitive material to avoid confusion. Particular care is also needed with any information with a classification marking above 'official';[16] this will need to be passed to either the sponsoring department or Cabinet Office until a time when the sensitivity has diminished to a suitable level to allow for general archiving.

Quote

'An important part of the archiving process is to ensure that any decisions taken by the Inquiry as to confidentiality are respected by the archiver, or the supervising department holding the Inquiry's papers. Otherwise there is a risk that material properly withheld from the public domain by the Inquiry is released subsequently in error, or in ignorance of the Inquiry's decisions.'

Sir Robert Francis QC, Chair of the Mid Staffordshire NHS Foundation Trust Public Inquiry

Issue – What about the cost of archiving?

The cost of closing down an inquiry can come as a shock if the inquiry team has not planned appropriately. The cost of closing down an inquiry should have been scoped at the outset of the inquiry and, as stated above, decisions made during the life of the inquiry should be made with the closing-down processes in mind.

[16] See n 15. Most public sector documents, where no specific risks apply, are classified 'Official'.

If the correct policies and procedures are in place at the beginning of the inquiry, and if they are complied with during the evidence-gathering stage, the cost of closing down the inquiry can be significantly reduced.

Lessons Learned

The closure of an inquiry is the appropriate time to reflect on the work of an inquiry and conducting a review of the lessons learned can be a very valuable exercise, particularly for those who may find themselves involved in other inquiries in the future. There may be some elements that, on reflection, could have been approached differently and others that worked particularly well.

There is very limited government guidance available on the running of public inquiries, in the form of draft guidance from the Cabinet Office.[17] That guidance states that

> on conclusion of the inquiry [the inquiry secretary should] submit a 'Lessons Learned' report to the Cabinet Office Propriety and Ethics Team. The report should include details of success and failures of the process and handling and will be used to help inform the setting up of future inquiries.[18]

However, this has not been common practice and there are very few such reports in existence; where they do exist they are not made publicly available. In 2014 there was a renewed call for such papers to be produced and used to provide detailed guidance for secretaries of subsequent inquiries,[19] although this still appears to be rarely done.

No two inquiries are ever the same; however, the structural outline and setup of a well-run inquiry, and procedures and protocols followed, can be used time and time again. Lessons learned and efficiencies should be recorded and shared, not only with subsequent secretaries of subsequent inquiries, but also with the inquiry teams, legal representatives and participants to assist the smooth running of the future inquiries.

[17] Cabinet Office, *Inquiries Guidance: Guidance for inquiry chairs and secretaries, and sponsor departments: Draft version* (2012), available at www.parliament.uk/documents/lords-committees/Inquiries-Act-2005/caboffguide.pdf (accessed 12 August 2020).

[18] Cabinet Office, *Inquiries Guidance* (n 17) 23.

[19] House of Lords Select Committee on the Inquiries Act 2005, *The Inquiries Act 2005: post-legislative scrutiny, Report of Session 2013–14* (TSO, 2014), HL Paper 143 paras 162–164.

INDEX